Real Reading 4

Real Reading 4

Creating an Authentic Reading Experience

Alice Savage • David Wiese

Lynn Bonesteel
Series Editor

Paul Nation
Series Consultant

PEARSON
Longman

Real Reading 4: Creating an Authentic Reading Experience

Pearson Education, 10 Bank Street, White Plains, NY 10606

Staff credits: The people who made up the **Real Reading 4** team, representing editorial,
production, design, and manufacturing, are Nancy Flaggman, Ann France, Dana Klinek,
Amy McCormick, Martha McGaughey, Joan Poole, Robert Ruvo, Debbie Sistino, and
Jennifer Stem.

Cover art: Shutterstock.com
Text composition: TSI Graphics
Text font: Helvetica Neue
Illustrations: TSI Graphics—pages 2, 31; Gary Torrisi—pages 19, 20, 26, 38, 44, 137, 152,
170, 179
References: see page xx
Photo Credits: see page xxii
Text Credits: see page xxiii

Library of Congress Cataloging-in-Publication Data

Bonesteel, Lynn.
  Real reading : creating an authentic reading experience / Lynn Bonesteel.
      p. cm.
  Includes index.
  ISBN-10: 0-13-606654-2 (Level 1)
  ISBN-10: 0-13-814627-6 (Level 2)
  ISBN-10: 0-13-714443-1 (Level 3)
  ISBN-10: 0-13-502771-3 (Level 4))
  [etc.]
  1. English language--Textbooks for foreign speakers. 2. Reading comprehension.
  3. Vocabulary. I. Title.
  PE1128.B6243 2010
  428.6'4--dc22

                                                                2010017172

PEARSON LONGMAN ON THE **WEB**

Pearsonlongman.com offers online
resources for teachers. Access our Companion
Websites, our online catalog, and our local
offices around the world.

Visit us at **pearsonlongman.com**.

ISBN 10: 0-13-502771-3
ISBN 13: 978-0-13-502771-4

Printed in the United States of America
4 5 6 7 8 9 10—V011—15 14 13

CONTENTS

Acknowledgments

We would like to express our appreciation to all of those who made this project possible. We want to extend a special thanks to Series Editor Lynn Bonesteel for her tireless efforts to invigorate this series with solid research and engaging material. She was always there for us, always kind, and always ready to lend a hand. At Pearson, we'd like to thank Debbie Sistino for her mentorship, Dana Klinek for her constant support, Pietro Alongi for believing in the project in the first place, Joan Poole and Martha McGaughey for their careful attention to detail, and Amy McCormick, Robert Ruvo, Ann France, and Aerin Csigay for creating a beautifully designed and illustrated book. We would also like to thank Paul Nation, whose conception of an authentic reading experience was the inspiration for this series.

Alice Savage and David Wiese

I would like to thank David Wiese for his great ideas and professionalism. It was a pleasure to work with you. A special thanks also goes to the administrators, faculty, and students at Lone Star College System for providing an extraordinary community that has allowed me to grow and learn. Finally, Masoud, Cyrus, and Kaveh, you are my inspiration.

Alice Savage

I would also like to thank Alice Savage, whose good humor and creativity made the *Real Reading* collaboration a pleasure, and John Beaumont, who introduced me to so many of the above people. Finally, I would like to thank my parents, Ken and Julie; my lovely wife, Gessi; and my family and friends for their unconditional love and support over so many years.

David Wiese

Reviewers

William Brazda, Long Beach City College, Long Beach, CA; **Abigail Brown**, University of Hawaii, Honolulu, HI; **David Dahnke**, North Harris Community College, Houston, TX; **Scott Fisher**, Sungshin Women's University, Seoul, Korea; **Roberta Hodges**, Sonoma State American Language Institute, Sonoma, CA; **Kate Johnson**, Union County College Institute For Intensive English, Elizabeth, NJ; **Thomas Justice**, North Shore Community College, Danvers, MA; **Michael McCollister**, Feng Chia University, Taiching, Taiwan; **Myra Medina**, Miami-Dade Community College, Miami, FL; **Lesley Morgan**, West Virginia University, Morgantown, WV; **Angela Parrino**, Hunter College, New York, NY; **Christine Sharpe**, Howard Community College, Columbia, MD; **Christine Tierney**, Houston Community College, Houston, TX; **Kerry Vrabel**, GateWay Community College, Phoenix, AZ.

INTRODUCTION

Real Reading 4 is the fourth book in a four-level (beginning, low intermediate, intermediate, and high intermediate) intensive reading series for learners of English. The books in the series feature high-interest readings that have been carefully written or adapted from authentic sources to allow effective comprehension by learners at each level. The aim is for learners to be able to engage with the content in a meaningful and authentic way, as readers do in their native language. For example, learners who use *Real Reading* will be able to read to learn or feel something new, to evaluate information and ideas, to experience or share an emotion, to see something from a new perspective, or simply to get pleasure from reading in English. High-interest topics include superstitions, shyness, neuroscience, sports, magic, and technology, among others.

> THE *REAL READING* APPROACH

To allow for effective comprehension, the vocabulary in the readings in the *Real Reading* series has been controlled so that 95–98 percent of the words are likely to be known by a typical learner at each level. The vocabulary choices were based on analyses of the General Service Word List (GSL) (Michael West, 1953), the Academic Word List (AWL) (Averil Coxhead, 2000), and the Billuroğlu-Neufeld List (BNL) (Ali Billuroğlu and Steve Neufeld, 2007).

Research has shown that as they read a text, good readers employ a variety of skills.[1] Thus, essential reading skills, such as predicting, skimming, making inferences, and understanding text references, are presented, practiced, and recycled in each level of *Real Reading*, with level-appropriate explanations and practice. The goal is for learners to become autonomous readers in English; the reading skills are the tools that will help learners achieve this goal.

Vocabulary development skills and strategies are prominently featured in every chapter in *Real Reading*. The importance of vocabulary size to reading comprehension and fluency has been well documented in the research on both first and second language acquisition.[2] Thus, in the *Real Reading* series, learners are given extensive practice in applying level-appropriate skills and strategies to their acquisition of the target words in each chapter. This practice serves two purposes: First, because the target words have been selected from among the most
- frequent words in general and academic English, learners who use the books are exposed to the words that they will encounter most frequently in English texts.
- Second, through repeated practice with vocabulary skills and learning strategies, learners will acquire the tools they need to continue expanding their vocabulary long after completing the books in the series.

---

[1] Nation, I.S.P. *Learning Vocabulary in Another Language*. Cambridge, England: Cambridge University Press. 2001.

[2] Nation, I.S.P. *Teaching Vocabulary: Strategies and Techniques*. Boston, MA: Heinle, Cengage Learning. 2008.

VOCABULARY: FROM RESEARCH TO PRACTICE
By Paul Nation

Real Reading puts several well-established vocabulary-based principles into practice.

1. There is the idea that meaning-focused input should contain a small amount of unknown vocabulary but that this amount should be limited so that the learners can read for understanding without being overburdened by a large number of unknown words. Research suggests that somewhere around two percent of the running words in a text may be initially unknown and still allow a reasonable level of comprehension. If the number of unknown words is too large, then the learners cannot participate in an authentic reading experience. That is, they cannot read the text and react in the same way as a native speaker would. The texts in *Real Reading* have been developed so that learners are likely to gain a high level of comprehension while encountering some new words that they can begin to learn.

2. The activities in *Real Reading*, along with the texts, provide learners with the opportunity to thoughtfully process the unknown vocabulary that they encounter. In most of the exercises, the contexts for the target words are different from the contexts provided in the texts. This helps stretch the meaning of the new words and makes them more memorable. The various exercises also require the target words to be used in ways that will help learning.

3. *Real Reading* includes a systematic approach to the development of important vocabulary learning strategies. The ultimate goal of instructed vocabulary learning should be to help learners become autonomous language learners. An important step in this process is gaining control of effective vocabulary learning strategies, such as using word cards, using word parts, and using a dictionary. *Real Reading* includes vocabulary strategies in every unit. The strategies are broken down into their components, practiced and recycled in the vocabulary practice pages at the back of the books.

4. The sequencing of the vocabulary in *Real Reading* has been carefully designed so that the new items will not interfere with each other. That is, presenting the target words together with new vocabulary that belongs to the same lexical set or consists of opposites or synonyms greatly increases the difficulty of vocabulary learning. It is much more helpful if the unknown vocabulary fits together in ways that are similar to the ways the words occur in the texts.

5. Finally, a well-balanced language course provides four major kinds of opportunities for vocabulary learning. A unique feature of *Real Reading* is its use of these research-based principles. First, there is the opportunity to learn through *meaning-focused input*, where the learners' attention is focused on the message of what they are reading or listening to. Second, there is an opportunity to learn through *meaning-focused output*, where the learners are intent on conveying messages. Third, there is the opportunity to learn through *language-focused learning*, where learners give deliberate attention to language features. Fourth, there is the opportunity to *develop fluency* with what is already known. In a variety of ways, the *Real Reading* textbooks provide these opportunities. Their main focus is on deliberate learning through conscious attention to vocabulary, and through the use of specially designed exercises.

THE *REAL READING* UNIT

THINK BEFORE YOU READ

Each unit begins with a captivating opener that introduces students to the unit theme, elicits vocabulary relevant to the theme, and includes discussion questions to activate students' prior knowledge and stimulate interest.

PREPARE TO READ
This section previews words and phrases that students will encounter in the reading. Students reflect on what they already know and then answer questions about the topic.

READING SKILLS Every unit has one or two reading skills, which include previewing and predicting; understanding topics, main ideas, and details; and understanding cause and effect, among others.

READ The readings feature a wide variety of high-interest, contemporary topics, including business, science and nature, music and the visual arts, culture and society, sports and exercise, and health and nutrition, as well as a variety of genres, including newspaper and magazine articles, blogs, Web sites, newsletters, travel logs, personal essays, poetry, and short stories. Vocabulary is tightly controlled at each level, and target words are recycled from one chapter to the next within a unit, from unit to unit, and from one level to the next.

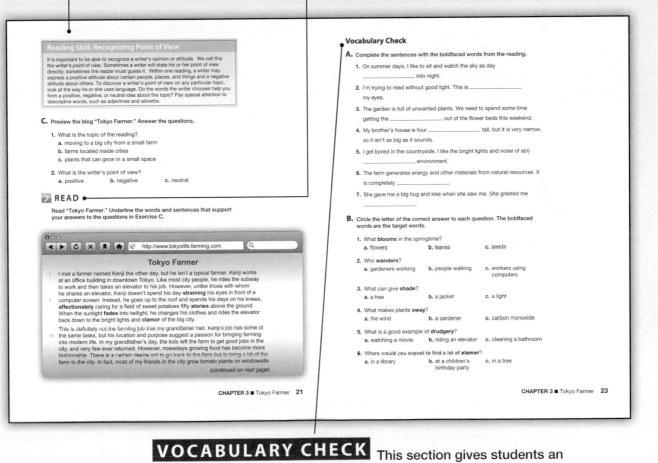

Reading Skill: Recognizing Point of View

It is important to be able to recognize a writer's opinion or attitude. We call this the writer's *point of view*. Sometimes a writer will state his or her point of view directly; sometimes the reader must guess it. Within one reading, a writer may express a positive attitude about certain people, places, and things and a negative attitude about others. To discover a writer's point of view on any particular topic, look at the way he or she uses language. Do the words the writer chooses help you form a positive, negative, or neutral idea about the topic? Pay special attention to descriptive words, such as adjectives and adverbs.

C. Preview the blog "Tokyo Farmer." Answer the questions.

1. What is the topic of the reading?
   a. moving to a big city from a small farm
   b. farms located inside cities
   c. plants that can grow in a small space

2. What is the writer's point of view?
   a. positive   b. negative   c. neutral

READ

Read "Tokyo Farmer." Underline the words and sentences that support your answers to the questions in Exercise C.

Tokyo Farmer

http://www.tokyolife.farming.com

I met a farmer named Kenji the other day, but he isn't a typical farmer. Kenji works at an office building in downtown Tokyo. Like most city people, he rides the subway to work and then takes an elevator to his job. However, unlike those with whom he shares an elevator, Kenji doesn't spend his day **straining** his eyes in front of a computer screen. Instead, he goes up to the roof and spends his days on his knees, **affectionately** caring for a field of sweet potatoes fifty **stories** above the ground. When the sunlight **fades** into twilight, he changes his clothes and rides the elevator back down to the bright lights and **clamor** of the big city.

This is definitely not the farming job that my grandfather had. Kenji's job has some of the same tasks, but his location and purpose suggest a passion for bringing farming into modern life. In my grandfather's day, the kids left the farm to get good jobs in the city, and very few ever returned. However, nowadays growing food has become more fashionable. There is a certain desire not to go back to the farm but to bring a bit of the farm to the city. In fact, most of my friends in the city grow tomato plants on windowsills

(continued on next page)

CHAPTER 3 ■ Tokyo Farmer **21**

Vocabulary Check

A. Complete the sentences with the boldfaced words from the reading.

1. On summer days, I like to sit and watch the sky as day _____ into night.

2. I'm trying to read without good light. This is _____ my eyes.

3. The garden is full of unwanted plants. We need to spend some time getting the _____ out of the flower beds this weekend.

4. My brother's house is four _____ tall, but it is very narrow, so it isn't as big as it sounds.

5. I get bored in the countryside. I like the bright lights and noise of a(n) _____ environment.

6. The farm generates energy and other materials from natural resources. It is completely _____.

7. She gave me a big hug and kiss when she saw me. She greeted me _____.

B. Circle the letter of the correct answer to each question. The boldfaced words are the target words.

1. What **blooms** in the springtime?
   a. flowers   b. leaves   c. seeds

2. Who **wanders**?
   a. gardeners working   b. people walking   c. workers using computers

3. What can give **shade**?
   a. a tree   b. a jacket   c. a light

4. What makes plants **sway**?
   a. the wind   b. a gardener   c. carbon monoxide

5. What is a good example of **drudgery**?
   a. watching a movie   b. riding an elevator   c. cleaning a bathroom

6. Where would you expect to find a lot of **clamor**?
   a. in a library   b. at a children's birthday party   c. in a tree

CHAPTER 3 ■ Tokyo Farmer **23**

VOCABULARY CHECK This section gives students an opportunity to focus on the meaning of the target vocabulary before completing the comprehension activities.

THE *REAL READING* UNIT (continued)

READING GOAL
The reading goal gives students a purpose for rereading the text before completing the comprehension activities. Reading goals include completing a graphic organizer, giving an oral or written summary of a text, retelling a story, identifying the writer's point of view, and giving an opinion on the content of a text, among others.

COMPREHENSION CHECK
Engaging and varied exercises help students achieve the reading goal. Target vocabulary is recycled, giving students additional exposure to the high frequency words and expressions.

▶ READ AGAIN

Read "Meat Under Fire" again and complete the comprehension exercises. As you work, keep the reading goal in mind.

> 📖 READING GOAL: To evaluate different perspectives on an issue and take a position

Comprehension Check

A. Are the statements facts or opinions? Write *F* (fact) or *O* (opinion).

___O___ 1. Animals raised for food suffer.

_____ 2. There is a connection between eating lots of red meat and getting heart disease.

_____ 3. Raising cattle for food is an inefficient use of land.

_____ 4. Land used to grow plants can produce more food than land used to raise animals.

_____ 5. To make new space for raising cattle, forests must be cut down.

_____ 6. Methane gas contributes to global warming.

_____ 7. Throughout history people have eaten meat.

_____ 8. Cave paintings showing ancient people celebrating hunting animals are beautiful.

_____ 9. Free-range chickens eat a healthy, natural diet.

_____ 10. Someday we will prefer animal-free meat products.

_____ 11. It is good manners to provide meat-free dishes at parties.

_____ 12. If people stop eating meat, the planet's environmental problems will be solved.

B. Work with a partner. Compare your answers from Exercise A. Underline the places in the text where you find the answer to each question.

C. Complete the chart on the next page with information from the reading. Then add your own opinion in the third column.

Argument/Problem	Solution	Your opinion
1. In the meat industry, animals are not treated humanely.	*Raise animals humanely. Consumers can choose to pay more.*	
2. Meat contributes to disease.	*Eat less meat.*	
3. Raising cattle for meat is an inefficient use of land, water, and fossil fuels.		
4. Meat consumption contributes to global warming.		

D. Write a short paragraph summarizing the opinions in the article. What do you agree with? What do you disagree with? Explain.

_____

_____

_____

_____

_____

_____

_____

▶ DISCUSS

Work in groups of four. One of you will be the talk show host. Three of you will be guests, each choosing and playing the role of one of the guests in the list. (One of the guest roles will not be chosen.) The person who is the talk show host should ask the guests questions related to the reading (e.g., "How do you feel when you see someone eating meat?")

Guests: chicken farmer, vegetarian, environmentalist, chef

DISCUSS
A variety of activities for small group or pair work encourages students to use vocabulary from the current unit as well as previous units.

VOCABULARY SKILL BUILDING

This section offers presentation and practice with skills such as identifying parts of speech, learning and using derived forms of target words, learning common affixes and roots, and recognizing common collocations, among others.

LEARN THE VOCABULARY

This final section of each unit challenges students to practice strategies and techniques outlined by Paul Nation that will help them to acquire not only the target vocabulary but also vocabulary beyond the text. Activities include learning from word cards, guessing meaning from context, discovering core meaning, using a dictionary, and learning word parts, among others.

▶ VOCABULARY SKILL BUILDING

Vocabulary Skill: The Prefixes anti-, de-, and re-

A prefix is a word part that is added to the beginning of some words. Prefixes change the meaning of a word but not the form.

- *Anti-* means against. It can be added to nouns and adjectives.
- *De-* shows that something is the opposite, taken away, or made smaller. It can be added to verbs.
- *Re-* means to do again in a better way or to bring something back to the way it was before.

EXAMPLE	MEANING
antibacterial	something that fights against/kills harmful bacteria
defrost	to warm something so that it is no longer frozen
restock	to bring in more supplies to replace those that have been used

A. Write the letter of the correct definition next to the word. Be careful. There are four extra definitions.

_____ 1. reheat
_____ 2. anti-meat
_____ 3. debone
_____ 4. redo
_____ 5. antiwar
_____ 6. reshape
_____ 7. reopen
_____ 8. restart
_____ 9. devalue
_____ 10. debug

a. to remove a problem from a system
b. to stop a project before it is complete
c. to form, shape, or organize again or in a different way
d. to make a meal or drink hot again
e. to remove the shape from something
f. to do something again
g. to begin something, such as a project or machine, again
h. to kill bugs
i. to remove the heat from something
j. to open something a second time after it has been closed
k. to be against war
l. to take the bones out of a fish or a piece of meat
m. to be against eating meat
n. to change something so that it is not worth as much

Learn the Vocabulary

Strategy

Using Word Cards: Changing Order and Grouping

You can change the order of your word cards. If you always study the words in the same order, it will be hard to remember each word on its own. You should change the order of your cards every time you study them.

You can also group them in many different ways. For example, you can make two groups of cards, one for words that you remember easily and the other for words that you often forget. Then you can review the words you forget more often than the other words. A third way to group cards is to select the words that you will need for your daily life and put those in a special group to study.

A. Make cards for the words from Chapters 19 and 20 that were new to you when you started the unit. Include target words and words that you wrote on page 236.

B. Review your new cards one time with a partner. As your partner quizzes you, he or she will put your cards into two groups: one group for the words you remembered and one group for the words you didn't remember. Review the words you didn't remember a second time.

C. Add your cards from Units 1–9 to the new cards. Now look through all your cards. Choose twenty to thirty words that you think are the most useful for you in real life. For the next three days, review these words twice a day. Review the second group of cards (the remaining words) once a day. Remember to change the order of the cards in each group before you review them. Each time you review your cards, make a check (✓) in the chart.

Day one	Day two	Day three
Group 1: _____ / _____	Group 1: _____ / _____	Group 1: _____ / _____
Group 2: _____	Group 2: _____	Group 2: _____

D. After three days, put the two groups back together, change the order, and review all of the cards with your partner in class. How many words did you remember this time?

E. Go back to the vocabulary list at the beginning of each chapter. What did you learn about the target words? Add your numbers to the lists.

Vocabulary Practice 10, see page 246.

THE *REAL READING* UNIT (continued)

FLUENCY PRACTICE

Four fluency practice sections address learners' extensive reading needs. Learners practice fluency strategies, read passages, check comprehension, and calculate their reading times. Fluency progress charts are provided at the back of the book for students to record their reading times and Comprehension Check scores.

VOCABULARY PRACTICE

These pages appear at the back of the book and reinforce understanding of the target vocabulary, vocabulary skills, and vocabulary learning strategies.

FLUENCY PRACTICE 4

Fluency Strategy

To become a more fluent reader, you need to read materials in English as frequently as possible, ideally every day. The material should be very easy for you, but you need to read extensively. Choose longer readings over short ones. Ask your teacher to help you find readings that are at the appropriate level of difficulty. Guided readers—simplified versions of classic novels—are a good place to start. There are also many magazines, websites, and newspapers with an appropriate reading level for fluency practice. Set yourself a goal of a certain number of pages every week. For example, you can start by reading fifty pages a week. Then increase the number of pages by ten pages every week, so that in the second week you are reading sixty pages, seventy in the third week, and so on.

▶ READING 1

Before You Read

Preview "A Cleaner Way to Shop?" on the next page. Then circle the letter of the correct answer to each question.

FLUENCY PRACTICE 4

	Words per Minute	
	First Try	**Second Try**
Reading 1		
Reading 2		
Comprehension Check Score _____%		

VOCABULARY PRACTICE 3

THINK ABOUT MEANING

Look at each group of words. Cross out the one word in each group that does not belong.

1. helpless	weak	vulnerable	kind
2. writhe	shake	sing	twist
3. jerk	move	twitch	sit
4. moan	groan	purchase	sigh
5. authoritative	wonderful	powerful	strong
6. proceed	continue	take	go
7. remedy	solve	fix	expect
8. wail	cry	chew	scream
9. grief	sorrow	excitement	sadness
10. steady	balance	adjust	sell

PRACTICE A SKILL: Understanding Phrasal Verbs

Circle the word or phrase that correctly completes each sentence.

1. A child / chair can straighten up.
2. A student tries to figure out problems / skills.
3. A passenger can whip out a ticket / suitcase.
4. People sometimes lose track of their phones /services.
5. It is difficult for a child to cut down on sweets / trees.
6. You need to bend down to pick up a rock / see a sunset.
7. A good student does not settle for a bad grade /a lot of homework.
8. The losers in a race usually give up hope / problems early on.
9. When their children act up, parents are usually happy /upset.
10. Students get tired of studying /getting good grades.

PRACTICE A SRATEGY: Guessing Meaning from Context

Review the phrasal verbs you studied in this unit. Type each phrasal verb into a search engine to find example sentences. Write the sentences on your word cards. Think about what the phrasal verb means in the sentences.

Vocabulary Practice 3   239

REAL READING COMPONENTS

- **MP3 Audio CD-ROM:** Each level has a bound-in MP3 Audio CD-ROM with recordings of all target vocabulary and readings.

- **Teacher's Manual:** The online Teacher's Manual provides a model lesson plan and includes the Student Book Answer Key. The Teacher's Manual is available at www.pearsonlongman.com/realreading.

- **Tests:** The Online Tests consist of a reading passage followed by comprehension, vocabulary, and vocabulary skill questions for each unit. An answer key is included. The Tests are available at www.pearsonlongman.com/realreading.

HOW TO USE THE LESSON PLAN

Overview of Unit Format

Each unit of Real Reading 1 consists of two thematically related chapters. Compelling readings in a variety of genres have been carefully written or adapted from authentic sources and feature a principled approach to vocabulary development.

- Chapters consist of pre-reading and post-reading activities, including a reading skill, a reading goal, comprehension questions, and discussion activities.
- Reading and vocabulary skill building and vocabulary learning strategies based on Paul Nation's research help students become more confident and successful in preparation for academic reading and reading on standardized tests.

Suggested Methods of Instruction

This lesson plan can serve as a generic guide for any chapter in the student book.

- Suggested methods for delivering instruction for each section or activity in a chapter are presented.
- Alternative ways to handle each activity are provided under the heading *Variations*. These options allow instructors to vary the way they treat the same activity from chapter to chapter and in so doing to identify the methods that work best for a specific class or individual students.

Think Before You Read

The activities in this section are designed to prepare students for the topics, themes, and key vocabulary in the readings.

A. and B. *(approximately 10 minutes)*

1. Give students a few minutes to read the discussion questions. Answer any questions.
2. Have students form pairs to discuss their answers. Tell them they will report at least one of their answers to the class.

After 10 minutes, ask several students to share their answers.

Variations

- After students have discussed the questions, ask them to write for 1–3 minutes in answer to the questions. Have students exchange their writing with a partner or group member and compare their ideas.
- Ask students to answer the discussion questions in writing at home. Have them read their partner's or group members' answers in class and discuss their answers.
- Assign one discussion question per pair or small group. Have each pair or group discuss the question and report their ideas to the class.
- Choose one discussion question and have each student do a one-minute freewrite to expand ideas generated from the discussion. The students' writing can be passed around the class or reviewed in small groups to encourage further feedback and discussion. The activity may also serve as a closure to the discussion.

Real Reading Teacher's Guide 1

NAME: _____ DATE: _____ SCORE _____ /40

UNIT 1
TEST

Synchronized Swimming

It's part swimming, part gymnastics, and part dance. It's synchronized swimming, one of the more unusual sports in the Olympic Games. Many people love to watch it. The swimmers move their bodies in and out, forward and back, on the surface and under water. They move in perfect time with each other and the music.

Synchronized swimming was first called "water ballet." It's easy to see why. It's like ballet. And like ballet, it seems easy, but it isn't. The swimmers seem natural and relaxed, but they have to train for a long time. Many exercises are done under water, so they have to hold their breath for as long as two minutes. It takes a lot of strength, power, and energy.

Synchronized swimming first began in Europe in the 1890s. At that time, swimmers often trained outside, in rivers or in lakes. The first synchronized swimmers were men. But by the middle of the 20th century, most synchronized swimmers were women. Swimmers sometimes performed in the theater, where they swam in large water tanks on the stage! Later, some Hollywood musicals used synchronized swimmers. The actress Esther Williams starred in movies such as *Bathing Beauty* in 1944 and *Million Dollar Mermaid* in 1952.

Synchronized swimming became an Olympic sport in 1984. In the Olympic Games, swimmers work in teams of nine athletes, or in pairs. They show their skills by doing special movements above and below the water. They do not touch the bottom of the pool. Instead, they move their hands like flippers and kick their feet. This helps them stay up in the water. Like all Olympic athletes, they work very hard. Their dream is the same: to win a medal for their country in the Olympic Games.

Part 1
Comprehension
Circle the letter of the correct answer to complete each sentence.

1. In the Olympics, synchronized swimming is done _____.
   a. on land   b. to music   c. by one person

2. According to the article, synchronized swimming looks _____.
   a. easy   b. difficult   c. dangerous

3. Swimmers have to hold their breath because they need to _____.
   a. be underwater b. train outside   c. swim on the surface

4. Synchronized swimming was first done by _____.
   a. children   b. men   c. women

5. In the early part of the twentieth century, people watched synchronized swimming _____.
   a. in the Olympics   b. in the theater   c. at the beach

6. In the Olympics, the swimmers cannot _____.
   a. kick their feet b. move their hands   c. touch the bottom

Total: _____ / 6

2   *Real Reading Tests*

SCOPE AND SEQUENCE

Vocabulary Skill	Vocabulary Strategy
Nouns, Verbs, Adjectives, and Adverbs	Making Word Cards
Similes vs. Metaphors	Finding the Core Meaning of Words
Phrasal Verbs	Learning Phrasal Verbs Through Example Sentences
Nouns as Adjectives and Verbs	Guessing Meaning from Context
Numerical Prefixes	Using Word Cards: Different Types of Cards for Different Types of Learning
The Prefixes *anti-*, *de-*, and *re-*	Choosing Which Words to Study

SCOPE AND SEQUENCE

Vocabulary Skill	Vocabulary Strategy
The Prefixes *inter-* and *extra-*	Using Word Cards: Adding Pictures to Examples Sentences
Roots	Using Word Parts to Guess Meaning
Onomatopoeia	The Keyword Technique
Collocations	Using Word Cards: Changing Order and Grouping
The Prefix *multi-*	Using Different Learning Styles
Expressions	Using an Online Concordancer to Learn More about Idioms and Expressions

References

ABC News. (2010). *Earth 2100: The Final Century of Civilization?* Retrieved September 1, 2009, from http://abcnews.go.com/Technology/Earth2100/story?id=7697237&page=1

Advocacy for Animals. (2009). *The return of the mountain lion.* In *Encyclopedia Britannica.* Retrieved August 7, 2009 from http://advocacy.britannica.com/blog/advocacy/2009/05/the-return-of-the-mountain-lion-the-wild-confronts-the-tame/

Buettner, D. (2008). *Blue zones: lessons for living longer from the people who've lived the longest.* National Geographic Books.

Chester, Tom. *Mountain lion attacks on people in the U.S. and Canada.* (2006). Retrieved August 7, 2009, from http://tchester.org/sgm/lists/lion_attacks.html

Jot House (2010). *Jot House: About.* Retrieved August 2, 2009, from http://www.jothouse.com/#model02

Microsoft. (2010). *2007 Microsoft Office system pricing and upgrade information.* Retrieved September 18, 2009, from: http://office.microsoft.com/en-us/products/FX101754511033.aspx

NASA Ames Research Center. (2010, May 9). *NASA, Kepler: About.* Retrieved July 25, 2009, from http://kepler.nasa.gov/about/

National Air Traffic Controllers Association. (2010). *Air traffic controller profiles.* Retrieved September 17, 2009, from http://www.natca.org/about/controllerprofilesmain.msp

Pilot Medical Solutions. (2008). *FAA medical certifications / allergy and cold medications.* Retrieved September 18, 2009, from http://www.leftseat.com/coldmeds.htm

Pimentel, David. (1994). *Food, land, population, and the U.S. economy,* Mario Giampietro Istituto of Nazionale della Nutrizione, Rome. Retrieved September 2, 2009, from http://dieoff.org/page40.htm

Prasso, Sheridan. Saving the world with a cup of yogurt. (January 29, 2007). *Fortune.* Retrieved September 18, 2009, from http://www.sheridanprasso.com/fortune_yunus_yogurt.htm

Rose, Charlie. *A conversation with architect Sarah Susanka.* (1999, March 29). Retrieved July 30, 2009,from charlierose.com: http://www.charlierose.com/view/interview/4371

References

Sacks, O. (2007). *Musicophilia: tales of music and the brain.* Canada: Alfred A. Knopf.

Shafter, Jay. (2010). *Tumbleweed tiny house company.* Retrieved August 2, 2009 from http://www.tumbleweedhouses.com/

TED. (June 2008). *Adam Grosser and his sustainable fridge.* Ted Conferences LLC. Retrieved September 20, 2009, from http://www.ted.com/talks/adam_grosser_and_his_sustainable_fridge.html

The United Nations. (2003). *World population in 2030.* New York: Retrieved September 1, 2009, from http://www.un.org/esa/population/publications/longrange2/Long_range_report.pdf

U.S. Energy Information Administration. (July 2008). *Annual oil market chronology.* Retrieved September 2, 2009, from http://www.eia.doe.gov/emeu/cabs/AOMC/Overview.html

U.S. Geological Survey. (December 2007). *Energy and minerals for America's future.* Retrieved September 2, 2009, from http://pubs.usgs.gov/fs/2007/3109/fs2007-3109.pdf

Womack, Brian. Google to challenge Microsoft with operating system. (May 10, 2009). *Bloomberg News.*Retrieved September 18, 2009, from http://www.bloomberg.com/apps/news?pid= 20601087&sid=aTd2k.YdQZ.Y

Photo Credits

Page 1 (left) Shutterstock.com, (middle) Shutterstock.com, (right) Shutterstock.com; **p. 12** (left) Shutterstock.com, (right) Tetra Images/Corbis; **p. 37** Copyright 2010 photolibrary.com; **p. 60** (top left) Shutterstock.com, (middle left) Shutterstock.com, (middle right) Shutterstock.com, (right) Shutterstock.com; **p. 62** Radius Images/ Corbis; **p. 66** Michele Falzone/Alamy; **p. 68** iStockphoto.com; **p. 78** (left) Shutterstock.com, (middle left) Shutterstock.com, (middle right) Blend Images/ Alamy, (right) Shutterstock.com; **p. 79** Dreamstime.com; **p. 85** Shutterstock.com; **p. 96** (left) Shutterstock.com, (right) Shutterstock.com; **p. 97** Copyright 2010 photolibrary.com; **p. 104** Shutterstock.com; **p. 122** Shutterstock.com; **p. 123** (left) Steve Bly/Alamy, (right) Shutterstock.com; **p. 129** Shutterstock.com; **p. 132** Shutterstock.com; **p. 138** Shutterstock.com; **p. 139** (left) Wenn/Newscom, (right) Wenn/Newscom; **p. 140** Shutterstock.com; **p. 146** Mike Clarke/AFP/Getty Images; **p. 156** Shutterstock.com; **p. 157** Shutterstock.com; **p. 163** (right) National Maritime Museum, Greenwich, London; **p. 188** Wenn/Newscom; **p. 195** Edward Bock/Corbis; **p. 196** Michael Dwyer/Alamy; **p. 202** Shutterstock.com; **p. 212** (left) Photos.com, (right) Dreamstime.com; **p. 213** Andres Stapff/Reuters/Corbis; **p. 220** MCT/Newscom.

Text Credits

The Science of Sound

> THINK BEFORE YOU READ

A. Work with a partner. Look at the pictures. Ask and answer the questions. If you don't know a word in English, ask your partner or look in your dictionary. Then write your new words on page 235.

1. What do you see in the pictures? Describe the details.

2. What type of music do you think each person is listening to?

3. What types of music do you like? Which types do you not like?

B. Ask other students in your class the questions in the chart. For each question, find one person who answers *yes*.

Question	Name of student who answers *yes*
Do you listen to music while you drive or take public transportation?	
Do you listen to music while you study?	
Can you play a musical instrument?	
Do you listen to music in English?	

Earworms

> PREPARE TO READ

A. Look at the words (and phrases) in the list. Write the number(s) next to each word to show what you know. You may be able to write more than one number next to some of the words. You will study all of these words in this chapter.

1. I can use the word in a sentence.

2. I know <u>one meaning</u> of the word.

3. I know <u>more than one meaning</u> of the word.

4. I know how to pronounce the word.

B. Work with a partner. Look at the pictures. Ask and answer the questions. If you don't know a word in English, ask your partner or look in your dictionary. Then write your new words on page 235.

1. What do you see in the pictures? Describe the details.

2. What problem does the man have? How is he feeling?

3. Have you ever had this problem? Explain.

_____ catchy

_____ consciousness

_____ device

_____ familiar

_____ function

_____ get rid of

_____ hum

_____ infect

_____ invade

_____ itch

_____ phenomenon

_____ subjected

_____ susceptible

_____ tune

Reading Skill: Understanding Basic Text Organization

Many texts in English are organized in a predictable way. If you understand this basic organization, you will be able to find the most important information quickly in many different kinds of texts.

- **The Hook**
  Many texts begin with a hook. A hook attracts your attention and makes you want to keep reading. The hook could be one or two sentences or a whole paragraph. Often the hook is an interesting story about a real person or event or a surprising fact.

- **The General Topic and Main Idea**
  After the hook, the writer introduces the general topic of the reading. This introduction is usually in the first or second paragraph of the reading, depending on how long the hook is. At the end of the introduction, the writer often gives the main idea of the text. Sometimes the main idea is more than one sentence.

- **The Main Points that Support the Main Idea**
  Each main point is developed in one or more paragraphs after the introduction. Some main points are developed in one paragraph. Other main points are more complex and require two or more paragraphs.

- **Supporting Examples and Details**
  Examples and details reinforce the main ideas. They make the writing more convincing and more interesting.

- **The Conclusion**
  The conclusion brings together all of the information and ends the text smoothly. The conclusion is usually one or two paragraphs. In the conclusion, the author might restate the main idea, give a suggestion, or make a prediction.

C. Read the first three paragraphs of the textbook reading "Earworms." Answer the questions.

1. What type of hook does the reading contain?
   a. an historical background of the subject
   b. a surprising fact
   c. information about a real person

2. What is the general topic of the reading?
   a. annoying portable audio devices
   b. earworms
   c. psychology

3. What is the main idea of the text?
   a. Portable audio devices have changed how we listen to music.
   b. There are explanations for why earworms occur.
   c. Psychological problems can be passed from person to person.

➤ READ

Read "Earworms." Decide if the conclusion restates the main idea, gives a suggestion, or makes a prediction.

❧ Earworms ☙

1   In 1882, the American writer Mark Twain published a short story about an annoying jingle[1] that kept repeating itself in his mind. In the story, Twain is able to **get rid of** the **tune** by passing it on to someone else. However, today, this **phenomenon** of music stuck in the head is quite common and affects up to 99
5   percent of the population. Researchers are just beginning to identify the reasons these catchy tunes, also known as *earworms,* have become so common.

But first, a little background: What exactly is an earworm? An earworm begins when a person hears a tune—on the radio, on an iPod®, on television, in a movie. Later a piece of the song returns to the person's mind and begins repeating itself.
10   This earworm may stay with the person for days, starting at odd times when the mind is at rest. It may also appear when the person has an experience that he or she associates with the song. For example, a person might hear a tune while watching an exciting basketball game. Later, while the person is playing basketball, the tune might return as an earworm. Earworms can also **infect** other
15   people. If a person with the earworm starts **humming** the tune, people nearby who are also **familiar** with the tune can catch the earworm.

Neurologist[2] and author Oliver Sacks suggests that earworms may be a product of modern life. Sacks notes that these days, people listen to portable[3] audio **devices** when they are driving, exercising, or doing homework. Even without
20   earbuds,[4] people are **subjected** to tunes on telephones, in elevators, and in offices, so it shouldn't be surprising that this supposedly harmless background noise attaches itself to their brains. The likelihood that an earworm will infect a person is greater today simply because there are more tunes out there than in the past.

In fact, earworms have become so frequent that the study of this phenomenon
25   has now become a topic of academic research. According to James Kellaris, a consumer psychologist at the University of Cincinnati, an earworm is a sort of brain **itch**. He says that tunes, especially if they are **catchy** or repetitive, can affect the brain in the same way that histamines[5] create an itch in the body. The brain repeats the tune as a way of scratching the itch. For some people, this
30   can last a few hours, but for others, it may go on for days. Kellaris recommends listening to a song all the way through to help make the song go away. If that doesn't work, however, he suggests that the person be patient and wait for the earworm to go away on its own, as most itches eventually do.

---

[1] **jingle:** a short song used in advertisements

[2] **neurologist:** a person who studies the nervous system and its diseases

[3] **portable:** carried or moved easily

[4] **earbuds:** small earphones inserted into the ears

[5] **histamines:** chemical compounds that increase the flow of blood in your body and are involved in allergic reactions

Why does the brain itch? It seems that music has a powerful effect on the human **consciousness**. Sad music causes people to cry, while relaxing music relieves stress. Music written for scary movies creates fear, and dance music gets people up and moving. Studies show that loud and fast music even causes people to drive faster. These psychological and behavioral effects speak to the deep associations that humans have with musical sounds.

The power of music has not gone unnoticed by the advertising industry, and it is partly responsible for the creation of earworms as well. Since the early days of radio, jingle writers have studied ways to make songs stick. Music that is catchy or repetitive has a greater chance of staying in the mind. And when an effective jingle reappears in the mind as an earworm, the brain replays not only the tune but also the words and products that the jingle-writer is trying to sell. In fact, Petr Janata, a cognitive neuroscientist who has studied music and the brain, says that music can **function** like a movie soundtrack.[6] As this soundtrack plays, it creates a sort of "mental movie" in the mind. Such findings might suggest that earworms can help advertisers by reminding the consumer of their product. However, whether or not advertisers' jingles will be effective is difficult to say. Already, some people have raised protests. In one Michigan neighborhood, residents requested that an ice cream truck not play its catchy tune when it drove through their neighborhood. They did not like the way the song continued in their minds even after the truck had left their neighborhood.

A final factor in earworms is the individual: Some people are more likely to get them than others. Kellaris says that musicians tend to be more **susceptible** to earworms, perhaps because of their sensitivity to music. Women are also more susceptible than men. However, different brains have different responses, so it is not possible to predict which tunes will become earworms for which people.

With these recent scientific findings, more and more people are becoming aware of earworms and the ways that they can be used to influence memory. As researchers in science and industry begin to explain what causes them and how they work, advertisers and musicians will use this knowledge to make their tunes stand out in an increasingly noisy environment. It is entirely possible that some day consumers will need to defend themselves against music that seems to **invade** private mental space.

---

[6] **soundtrack:** the recorded music from a movie

Vocabulary Check

A. Circle the letter of the correct answer to complete each sentence.

1. When you pass your cold on to your friends, you _____ them.
   a. get rid of　　　**b.** invade　　　**c.** infect

2. A "smart phone" _____ as a phone and as a mini-computer.
   a. infects　　　**b.** functions　　　**c.** hums

3. Every summer, tourists _____ the beach town, and it becomes too crowded.
   a. invade　　　**b.** infect　　　**c.** get rid of

4. Our new apartment was very small, so we _____ our extra sofa.
   a. subjected　　　**b.** got rid of　　　**c.** infected

5. My classmate looked _____. I knew that I had seen her before.
   a. susceptible　　　**b.** catchy　　　**c.** familiar

6. You will be _____ to colds if you don't exercise regularly.
   a. catchy　　　**b.** familiar　　　**c.** susceptible

7. A lot of commercials play a familiar _____ so that you remember them.
   a. device　　　**b.** phenomenon　　　**c.** tune

B. Circle the letter of the correct answer to complete each sentence. The boldfaced words are the target words.

1. I had an **itch** on my face, and I wanted to _____ it.
   a. scratch　　　**b.** hide　　　**c.** put ice on

2. One **device** many students use is a(n) _____.
   a. uniform　　　**b.** tutor　　　**c.** laptop

3. We were **subjected** to a _____.
   a. wonderful meal　　　**b.** long, boring speech　　　**c.** new idea

4. Tunes stick in the mind because they are **catchy** or _____.
   a. repetitive　　　**b.** hard to perform　　　**c.** advertisements

5. An example of a natural **phenomenon** is a(n) _____.
   a. storm　　　**b.** painting　　　**c.** engineer

6. I do not know the words, but I can **hum** the _____.
   a. message　　　**b.** tune　　　**c.** article

7. The book changed my political **consciousness**, or my _____.
   a. awareness　　　**b.** phenomenon　　　**c.** effect

► READ AGAIN

Read "Earworms" again and complete the comprehension exercises. As you work, keep the reading goal in mind.

📖 **READING GOAL:** To understand basic text organization

Comprehension Check

A. Read the statements about the reading. Write *T* (true) or *F* (false). If it is not possible to tell, write *?*.

_____ 1. Earworms are not very common in the modern world.

_____ 2. An earworm is always an entire song.

_____ 3. If you listen to a song during an important life experience, that song is more likely to become an earworm.

_____ 4. Our friends can pass their earworms on to us.

_____ 5. Oliver Sacks believes that people can stop earworms by listening to more music.

_____ 6. James Kellaris believes that the brain reacts to earworms in a way that is similar to the body reacting to a mosquito bite.

_____ 7. Scientists have found a way to make earworms disappear.

_____ 8. Music affects the mind but not behavior.

_____ 9. Listening to music while studying can help people do better on tests.

_____ 10. More men get earworms than women.

_____ 11. Learning how earworms work is important to the advertising industry.

B. Put the main ideas from the reading into the correct sequence. Write *1* next to the first idea, *2* next to the second, and so on.

_____ a. a brain-based explanation of why earworms occur

_____ b. a definition of an earworm

_____ c. a sociological explanation of why earworms occur more frequently now

_____ d. an explanation of how advertisers use knowledge of earworms

C. Complete the graphic organizer of the reading. Use your answers from Exercise B to help you.

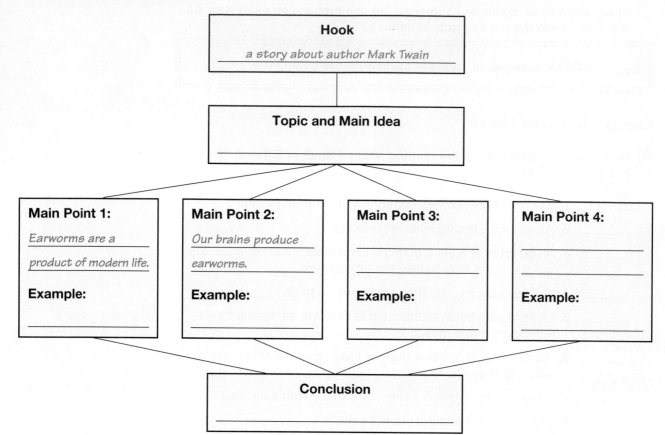

Hook

a story about author Mark Twain

Topic and Main Idea

Main Point 1:

Earworms are a
product of modern life.

Example:

Main Point 2:

Our brains produce
earworms.

Example:

Main Point 3:

Example:

Main Point 4:

Example:

Conclusion

D. Work with a partner. Compare your graphic organizers.

> DISCUSS

Work with a partner. Decide who is A and B. Then role-play.

A: You are suffering from an earworm. Explain your problem and how you

are feeling to B.

B: Listen to A's explanation. Then offer some advice based on the reading

and your own personal experience with earworms.

> VOCABULARY SKILL BUILDING

Vocabulary Skill: Nouns, Verbs, Adjectives, and Adverbs

To use a word correctly, you need to know its part of speech. *Nouns, verbs, adjectives,* and *adverbs* are the most common parts of speech in English.

Nouns are words for people, places, things, and ideas. The word *neurologist* is a noun.

Verbs show actions, experiences, or states of being. The words *listen* and *discuss* are verbs.

Adjectives describe nouns. The words *catchy* and *worried* are adjectives. Sometimes a noun is used as an adjective, as in *A song from a <u>car</u> commercial is driving me crazy.*

Adverbs describe verbs, adjectives, or an entire sentence. Adverbs are often formed by adding *-ly* to an adjective. Their placement in a sentence depends on what they are modifying. When they modify an entire sentence, they often appear at the beginning, as in <u>*Surprisingly*</u>*, she didn't get angry.*

Word Families

Many words in English belong to word families. In one word family, there can be several forms of a word. Words in the same word family often have the same base, or main part, but different endings, called *suffixes*. The suffix often changes the part of speech (noun, verb, adjective, adverb), but it usually does not change the core meaning of the word.

EXAMPLE:

music (noun)   *musical* (adjective)   *musically* (adverb)

Some words have the same form although they are different parts of speech.

EXAMPLE:

Red (noun) is my favorite color.

I like *red* (adjective) shoes.

The chart contains word families for words from the unit. Complete each sentence by choosing the correct form of the word in the row with the number that matches the number of the sentence.

Verb	Noun	Adjective	Adverb
1. annoy	annoyance	annoying	annoyingly
2.	brain	brainy	
3. distance	distance	distant	distantly
4.	expert expertise	expert	expertly
5. function	function	functional	functionally
6. hire	hire		
7. infect	infection	infectious	infectiously
8. itch	itch	itchy	
9.	music musician musical	musical	musically
10.	phenomenon phenomena (pl.)	phenomenal	phenomenally
11. repeat	repetition	repetitious	repeatedly
12. silence	silence	silent	silently

1. The noise coming from that machine is a terrible _____.

2. She always gets straight As in school. She is so _____.

3. We usually _____ ourselves from people we do not like.

4. Oliver Sacks has plenty of _____ when it comes to understanding music and the brain.

5. This computer is not fully _____. It still has problems with the sound.

6. The boss says that the new _____ is working very hard.

7. The "Numa Numa" song is the most _____ song I've ever heard. I can't stop humming it.

8. My ear is starting to _____. Maybe those headphones are irritating it.

9. My brother loved piano lessons as a child, and today he is a

_____.

10. He's a _____ singer. You must go hear him perform.

11. He has _____ been caught cheating. This is not the first time.

12. We need to _____ that dog. It has been barking all night.

How We Use Sound

▷ PREPARE TO READ

A. Look at the words in the list. Write the number(s) next to each word to show what you know. You may be able to write more than one number next to some of the words. You will study all of these words in this chapter.

1. I can use the word in a sentence.

2. I know <u>one meaning</u> of the word.

3. I know <u>more than one meaning</u> of the word.

4. I know how to pronounce the word.

B. Work with a partner. Look at the pictures. Ask and answer the questions. If you don't know a word in English, ask your partner or look in your dictionary. Then write your new words on page 235.

1. What do you see in the pictures?

2. What type of sound does each object make? What is the purpose of the sound?

_____ acoustic

_____ activate

_____ beam

_____ deafening

_____ frequency

_____ high-pitched

_____ innovation

_____ lethal

_____ offensive

_____ restore

_____ temporarily

Reading Skill: Previewing and Predicting

Before you read something, first get a general idea about the topic and main idea by *previewing*. To get an idea about the topic, read the title and any headings. Look at any pictures. Once you have identified the topic, think about what you already know about it. To get a sense of the main idea, read the last sentence of the first paragraph. Then read the first sentence of every paragraph. These sentences will help you guess, or *predict*, what the reading will be about.

C. Preview the Internet article "Technology Watch." Answer the questions.

1. What is the general topic of the reading?
   a. sound technicians
   b. audio technology
   c. electronic devices

2. What is the main idea of the reading?
   a. Sound technicians are sharing their knowledge and experience.
   b. There are surprising new innovations based on sound.
   c. Electronic devices are making modern life more convenient.

> READ

Read "Technology Watch." Underline the sentences where you find the answers to the questions in Exercise C.

---

http://www.technology.spotlight.com

HOW WE USE SOUND

1 **SPOTLIGHT: AUDIO TECHNOLOGY**
For people who are interested in sound, the field of audio technology is definitely making noise. In the past, sound technicians worked
5 in the back rooms of recording studios,[1] but many of today's sound professionals are sharing their knowledge and experience with professionals in other fields to create new products. The following are just a few

10 of the surprising **innovations** based on the phenomenon we call sound.

An Invisible Fence
Audio technology has a solution for dog owners who want to keep their dog on their
15 property without building a fence. There is now a dog collar that makes a **high-pitched** sound whenever the dog wearing it tries to leave the yard. Humans can't hear the sound,

(continued on next page)

---

[1] **recording studio:** a room where television and radio programs are made and broadcast or where music is recorded

but dogs, which can hear sounds in a much
higher **frequency** range than humans, hear
it and hate it. For dogs, the area beyond the
yard becomes associated with the high-
pitched noise. As a result, the dogs quickly
learn that they have to stay in the yard to
avoid the unpleasant sound.

A Nonlethal Weapon

Sound can also be used as a weapon.
Imagine that a police officer is chasing a car
thief on the highway. The thief makes a wrong
turn and crashes into a wall and then tries to
escape on foot. The officer does not want to
shoot the thief, but he can't let him get away.
The officer pulls out a special device, points
it at the suspect, and **activates** it. The thief
drops to the ground, and the police officer is
able to catch him. Amazingly, the thief isn't
hurt because the officer hasn't used a real
gun, but rather something called a Long
Range **Acoustic** Device (LRAD). This device
produces a **deafening** sound that is so painful
that it **temporarily** disables a person. At the
same time, the officer and bystanders[2] are
not affected because unlike regular sound
that spreads in many directions, the noise
from the LRAD is directed like a **beam** of light.
This beam of sound from the LRAD travels
only into the ears of the targeted individual.
Unfortunately, the LRAD may cause some
hearing loss, which makes it controversial,
but it is not **lethal**.

A Silence Machine

For those who are hungry for some peace and
quiet, sound can now create silence. Let's say
you are at the airport, and the little girl on the
seat next to you is humming a catchy jingle
from a breakfast cereal commercial. The girl
hums the familiar jingle over and over again,
and you are about to go out of your mind.
Thanks to the Silence Machine, an invention
by British scientist Selwyn Wright, you can get
rid of the **offensive** tune without offending the
little girl or her parents.

The Silence Machine functions by analyzing
the waves of the incoming sound and
creating a second set of outgoing waves.
The two sets of waves cancel each other out.
Simply activate the machine, point it at the
offending target, and your peace and quiet is
instantly **restored**.

A Sound Spotlight

Directed sound is a new technology that
allows companies to use sound in much the
same way spotlights are used in the theater.
A spotlight lights up only one section of a
stage; similarly, a "spotsound" creates a circle
of sound in one targeted area. This can be
useful for businesses such as restaurants
and stores because it offers a new way to
attract customers. Restaurants can offer a
choice of music along with the various food
choices on the menu, allowing customers
from business people to newly wedded
couples more control over the atmosphere in
which they are dining. Spotsound technology
is also beginning to appear in malls and even
some cars. Shoppers may soon hear voices
meant for their ears only, and drivers will be
able to listen to classical music instead of
being subjected to the loud music of their
children in the back seat.

Sound Images

In other areas, scientists are using sound
as a tool for research. Jack Kassewitz
and John Stuart Reid are using a sound
technology called *cymatics* to study the
language of dolphins. After they record the
sounds made by these ocean animals, they
use the technology to create visual images
for each sound. By analyzing the patterns,
they believe they may be able to translate
what dolphins are saying into a language that
humans can understand.

---

[2] **bystander:** someone who watches what is happening without participating

Vocabulary Check

Read the definitions. Write the boldfaced word from the reading next to the correct definition. Use the correct form of the word.

1. _____ = noise or music that is very loud

2. _____ = relating to sound and the way people hear things

3. _____ = a line of light, energy, etc., that you often cannot see

4. _____ = causing death, or able to cause death

5. _____ = the rate at which a sound wave moves up and down per second

6. _____ = continuing for only a limited period of time

7. _____ = returned to its former state or condition

8. _____ = voice or sound that is higher than usual

9. _____ = very rude or insulting and likely to upset people

10. _____ = makes something, especially an electrical system, start working

11. _____ = new ideas, methods, or inventions

> READ AGAIN

Read "Technology Watch" again and complete the comprehension exercises. As you work, keep the reading goal in mind.

> 📖 **READING GOAL:** To write a summary of the reading

Comprehension Check

A. On a separate sheet of paper, draw a simple picture of one of the technological innovations described in the reading. Include the most interesting features.

B. Work with a partner. Look at each other's drawing. Talk about the innovations you see in each drawing. Remember as many details as you can without looking back at the reading.

C. On a separate sheet of paper, make a diagram of the reading. Use the diagram on page 8 as a model. Include only the most important information: the main idea, the main points, and the most important examples and details.

D. Work with a partner. Compare your diagrams. Do they contain similar information? Did you leave out any important information? Did you include any unnecessary information? Change your diagram as needed.

E. Use the information from your diagram to write a one-paragraph summary of the reading. Do not look back at the reading.

_____

_____

_____

_____

_____

_____

_____

_____

_____

_____

❯ DISCUSS

Work in small groups. Ask and answer the questions.

1. How useful to society are the inventions in the reading? Rank them from 1 (most important to society) to 5 (least important to society). Write the numbers on the lines. Explain your opinions.

    _____ invisible fence

    _____ nonlethal weapon

    _____ silence machine

    _____ sound spotlight

    _____ sound images

2. Which of the inventions in the reading would you buy? Explain.

3. What are some other problems that have to do with noise or sound? Make a list of ideas (for example, traffic noise, hearing loss, etc.).

4. Of the problems on your list, which could be solved by a new invention? How would the invention work? Explain.

Learn the Vocabulary

acoustic (adj.)

relating to sound and the way people hear things

An _____ song is a song without electronic instruments.

A. Make cards for the words from Chapters 1 and 2 that were new to you when you started the unit. Include target words and words that you wrote on page 235. Make sure you spell the new words correctly!

B. Work with a partner. Take your partner's cards and show the back side of one of his or her cards (the side with the translation, drawing, or definition on it). You look at the front side of the card. Your partner will say and spell the word in English. If your partner makes a mistake, correct him or her. Then your partner will do the same with one of your cards. Continue until you review all of the cards.

C. Go back to the vocabulary list at the beginning of each chapter. What did you learn about the target words? Add your numbers to the lists.

Vocabulary Practice 1, see page 237.

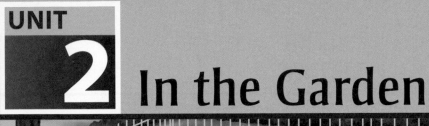

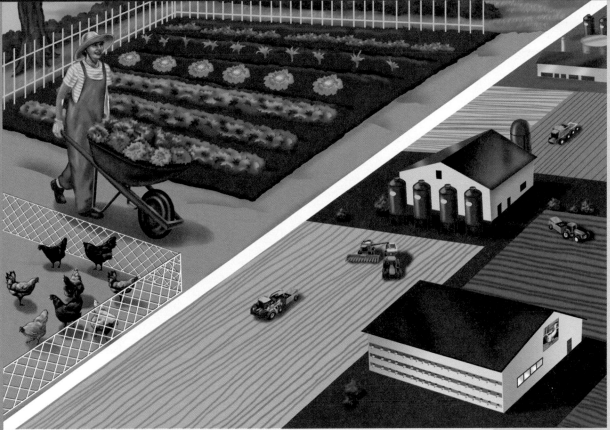

> THINK BEFORE YOU READ

A. Work with a partner. Look at the pictures. Ask and answer the questions. If you don't know a word in English, ask your partner or look in your dictionary. Then write your new words on page 235.

  1. What do you see in the pictures? Describe the details.

  2. How are the pictures different? Explain.

B. Work in small groups. Ask and answer the questions.

  1. What are the advantages and disadvantages of each type of farming?

  2. Is agriculture an important business in your home country? Explain.

  3. Would you like to have a private garden like the one in the picture? Explain.

Tokyo Farmer

> PREPARE TO READ

A. Look at the words in the list. Write the number(s) next to each word to show what you know. You may be able to write more than one number next to some of the words. You will study all of these words in this chapter.

1. I can use the word in a sentence.

2. I know <u>one meaning</u> of the word.

3. I know <u>more than one meaning</u> of the word.

4. I know how to pronounce the word.

B. Work with a partner. Look at the picture. Ask and answer the questions. If you don't know a word in English, ask your partner or look in your dictionary. Then write your new words on page 235.

1. What do you see in the picture? Describe the details.

2. What is unusual about the garden in the picture?

3. Is this a good place for a garden? Explain.

_____ affectionately

_____ bloom

_____ clamor

_____ drudgery

_____ fade

_____ self-sustaining

_____ shade

_____ story

_____ strain

_____ sway

_____ urban

_____ wander

_____ weed

C. Preview the blog "Tokyo Farmer." Answer the questions.

1. What is the topic of the reading?

   a. moving to a big city from a small farm

   b. farms located inside cities

   c. plants that can grow in a small space

2. What is the writer's point of view?

   a. positive   **b.** negative   **c.** neutral

> READ

Read "Tokyo Farmer." Underline the words and sentences that support your answers to the questions in Exercise C.

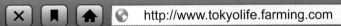

http://www.tokyolife.farming.com

Tokyo Farmer

1   I met a farmer named Kenji the other day, but he isn't a typical farmer. Kenji works at an office building in downtown Tokyo. Like most city people, he rides the subway to work and then takes an elevator to his job. However, unlike those with whom he shares an elevator, Kenji doesn't spend his day **straining** his eyes in front of a
5   computer screen. Instead, he goes up to the roof and spends his days on his knees, **affectionately** caring for a field of sweet potatoes fifty **stories** above the ground. When the sunlight **fades** into twilight, he changes his clothes and rides the elevator back down to the bright lights and **clamor** of the big city.

This is definitely not the farming job that my grandfather had. Kenji's job has some of
10   the same tasks, but his location and purpose suggest a passion for bringing farming into modern life. In my grandfather's day, the kids left the farm to get good jobs in the city, and very few ever returned. However, nowadays growing food has become more fashionable. There is a certain desire not to go back to the farm but to bring a bit of the farm to the city. In fact, most of my friends in the city grow tomato plants on windowsills

(continued on next page)

15 or balconies. Now, when people say "farmer," I think of young, cool, **urban** Kenji, a guy with a little dirt under his fingernails as well as a downtown address.

In addition to being fashionable, these rooftop farms benefit residents and the environment. The sweet potatoes across Kenji's roof garden provide food, and their broad leaves also provide **shade**, which keeps the roof cooler. People in the building
20 do not use air-conditioning as often, so less energy is needed, which in turn means the air control systems produce less heat and less pollution. It's a win-win situation.

The plants also take carbon monoxide[1] from traffic and industry and turn it into good, clean oxygen. This simple yet elegant process for cleaning the air may be a small step, but it is a step in the right direction. If rooftop farms become more popular, cities could
25 soon be covered with oxygen-producing green zones high above the noise and bustle of everyday urban life.

In addition to providing environmental benefits, rooftop farms contribute to the economy. Plants need to be fed and watered, and they need someone to pull **weeds**, so employees like Kenji are paid to help building owners set up and maintain farms on
30 their roofs as well as offer advice on what to plant. (Sweet potatoes are good because
31 they love the hot sun and don't mind the wind.)

The employment agency Pasona 2 is hoping that farming—urban or otherwise—will become a popular career option. Pasona 2 started an agricultural training program in the basement of their downtown office in Tokyo's Otemachi district. If you walked in the
35 building's front doors, you would never imagine that young people study agriculture there—not on the roof, but in the basement. Take the elevator down two floors, and you will see roses **blooming**, tomato seedlings climbing up their wire frames, and lettuces and pumpkins stretching their leaves toward lights in the ceiling. Another room has rice plants **swaying** in the breeze created by white-coated workers who **wander**
40 back and forth between the rooms, pushing buttons and adjusting the climate.

City farming also makes political sense. Japan imports 60 percent of its food, and there have been recent concerns about food safety. The possibility of producing food locally might mean greater control over food production and will certainly cut down on the cost of transporting it. Tokyo's environmentally friendly governor shares the vision
45 of a more **self-sustaining** urban agriculture. He is encouraging building owners in the capital to get rid of things they don't need on roofs, in basements, and on unused floors and to introduce urban farms in these places.

Reading about what's going on in Tokyo makes me re-evaluate life in the city. What is **drudgery** anyway? Is it pushing a wheelbarrow through mud in the hot sun? Or is it
50 sitting in a cubicle[2] staring at a computer? As a typical urbanite with a typical desk job, I get tired of sitting all day. It would be a nice break to go up on the roof and get my hands in the dirt. If my company ever decides to create a rooftop garden, I will be more than happy to volunteer a few hours of planting or weeding. I might even try a career change and get a full-time job on the roof. I like knowing that food grows nearby and
55 that farms can exist within walking distance. For years, cities have been gobbling up[3] farmland. Now the farms are returning, and that can be only a good thing.

---

[1] **carbon monoxide:** a poisonous gas

[2] **cubicle:** a small, partly enclosed part of a room in an office

[3] **gobble up:** use a supply of something quickly

Vocabulary Check

A. Complete the sentences with the boldfaced words from the reading.

1. On summer days, I like to sit and watch the sky as day
   _____fades_____ into night.

2. I'm trying to read without good light. This is _____straining_____
   my eyes.

3. The garden is full of unwanted plants. We need to spend some time
   getting the _____weeds_____ out of the flower beds this weekend.

4. My brother's house is four _____stories_____ tall, but it is very narrow,
   so it isn't as big as it sounds.

5. I get bored in the countryside. I like the bright lights and noise of a(n)
   _____urban_____ environment.

6. The farm generates energy and other materials from natural resources. It
   is completely _____self-sustaining_____.

7. She gave me a big hug and kiss when she saw me. She greeted me
   _____affectionately_____.

B. Circle the letter of the correct answer to each question. The boldfaced
words are the target words.

1. What **blooms** in the springtime?
   a. flowers   **b.** leaves   **c.** seeds

2. Who **wanders**?
   a. gardeners working   **b.** people walking   **c.** workers using computers

3. What can give **shade**?
   a. a tree   **b.** a jacket   **c.** a light

4. What makes plants **sway**?
   a. the wind   **b.** a gardener   **c.** carbon monoxide

5. What is a good example of **drudgery**?
   a. watching a movie   **b.** riding an elevator   **c.** cleaning a bathroom

6. Where would you expect to find a lot of **clamor**?
   a. in a library   **b.** at a children's birthday party   **c.** in a tree

Read "Tokyo Farmer" again and complete the comprehension exercises. As you work, keep the reading goal in mind.

> 📖 **READING GOAL:** To summarize the author's attitude about urban farms

Comprehension Check

A. What can you guess is true about the author? Check (✓) the statements.

_____ **1.** She lives in a city.

_____ **2.** She lives in Tokyo.

_____ **3.** She is a farmer.

_____ **4.** Her grandfather was a farmer.

_____ **5.** Her friends grow their own vegetables.

_____ **6.** She is a self-employed writer.

_____ **7.** She works in an office.

B. Study the sentences from the reading. Does the author have a positive or negative attitude about the boldfaced words? Write *P* (positive) or *N* (negative). Then underline the descriptive word(s) in the sentence that shows the author's attitude.

___*P*___ **1.** These days, when I say "farmer," I am just as likely to be thinking of young, <u>cool</u>, urban **Kenji** as of my grandfather.

_____ **2.** Instead, he spends his days on his knees, affectionately **caring for a field of sweet potatoes** fifty stories above the ground.

___*N*___ **3.** Kenji doesn't spend his day straining his eyes **in front of a computer screen**.

_____ **4.** His location and purpose suggest a passion for **bringing farming into modern life**.

_____ **5.** In Tokyo, **city farms** offer residents a lot of benefits.

_____ **6.** This simple yet elegant **process for cleaning the air** may be a small step, but it is a step in the right direction.

_____ **7.** Cities could soon be covered with oxygen-producing green zones high above the noise and bustle of **everyday urban life**.

_____ **8.** Tokyo's environmentally-friendly **governor** shares the vision of a more self-sustaining urban agriculture.

_____ **9.** I will be more than happy to **volunteer** a few hours of planting or weeding.

___N___ **10.** For years, **cities** have been gobbling up farmland.

C. Work with a partner. Do not look back at the reading. List the positive things the author says about urban farms. Then check your answers in the text.

_____   _____

_____   _____

_____   _____

_____   _____

D. Use the information from Exercise C to write a one-paragraph summary of the reading. Do not look back at the reading.

_____

_____

_____

_____

_____

_____

_____

_____

_____

_____

_____

> DISCUSS

Work in small groups. Design an urban garden for the roof of the building where your classroom is located. Follow the steps.

- Decide what benefits the roof garden will have.

- Decide which plants you will grow in your roof garden.

- Draw a picture of your planned roof garden.

- List a few problems you might have while building the roof garden and decide how you will solve them.

My Invisible Garden

 PREPARE TO READ

A. Look at the words (and phrases) in the list. Write the number(s) next to each word to show what you know. You may be able to write more than one number next to some of the words. You will study all of these words in this chapter.

1. I can use the word in a sentence.

2. I know <u>one meaning</u> of the word.

3. I know <u>more than one meaning</u> of the word.

4. I know how to pronounce the word.

B. Work with a partner. Ask and answer the questions. If you don't know a word in English, ask your partner or look in your dictionary. Then write your new words on page 235.

1. Where are the women in the picture? What are they doing? Describe the details.

2. What is the woman on the left thinking about? How does she feel?

3. Do you have any hobbies? Why do they interest you?

_____ affair

_____ bring up

_____ dose

_____ gorgeous

_____ in exchange for

_____ lose track of

_____ mineral

_____ profound

_____ recount

_____ rough

_____ settle for

_____ shot (a photograph)

_____ trail off

_____ transplant

_____ uncomprehendingly

Reading Skill: Understanding Figurative Language

A *figurative* word or expression is used in a different way from its usual meaning to give you a picture or idea in your mind. Note that when a word is used figuratively, its part of speech may change, as in the examples below.

EXAMPLES:

Weed used with its usual meaning (noun)

I removed the weeds from my garden. = I removed wild plants growing where they are not wanted.

Weed used figuratively (verb)

After interviewing the job applicants, the manager was able to weed some out. = After the manager interviewed the job applicants, he was able to remove some of them from consideration.

Usually there is a connection between a word's usual and figurative meanings. Using *weed* figuratively gives you the idea in your mind that something unwanted is being removed, like a plant from a garden.

C. Read the first paragraph of the essay "My Invisible Garden" on the next page. Answer the questions.

1. Which meaning of *funny* is expressed in the paragraph?

_____ **a.** amusing, making you laugh (usual meaning)

_____ **b.** strange, unusual, or difficult to explain (figurative meaning)

2. What is the connection between the usual and figurative meanings of *funny*? Write your ideas.

_____

_____

READ

Read "My Invisible Garden." As you read, think about whether words are being used in their usual way or figuratively.

ᔐ My Invisible Garden ᕀ

1   Sometimes my friend gives me a funny look when I talk about my garden. I was late for dinner one night because I'd **lost track of** the time, and I tried to explain how it is, in the garden, at twilight.[1]

    "I was mulching[2] my potatoes . . . and wondering if marsh hay[3] was too salty
5 or if all those **minerals** from the sea would be good for them. And then I realized that I still have this fear of plants, you know, because I haven't grown potatoes before . . ."

    My voice **trailed off**. The restaurant was noisy, and we were supposed to order quickly, because the kitchen was about to close. I thought of the wind blowing
10 over my potato plants. . . .

    "And guess what? My cleome[4] self-seeded."

    "I think I'll have the tortellini,"[5] my friend said.

    "They look like little hands," I . . . went on. "That's how I tell them from the weeds."

15 She smiled, affectionately, but **uncomprehendingly**. The funny look. The way I nod at new mothers, friends of mine, when they talk about their children. I know they're **recounting** something passionate, something I even want to experience, but I can't relate to the words.

    Other mothers can, just as other gardeners know what happens when you start
20 out mulching potatoes and stop to . . . notice a . . . bird with a strange marking or see, long after you had given up all hope, that the cleome is up.

    That evening for instance, as the light faded, and the tree branches grew black against the pink sky, I knew it was getting on toward dinnertime, but I felt so peaceful sitting like a child in the warm earth. It was dark as I strained my eyes,
25 searching out . . . parsley[6] seedlings among the weeds.

    I'd wandered by the parsley patch looking for my watering can, intending to give the potatoes a **dose** of sea kelp[7] . . . before going to dinner. I'd given up on the parsley, a flavorful, single-leafed Italian variety I'd direct-seeded, and figured I'd have to **settle for** buying some plants at my local nursery. All they sell is the
30 curly-leafed stuff, which doesn't taste half as sweet. But as I went by, I bent over, just for a look, and there in the twilight I spied a bit of parsley. . . .

---

[1] **twilight:** the time when day is just starting to become night

[2] **mulch:** cover the soil with old leaves to improve its quality

[3] **hay:** long grass from low-lying wetland that has been cut and dried for use in mulching

[4] **cleome:** a type of plant with flowers shaped like spiders

[5] **tortellini:** a type of ring-shaped pasta stuffed with meat or cheese

[6] **parsley:** a small plant with curly leaves with a strong taste, used in cooking or as decoration on food

[7] **kelp:** a large brown plant that grows in the ocean

I was so happy to see them, these little jokes on my lack of faith, that I had to sit right down and pull a few weeds. Give the parsley some air and light **in exchange for** coming up. And it wasn't easy, because each seedling was about as

35 big as a flea,[8] lost in weeds as thick as a . . . fur coat. So I slowed down a little, and paid attention to what my fingers had hold of—weed or parsley—and it got a little later, and a little later.

I'd always thought of weeding as such drudgery. And it was, in my father's garden. Work, pure and simple. Because it was his garden, his vision. It had

40 nothing to do with mine.

But now that I have my own garden, I realize that it exists on two planes.[9] It grows on an earthly plane, of course. . . . But it also exists, in a more **profound** way, in my mind, where it has been growing for many years now. . . . It's a garden that I carry with me like a happy secret, as I go about the clamorous world

45 outside the garden gate.

"I think I'll have the clam sauce, white," I said, closing the menu. I smiled at my friend and saw by her face that she'd had a **rough** day. But what I was really seeing, with my mind's eye, was the cleome. A sea of tall pink and white spidery blossoms, swaying on the evening breeze.

50 "So how did it go today?" I asked, thinking how, if I got up early, I'd have time to **transplant** the baby cleome.

It wasn't that I didn't care what my friend was saying; it's just that the garden, especially in summer, comes in and out of the mind like a love **affair**. The knowledge that something's waiting for me when I get home. . . .

55 There was a lull in the conversation, and I started talking about my garden again.

"You've got to see these little lettuces growing all around my broccolis. And there's this perennial[10] I don't even know the name of that somebody gave me last year, just a transplant, and now it's this wonderful huge **gorgeous** purple

60 thing . . ."

I stopped. Enough was enough.

"It's OK," my friend said. She feels the same way about trying to take the perfect picture. Her photographer's eye has a vision that reaches beyond the realities of rain or technical snags[11] or falling off a wall and missing the **shot** of a

lifetime.

65 "I like people who are passionate about things," she said. And when you're passionate about something, you often, mistakenly, try to get the other person to understand. You keep **bringing up** little details and profound events, thinking that maybe this time the person will get it, will see what you see. . . .

When my friend wanders by my garden on a perfect beach day, she sees the

70 usual state of affairs. The peas are tumbling . . . over their fence. The parsley still needs weeding. Something has completely eaten the carrots. That gorgeous purple perennial has stopped blooming. And there I am, a mess. Sweaty and dirty, pushing a wheelbarrow back and forth.

---

[8] **flea:** a very small insect without wings that jumps and bites animals and people to eat their blood

[9] **plane:** a level of thought

[10] **perennial:** a plant that lives for more than two years

[11] **snag:** a disadvantage or problem that is not very serious

Vocabulary Check

A. Circle the letter of the correct answer to complete each sentence. The boldfaced words are the target words.

1. When someone looks at you **uncomprehendingly**, he or she probably _____.

   a. disagrees
   b. does not understand
   c. likes you

2. You are most likely to **lose track of** the time when you are _____.

   a. bored
   b. late for something
   c. interested in your work

3. He keeps **bringing up** the possibility of growing our own food because he _____.

   a. needs work
   b. wants to discuss the idea
   c. wants to avoid the idea

4. The tree looked **gorgeous** after _____.

   a. the fire damaged it
   b. the leaves turned orange
   c. we cut it down

5. When her voice **trailed off**, I knew that she was _____.

   a. thinking about something else
   b. trying to make me understand
   c. starting to get excited

6. I hoped to buy my neighbor's farm and expand, but I **settled for** _____.

   a. a bigger farm
   b. a smaller farm
   c. the job that I really wanted

7. My cousin **recounted** the story of the wild cat in the yard because _____.

   a. we had not heard it yet
   b. she had not told it before
   c. it was a secret

8. I offered to work in the garden **in exchange for** _____.

   a. Saturday
   b. the chance to be outside
   c. some of the vegetables

9. When someone says she is having a love **affair** with her garden, it means she _____.

   a. is passionate about gardening
   b. loves a gardener
   c. meets her true love in a garden

10. Some **minerals** are good for plants because they _____.

    a. have beautiful flowers
    b. help them to grow
    c. keep birds away

B. Read the definitions. Write the boldfaced word from the reading next to the correct definition.

1. _____ = a measured amount of a medicine

2. _____ = important and having a strong influence or effect

3. _____ = difficult, or not fair or kind

4. _____ = a photograph of a particular thing

5. _____ = to move a plant from one place and plant it in another

▷ READ AGAIN

Read "My Invisible Garden" again and complete the comprehension exercises. As you work, keep the reading goal in mind.

> 📖 **READING GOAL:** To identify the figurative uses of language

Comprehension Check

A. Study the descriptions of the plants in the reading. Then find each plant in the picture of the author's garden. Write the letter of the plant next to its correct name.

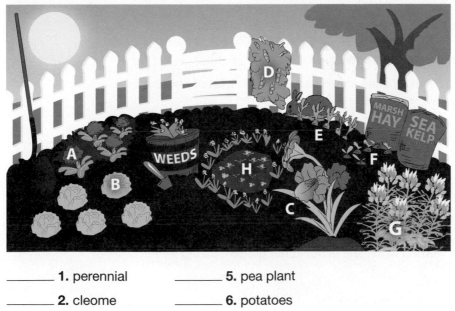

_____ **1.** perennial   _____ **5.** pea plant

_____ **2.** cleome   _____ **6.** potatoes

_____ **3.** parsley   _____ **7.** lettuces

_____ **4.** broccoli   _____ **8.** carrots

B. Work with a partner. Compare your answers from Exercise A. Underline the details in the reading that help you identify each plant in the picture.

C. Look at the sentences from the reading. Write *U* next to the sentences in which the underlined words are used <u>in their usual way</u>. Write *F* next to the sentences that contain <u>figurative language</u>.

_____F_____ **1.** Sometimes my friend gives me a <u>funny</u> look when I talk about my garden.

_____ **2.** "They look like <u>little hands</u>," I went on. "That's how I tell them from the weeds."

_____ **3.** The light <u>faded</u>, and the tree branches grew black against the pink sky.

_____ **4.** I felt so peaceful sitting like <u>a child</u> in the warm earth.

_____ **5.** I was so happy to see them, these little <u>jokes</u> on my lack of faith, that I had to sit right down and pull a few weeds.

_____ **6.** I'd always thought of weeding as such <u>drudgery</u>.

_____ **7.** And it wasn't easy, because each seedling was about as big as <u>a flea</u>, lost in weeds as thick as a fur coat.

_____ **8.** And it wasn't easy, because each seedling was about as big as a flea, lost in weeds as thick as <u>a fur coat</u>.

_____ **9.** "I think I'll have the clam sauce, white," I said, closing the <u>menu</u>.

_____ **10.** I smiled at my friend and saw by her face that she'd had a <u>rough</u> day.

_____ **11.** The peas are <u>tumbling</u> over their fence.

_____ **12.** That gorgeous purple perennial has stopped <u>blooming</u>.

D. Check (✓) the best summary of the reading.

_____ **1.** Although gardening makes a mess and requires a lot of physical effort, the author enjoys having fresh vegetables to eat.

_____ **2.** In the author's mind, her garden is a special place that needs her attention, but she recognizes that her friend does not share her point of view.

_____ **3.** In the author's mind, photography is not as interesting as gardening because photographs do not grow and develop in the same way as plants.

_____ **4.** Although it is important for her to spend time with friends, the author feels worried when she is not in her garden, caring for her plants.

> DISCUSS

Work small groups. Ask and answer the questions.

1. Do you have any unusual hobbies? Describe them.

2. Why do you enjoy these hobbies in particular?

3. Are there any hobbies that you can't understand why people enjoy? Explain.

4. Do you discuss your hobbies when you meet new people?

> VOCABULARY SKILL BUILDING

Vocabulary Skill: Similes vs. Metaphors

A **simile** is a type of comparison in which the writer uses *like* or *as* to create a connection between two things that might seem very different.

EXAMPLES:

. . . I felt so peaceful sitting **like** a child in the warm earth.

. . . each seedling was about **as** big **as** a flea, lost in weeds **as** thick **as** a . . . fur coat

A **metaphor** is another type of comparison in which the writer replaces literal language with figurative language. Sometimes a metaphor gives an object human characteristics or actions.

EXAMPLE:

A **sea** of tall pink and white **spidery** blossoms, swaying on the evening breeze . . .

The literal expression of this metaphor would be "A field of tall, thin, pink and white blossoms . . ."

A. Read the sentences. Notice the underlined words. Write *S* for simile, *M* for metaphor, or *X* for neither.

_____ 1. Sound designers have created an <u>invisible fence</u> with sound.

_____ 2. For people who are interested in sound, the field of audio technology is definitely <u>making noise</u>.

_____ 3. An earworm is <u>like an itch</u>.

_____ 4. He <u>rides the subway</u> to work.

_____ 5. Sweet potatoes are good because <u>they love</u> the hot sun and <u>don't mind</u> the wind.

_____ 6. You will see <u>roses blooming</u>.

(continued on next page)

_____ **7.** One room has rice plants <u>swaying in the breeze</u> created by workers in white lab coats.

_____ **8.** For years, cities have been <u>gobbling up farmland</u>.

_____ **9.** It's a garden that I carry with me <u>like a happy secret</u> . . .

_____ **10.** It's just that the garden, especially in summer, comes in and out of the mind <u>like a love affair</u>.

_____ **11.** I <u>started talking</u> about my garden again.

_____ **12.** The peas are <u>tumbling</u> . . . over their fence.

B. Complete the sentences with your own ideas to create similes and metaphors.

Similes

1. Her face was as white as _____

_____.

2. The garden looked like _____

_____.

3. Sitting in the passenger seat while he was driving was like _____

_____.

Metaphors

1. The angry wind _____

_____.

2. Her smile warmed _____

_____.

3. The flowers danced _____

_____.

Learn the Vocabulary

Strategy

Finding the Core Meaning of Words

In English there is often more than one meaning for a word listed in the dictionary. However, most of the definitions are actually based on one core meaning of the word. If you understand what the core meaning is, then you will be able to understand the word when it is used in many different contexts.

A. Work in small groups. Read the definitions and the example sentences and complete the tasks in Columns 1 and 2. Then complete the task in Column 3.

Column 1	Column 2	Column 3
bloom: definition 1 a) If a plant blooms, it produces flowers. b) If a flower blooms, it opens. *The azaleas bloomed early this year.* Task: Tell the names of plants that bloom in the area where you live.	_bloom:_ definition 2 to become happy and healthy or successful *The experiment bloomed into a $50 million business.* Task: Describe the last time someone you know bloomed as a result of a happy event.	Core meaning of _bloom_ Task: Say what the similar features/ideas are in Columns 1 and 2.
fade: definition 1 to gradually disappear *Over the years her beauty faded a little.* Task: Name a wish that you had that faded away over time.	_fade:_ definition 2 to lose color or brightness *The curtains faded in the sun.* Task: Name two things that can cause clothing to fade.	Core meaning of _fade_ Task: Say what the similar features/ideas are in Columns 1 and 2.
strain: definition 1 to injure a muscle or other part of your body by making it work too hard *James strained his right knee playing football.* Task: Name the parts of your body that are easily strained.	_strain:_ definition 2 to try very hard to do something using all your physical or mental strength *I strained to remember where I had met him before.* Task: Talk about a time you strained to remember someone's name.	Core meaning of _strain_ Task: Say what the similar features/ideas are in Columns 1 and 2.
transplant: definition 1 to move a plant from one place and plant it in another *I need to transplant the baby cleome so it will get more light.* Task: Give two reasons for transplanting plants.	_transplant:_ definition 2 to move something or someone from one place to another *This nightclub looks like a little bit of Las Vegas transplanted in Texas.* Task: Give an example of something that people from your culture continue to do after they are transplanted to the U.S.	Core meaning of _transplant_ Task: Say what the similar features/ideas are in Columns 1 and 2.

B. Look up the words that were new to you when you started the unit. Include target words and words that you wrote on page 235. If the word has more than one definition, read all of the definitions, and try to come up with the core meaning. Work with a partner. Compare your core meanings.

C. Make cards for the words from Exercise B. Write the core meaning under the translation, picture, or English definition of the word. When you review your cards, try to recall the core meaning as well as the definition, translation, or picture.

D. Go back to the vocabulary list at the beginning of each chapter. What did you learn about the target words? Add your numbers to the lists.

Vocabulary Practice 2, see page 238.

> THINK BEFORE YOU READ

A. Work with a partner. Look at the picture. Ask and answer the questions. If you don't know a word in English, ask your partner or look in your dictionary. Then write your new words on page 235.

    1. What do you see in the picture? Describe the details.

    2. How does the woman feel?

    3. Why do you think the children are acting that way?

B. Work in small groups. Ask and answer the questions.

    1. What rules did you have to follow as a child?

    2. Do children behave worse today than they did in the past? Explain.

    3. What can parents do to make their children behave well?

CHAPTER 5

Manners: Do Children Really Need Them?

▶ PREPARE TO READ

A. Look at the words (and phrases) in the list. Write the number(s) next to each word to show what you know. You may be able to write more than one number next to some of the words. You will study all of these words in this chapter.

1. I can use the word in a sentence.

2. I know <u>one meaning</u> of the word.

3. I know <u>more than one meaning</u> of the word.

4. I know how to pronounce the word.

B. Work with a partner. Look at the pictures. Ask and answer the questions. If you don't know a word in English, ask your partner or look in your dictionary. Then write your new words on page 235.

1. Why is the child crying?

2. Why does the father give him the toy? Is this a good thing to do?

3. What would you do in the father's situation?

_____ consideration

_____ grief

_____ helpless

_____ impulsive

_____ manipulate

_____ manners

_____ proceed

_____ reinforce

_____ scream at
the top of
(their) lungs

_____ slam

_____ wail

_____ writhe

C. Preview the magazine article "Manners: Do Children Really Need Them?" Check (✓) the organizational pattern that the reading follows.

_____ **1.** a fictional story

_____ **2.** an interview

_____ **3.** an essay

▷ READ

Read "Manners: Do Children Really Need Them?" As you read, pay attention to how the author answers the question in the title.

Manners: Do Children Really Need Them?

1   *Dr. Sheida Asgari is a pediatrician,[1] writer, and mother of two. In this conversation, she shares her thoughts about raising children in the twenty-first century.*

5   **Q:** Recently there has been a lot of discussion of parenting. The assumption seems to be that we don't really know how to raise children anymore. Do we?

Dr. Asgari: Of course we do. But bringing up
10 children is more complicated now. It isn't that children have changed that much; they are still emotional, **impulsive**, and curious little creatures who have always needed training to become productive members of society. What
15 has changed is that parents are facing new challenges in raising them.

Q: Like being busy and feeling guilty about not spending more time with them and being worried about their future all at the same time?
20 **Dr. Asgari:** Does that describe you as a parent?

Q: Yes, it does.

Dr. Asgari: That's me as well. I'm a working mother, which helps me to understand parents.
25 We have extremely busy lives, and we want to enjoy our limited time with our kids, but we also have responsibilities. Our duty as parents is to help our kids to be successful, which sometimes means we have to teach them
30 appropriate social behavior.

Q: So it sounds like you are talking about **manners**.

(continued on next page)

---

[1]**pediatrician:** a doctor who treats children

Dr. Asgari: Yes, children who have good manners can interact with adults, a basic life
35 skill for now and the future. In my practice, I have young patients who smile, look me in the eye, and shake my hand, which shows me that they already have one of the most important skills of being human: basic **consideration** for
40 others. On the other hand, I also have patients who never say hello, **scream at the top of their lungs**, and **slam** doors. . . . Clearly, they have not been taught one of the most important skills for a successful future, which
45 is appropriate social behavior.

Q: So if manners are the issue, what mistakes are parents making, and, perhaps more important, how can they start teaching their children good manners?

50 **Dr. Asgari:** As parents most of us are not strict enough when our children behave badly. Lots of parents give a warning and then do not do anything, which is a huge mistake. If we say we are going to punish a child for
55 bad behavior, we need to actually do it or our words will have no meaning. We also have to stop praising children for every little thing and, instead, be specific about recognizing good behavior when it is earned. It's the
60 difference between saying "You are wonderful" and "I noticed you thanked grandma today when she gave you a cookie."

Q: Some people say that it is impossible to spoil a child. What would you tell them?

65 **Dr. Asgari:** I would agree if we were discussing *babies* since you can't spoil a baby. Infants are completely **helpless**. Consequently, they do whatever they can to get what they need to survive. They **wail** loudly to call for
70 food when they are hungry, and they **writhe** and kick when they are in pain. However, the infant stage is short, and if those behaviors continue to work well for them as they grow older, there is no reason for them to change.
75 If they do not change, it will be impossible for them to have healthy relationships as adults.

We can expect more from toddlers[2] because they communicate quite well when it comes to dealing with things like hunger and pain.
80 At the age of two or three, they also develop skills for **manipulating** adults. For example, they may figure out that if they scream at the top of their lungs in a restaurant, Mom will get embarrassed and give them whatever
85 they want to shut them up. So what do they do? The minute they sit down at the table, they **proceed** to scream. Giving children what they want in exchange for misbehavior only makes things worse. It just **reinforces** the bad
90 behavior.

Q: But isn't it natural for kids to act out their feelings?

Dr. Asgari: I'm so glad you asked that. I think children need to express feelings like
95 **grief**, anger, fear, and hurt just as much as happiness. Those emotions are all part of life, and they'll have them in the future anyway. What I can do as a parent is show my girls that it is normal to have those feelings but also
100 teach them strategies for dealing with them in a way that will help them throughout their lives.

Q: But how can a child be angry and behave well at the same time?

105 **Dr. Asgari:** Well that's the great thing about manners. You're allowed to be angry with someone, but you can't hit her. You do not have to like your teacher, but you should treat him with respect. I realize that separating
110 feelings and behavior is difficult, but it is one of the skills that children are quite capable of learning at an early age.

Here's an example of how children do it by themselves. When my daughter plays hospital
115 with her friends, she follows the rules of the hospital, as she understands them. These are rules she will need for many types of future interactions, including the rules for asking people questions, listening carefully to their
120 answers, and responding politely.

Q: Is she going to be a doctor, too, do you think?

Dr. Asgari: If you ask her, she already is one.

---

[2] **toddler:** a very young child who is just learning to walk

Vocabulary Check

Complete the sentences with the boldfaced words from the reading.
Use the correct form of the words.

1. I wanted everyone to hear me, so I _____.

2. The child is not really hungry. He is crying because he is
_____ his mother into getting him a cookie.

3. Please don't _____ the door. Close it softly instead.

4. Although parents tell them to stop, many young children will
_____ to do dangerous things.

5. If Principal Williams smiles at a child who says *please*, he
_____ good behavior.

6. Chewing with your mouth open is an example of bad
_____.

7. The ambulance is so loud that I can hear the siren _____
from a mile away.

8. My five-year-old daughter can get dressed by herself. She is not
_____.

9. Children need to learn to handle powerful feelings such as the
_____ they might feel when a pet dies.

10. Many parents are pleasantly surprised when a child shows
_____ for the feelings of others.

11. When the baby began to kick and _____ in pain, the
parents got worried and called the doctor.

12. She's just a typical _____ little girl. She does things
without thinking about the consequences.

READ AGAIN

Read "Manners: Do Children Really Need Them?" again and complete the comprehension exercises. As you work, keep the reading goal in mind.

> 📖 **READING GOAL:** To understand the reading and make inferences

Comprehension Check

A. Write a one-sentence summary of the reading. Don't worry about checking your answer now. You'll do that later.

_____

_____

B. Answer the questions in your own words. Some of the answers are not in the reading. You will need to infer them.

1. How is parenting today more complicated than it was in the past?

_____

2. According to Dr. Asgari, what training do children need?

_____

3. What two examples of bad manners are given in the reading?

_____

4. Why is it not effective to tell a child, "You're a good boy / girl"?

_____

5. According to Dr. Asgari, how do parents sometimes encourage bad behavior?

_____

6. How are infants and toddlers different, according to the reading?

_____

7. According to Dr. Asgari, if a child hits people when angry, what should the parents do?

_____

8. What specific rules for showing courtesy do you think Dr. Asgari's daughter follows?

_____

C. Work with a partner. Circle the letter of the correct answer to each question.

1. What is the general topic of the reading?
   a. doctors
   b. parenting
   c. infants

2. What main ideas does the author have about the topic?
   a. Doctors need to have good manners, and they acquire them as children.
   b. Parenting involves teaching children good manners.
   c. Infants have no manners because they are helpless.

D. Now read the summary sentence you wrote in Exercise A. Did you mention the topic and main idea of the reading in your own words? Make any changes to your sentence that you feel are necessary.

E. Listen to your classmates read their revised summary sentences. Are they similar to yours?

❯ DISCUSS

Work in small groups. Read the scenarios. For each one, tell whether you think the adult did the right thing and what you think will happen next.

1. In a restaurant, a child is banging the table with a spoon. One parent tries to take the spoon away, and the child begins to scream. The parents give the child a new toy to play with instead.

2. At a playground two children are fighting over a toy. A teacher takes the toy from the children and says, "If you can't share, you can't play with the toy."

3. At a supermarket, a child refuses to put back a box of candy. The mother kneels down and hugs the child and then takes away the candy.

4. On the bus, a child is kicking the seat in front of her. To stop her, the parent points out the window and tells the child to look at something outside.

The Nanny Diaries

PREPARE TO READ

A. Look at the words (and phrases) in the list. Write the number(s) next to each word to show what you know. You may be able to write more than one number next to some of the words. You will study all of these words in this chapter.

1. I can use the word in a sentence.

2. I know <u>one meaning</u> of the word.

3. I know <u>more than one meaning</u> of the word.

4. I know how to pronounce the word.

B. Work with a partner. Look at the picture. Ask and answer the questions. If you don't know a word in English, ask your partner or look in your dictionary. Then write your new words on page 235.

1. Who are the people in the picture? Where are they?

2. Which people are the parents of the little boy?

3. The younger woman is a nanny. Is being a nanny a good job? Explain.

_____ authoritative

_____ clear (one's) throat

_____ field of vision

_____ jerk

_____ moan

_____ pleadingly

_____ poll

_____ propel

_____ remainder

_____ remedy

_____ sob

_____ steady

_____ straighten up

_____ with ease

C. Read the introduction and first two paragraphs of the excerpt from *The Nanny Diaries*. Answer the questions.

1. Who is the author?

2. Why won't taking care of Grayer be easy?

▶ READ

Read the excerpt from *The Nanny Diaries*. Find and underline reasons why taking care of Grayer won't be easy.

❧ *The Nanny Diaries* ❧

---

1 *The author is a young college student who accepts a job as a nanny for Grayer, the child of a rich New York family. The writer never gives Grayer's last name; she refers to his mother as Mrs. X. When she meets Grayer and his current nanny, Caitlin, at Grayer's school, she tries to help out but soon discovers that taking care of four-year-old*
5 *Grayer will not be easy.*

We head toward the park as Caitlin and Grayer chatter[1] away. She **propels** him forward **with ease**, though he can't be a light load with his sand toys, [and] school stuff. . . .

"Grayer, who's your best friend at school?" I ask.
10 "Shut up stupidhead," he says, kicking out at my shins.[2] I walk the **remainder** of the way well outside his **field of** stroller **vision**. . . .

We make it full circle back to the sandbox where another family . . . is playing.

"He's so cute. Is he your only child?" the mother asks. . . . I'm twenty-one. He's four.

15 "No, I'm his—"

"I told you to get out of here, you bad woman!" Grayer hurls[3] his stroller at me, screaming at the top of his lungs.

Blood rushes to my face as I retort with false confidence, "You . . . silly!"

I consider taking a playground **poll** as to whether I should "get out" and, if I
20 choose not to, does this, in fact, make me a "bad woman"?

Caitlin rights the stroller as if his throwing it were part of a fabulous game we're playing. "Well, looks to me like somebody has a bit of energy and wants me to catch him!" She chases him all over the playground, laughing deeply. He slides down the slide and she catches him. He hides behind the monkey bars
25 and she catches him. There is a lot of catching overall. I start to chase her as she chases him, but give up when he looks **pleadingly** into my eyes, **moaning** "STOaaaooop." I walk to a bench. . . .

(continued on next page)

---

[1] **chatter:** talk quickly in a friendly way without stopping
[2] **shin:** the front part of your leg between your knee and your foot
[3] **hurl:** throw something violently and with a lot of force

Three days later, just as I bend over to pick up the . . . little sneaker Grayer has hurled into the Xes' . . . entryway, the front door slams behind me with a loud bang. I **jerk** upright, still holding his shoe. . . .

I **steady** my voice and reach for a low, **authoritative** octave.[4]

"Grayer, open the door."

"No! I can stick my fingers out at you and you can't see. I got my thung thitikin out, too." He's sticking his tongue out at me.

[Grayer sticks his fingers through the crack underneath the door.]

"Nanny, try to catch my fingers! Do it! Do it! Come on, catch 'em!" I concentrate every muscle on not stepping on them.

"You're not even playing! I'm going to go take a bath. So don't ever come back here, OK? My mom said you don't ever have to come back." His voice gets quieter as he starts to move from the door. "Going to get in the tub.[5]"

"GRAYER!" I scream. . . . "Don't walk away from this door. Ummm, I have a surprise out here for you." . . . [T]he elevator door slides open and Mrs. X, her neighbor, and the doorman[6] all step out.

"Nanny! Naaanny, I don't want your surprise. So go away. Really, really, go, get out of here." . . . With a few "ahems[7]" the neighbor lets herself into her apartment and the doorman hands off the package he's been carrying and disappears back into the elevator.

I hold up Grayer's shoe.

. . . Mrs. X whips out her keys and proceeds to **remedy** the situation. "Well, then. Let's get this door open!" She laughs and unlocks the door. But she swings it open a little too quickly and catches one of Grayer's fingers.

"AHHhhhhhh. Nanny broke my hand! AAAAAHhhhhh—my hand is broke. Get out of HEERRrrreeee! GooOOOOoooo!" He throws himself onto the floor **sobbing**, lost in grief.

Mrs. X bends down, as if about to hold him, then **straightens up**.

"Well, looks like you really tuckered him out[8] at the park! You can go on ahead. I'm sure you have . . . homework to do. We'll see you Monday, then?" I reach carefully inside the doorway and put his shoe down in exchange for my backpack.

I **clear my throat**. "He just threw his shoe and I—"

At the sound of my voice Grayer lets out a fresh wail. "LEEAAAVVE! Ahhahhha." Mrs. X stares down at him as he writhes on the floor, smiles broadly, and pantomimes[9] that I should get the elevator. "Oh, and Nanny, C-a-i-t-l-i-n won't be returning, but I'm sure you have the hang of[10] everything by now."

I close their door and am alone. . . . I wait for the elevator and listen to Grayer scream. I feel as though the whole world is sticking its tongue out at me.

---

[4] **octave:** the range of musical notes between the first note of a musical scale and the last one

[5] **tub:** bathtub

[6] **doorman:** a man who works in a hotel or apartment building watching the door

[7] **ahem:** a sound you make in your throat when you want to attract someone's attention

[8] **tucker (someone) out:** make someone very tired

[9] **pantomime:** perform using only actions and not words

[10] **have the hang of:** understand how to do something

Vocabulary Check

A. Complete the sentences with the boldfaced words from the reading. Use the correct form of the word.

1. I _____ before I sing in order to improve my voice.

2. You will see a lot of tears when a child is _____.

3. If you hear a strange noise behind you, you will _____ your head around to see what is going on.

4. If a child is _____ softly, then he or she may feel pain, either emotional or physical.

5. I wish I had a solution so I could _____ the problem.

6. I have to _____ my voice so he will not know how angry I am.

7. If no one tells that child to _____ when he walks, he will end up looking like an old man.

B. Read the definitions. Write the boldfaced word from the reading next to the correct definition. Use the correct form of the word.

1. _____ = a confident and determined way of behaving or speaking that makes people respect and obey you

2. _____ = the whole area that you are able to see without turning your head

3. _____ = to drive or push something forward

4. _____ = a begging way of looking at someone if you want him or her to do something

5. _____ = the process of finding out what people think about something by asking many people the same question

6. _____ = the part of something that is left over after everything else is gone

7. _____ = without difficulty

Read the excerpt from *The Nanny Diaries* again and complete the comprehension exercises. As you work, keep the reading goal in mind.

> 📖 **READING GOAL:** To write a letter giving advice to the main character

Comprehension Check

A. Work with a partner. Don't look back at the reading. Put the events from the story into the correct sequence. Write *1* next to the first event, *2* next to the second, and so on.

_____ **a.** Nanny learns that Caitlin is leaving.

_____ **b.** Grayer locks Nanny out of the house.

_____ **c.** Nanny meets Grayer at school.

_____ **d.** Grayer tries to kick Nanny.

_____ **e.** Mrs. X opens the door for Nanny.

_____ **f.** Grayer throws his stroller at Nanny.

_____ **g.** Caitlin chases Grayer.

B. Circle the letter of the correct word or phrase that best describes each character in the reading.

1. Nanny
   a. authoritative   **c.** impulsive
   b. helpless   **d.** rough

2. Grayer
   a. considerate   **c.** affectionate
   b. manipulative   **d.** lazy

3. Mrs. X
   a. strict   **c.** uncomprehending
   b. effective   **d.** pleading

4. Caitlin
   a. easy-going   **c.** inexperienced
   b. dependable   **d.** sympathetic

5. Mrs. X's neighbor
   a. jealous   **c.** helpful
   b. disapproving   **d.** sad

C. You are a doctor who studies the best ways to teach children manners. On a separate sheet of paper, write a letter to Nanny. In your letter, give specific examples of how Grayer is misbehaving. Don't look back at the reading. Then, mention some things Nanny can do to improve Grayer's behavior.

> DISCUSS

Work in groups of three. Role-play one of the following situations.

1. Situation: Nanny and Grayer get on the elevator with the neighbor. Grayer steps on the neighbor's foot.

Nanny:

Grayer:

Neighbor:

2. Situation: Nanny and Grayer are at a restaurant. Grayer sees Caitlin at another table and wants to go to her.

Nanny:

Grayer:

Caitlin:

3. Situation: Nanny tells Mrs. X that Grayer hit another child at the playground. Grayer says he didn't do it.

Nanny:

Grayer:

Mrs. X:

4. Situation: Grayer climbs on the furniture and then falls down and hits his head. Nanny is putting ice on it when Mrs. X comes home.

Grayer:

Nanny:

Mrs. X:

> VOCABULARY SKILL BUILDING

Vocabulary Skill: Phrasal Verbs

A phrasal verb is a verb plus a particle that creates a meaning different from the original verb. *Up, down, in, into, out, on, off,* and *for* are some common particles.

Some phrasal verbs are transitive. They can be followed by an object.

EXAMPLE:

I **picked up** Grayer's shoe.

Some phrasal verbs are intransitive. They cannot be followed by an object.

EXAMPLE:

Grayer and Nanny didn't **get along**.

Some phrasal verbs are separable. The object can go between the verb and the particle.

EXAMPLE:

The plants also take carbon monoxide from traffic and industry and **turn *it* into** *clean oxygen. This is an example of* **turning *lemons* into** *lemonade.*

Some phrasal verbs are non-separable. The object always follows the phrasal verb.

EXAMPLE:

I would have to **settle for** the plants from the local nursery.

A. Circle the correct particle to complete the phrasal verb in each of the sentences.

1. The nanny bent (*out / down*) to tie her shoelace, and the child ran away.

2. Young children can figure (*on / out*) how to get what they want.

3. To cut down (*with / on*) spending, leave children at home when you go shopping.

4. Mrs. Smith whipped her wallet (*out / open*) and offered to pay for the damage.

5. People often lose track (*over / of*) their children in large department stores.

6. Parents should punish their children when they act (*down / up*).

7. If I read a good parenting book, I always pass it (*on / down*) to my friends.

8. Most kids will get tired (*about / of*) screaming after a while.

9. It is easy to give (*over / up*) and let children have their way.

10. Some parents are not willing to settle (*for / at*) an ordinary school for their kids.

B. Complete the passage with the phrasal verbs from the list. Use the correct form of the verb. (You will not use all of the phrasal verbs.)

act up	cut down on	get tired of	lose track of	straighten up
bend over	figure out	give up	pass (something) on	turn into
bring up	get rid of	go away	settle for	whip out

Parenting is big business, and sales of parenting books are going up. Some recently published books are promising to help mothers and fathers who are trying to (1)_____ how to raise their little ones.

If your child (2)_____ in public, you might want to read *Why Children Misbehave*. As a parent of difficult children, I found good tips for (3)_____ them _____ well-mannered young adults.

For those parents who are (4)_____ their children fighting with each other, *Brothers and Sisters* is a good choice. I found useful information in this book and then (5)_____ it _____ to my sister, who said it helped her find solutions for her two boys.

For parents who want to (6)_____ their children's complaining about boredom, there is the new book *40 Ways to Entertain Your Youngster*. It is something to take with you and (7)_____ when you are stuck in a bank or in traffic and you need a quick activity to keep your children busy.

Some parents may be ready to (8)_____ hope when faced with a difficult child, but it is not necessary to (9)_____ less than good behavior, and a quick trip to the parenting section at your local bookstore can supply you with new ideas. As parents we love our children, but it is our job to (10)_____ them _____ right, so that when the time comes, they are ready for adulthood.

Learn the Vocabulary

A. Read the definition and two example sentences from the dictionary. Try to write a sentence of your own that uses the boldfaced phrasal verb in a new context.

1.

> bend over / bend down: **move a part of your body so that it is not straight or so that you are not standing upright anymore**

Levy **bent over** to pick up the coins. I **bent down** to tie my shoelaces.

Your sentence: _____

_____

2.

> lose track of: **stop paying attention to someone or something so you do not know where he/she/it is or what is happening**

I **lost track of** my cousin after she moved to Seoul.

I had her address, but I **lost track of** it.

Your sentence: _____

_____

3.

go away: **leave a place or a person**

Nobody was home, so we **went away**.

I hate the rain. I hope it **goes away** soon.

Your sentence: _____

_____

4.

bring up: **take care of and influence a child until he/she is grown up**

Both her parents worked, so her grandmother **brought** her **up**.

She was **brought up** to respect others.

Your sentence: _____

_____

5.

figure out: **think about a problem or situation until you find the answer or understand what has happened**

We **figured out** the freeway system after about a month.

I have instructions for putting together the furniture, but I can't **figure** them **out**.

Your sentence: _____

_____

6.

pass (something) on: **tell someone else a piece of information that someone has told you**

She didn't say the job opening was a secret, so I **passed** the information **on** to my brother who is looking for work.

Is it OK to **pass on** the news of their engagement?

Your sentence: _____

_____

B. Go back to the vocabulary list at the beginning of each chapter. What did you learn about the target words? Add your numbers to the lists.

Vocabulary Practice 3, see page 239.

FLUENCY PRACTICE 1

> READING 1

Before You Read

Preview the reading on the next page. Answer the questions.

1. Are crows intelligent?

2. Can crows solve problems?

3. Do crows have social skills?

A. Read "Crows' Brains." Time yourself. Write your start and end times and your total reading time. Then calculate your reading speed (words per minute) and write it in the progress chart on page 249.

Start time: _____   **End time:** _____   **Total time:** _____ (in seconds)

Reading speed:
777 words ÷ _____ (total time in seconds) x 60 = _____ words per minute

Crows' Brains

1   Betty, an impulsive New Caledonian crow living in a research lab, was hungry. She could see a piece of meat at the bottom of a glass test tube, but without hands she was helpless
5   to reach it. In the wild, crows like Betty use twigs as tools to dig into trees to get insects. However, the only thing in Betty's cage was a piece of wire. She picked up the wire and bent it until she had created a hook. Then grabbing
10   the tool with her beak, she used it to remove the piece of meat from the test tube. The scientists in the lab watched in awe as Betty ate her lunch. They had known that crows could use objects like twigs to get food, but until they saw
15   Betty manipulate the wire, they hadn't known that crows could actually make tools. They had made a profound discovery. Clearly, crows were more intelligent than they had thought.

In another show of intelligence, a group of
20   urban crows in a Tokyo suburb learned a new way to get lunch. These brainy crows fly over intersections and drop nuts in the paths of cars. While the cars drive over the nuts, the crows wait for the light to change. When the light
25   turns red, the cautious crows take advantage of the fact that the streets will be safe temporarily. They fly down to join the pedestrians on the crosswalk and proceed to eat the nuts without fear of being run over. The strategy has become
30   widespread in the area as more crows learn it and then teach it to others, thus reinforcing the behavior.

After observing crow behavior in the laboratory and in the wild, scientists are now

35   convinced that the birds are not just acting instinctively. They are capable of planning and solving problems. They can even teach new behaviors to other crows.

In addition to tool building and problem
40   solving, crows also appear to have developed advanced social skills. University of Vermont researcher Bernd Heinrich made a case for a sort of crow language when he discovered that young crows clamor a great deal when feeding,
45   as opposed to older crows. Heinrich concluded that the younger birds were encouraging their friends to join them in defending the food from other hungry animals. In contrast, older crows preferred not to advertise the presence of food
50   so that they could eat quietly without worrying about competition from the rougher gangs of young crows.

In Switzerland, biologist Thomas Bugnyar observed a raven named Hugin remedy a
55   problem with a larger, stronger bird. Hugin had learned to open containers that contained breadcrumbs, but the other bird kept stealing them. The frustrated Hugin eventually came up with a plan. He pretended to open an empty
60   container, and when the larger bird came over to look for the bread, Hugin went to the right container, opened it, and ate his meal in peace.

The fact that Hugin understood that there was a difference between what he knew and
65   what the other crow knew was big news for researchers, as it suggested that crows were capable of higher order thinking. The fact that Hugin acted on that knowledge to get rid of

(continued on next page)

the other crow showed that crows are capable
70 of recognizing opportunities in much the same
way that humans do when they manipulate a
situation to their advantage.

These stories of crow genius caught the
attention of a writer named Joshua Klein.
75 He wondered if crows could be trained, so
he decided to do an experiment. Klein built
a device that he called a vending machine.
Inside the machine were nuts. Knowing that
crows are attracted to shiny things, he threw
80 coins on the ground around the machine,
which made the area a popular site for the
birds. After accidentally dropping coins into
the machine a few times and discovering that
nuts would appear, the crows soon learned how

85 the machine functioned. The crows started
intentionally picking up the coins and dropping
them into the machine in exchange for peanuts.

Klein's experiment in teaching crows how to
activate the vending machine, along with other
90 research, shows that crows can be trained, a
talent that is particularly useful in large cities,
where the environment is constantly changing.
While many city residents see crows as a noisy,
messy problem, Klein wonders what would
95 happen if we could find ways to accommodate
crows and even give them useful work. After all,
if crows can use a vending machine, why can't
they be trained to do other things? For example,
why can't they be trained to pick up garbage or
100 search for victims after a natural disaster?

B. Read "Crows' Brains" again, a little faster this time. Write your start and
end times and your total reading time. Then calculate your reading speed
(words per minute) and write it in the progress chart on page 249.

Start time: _____   **End time:** _____   **Total time:** _____ (in seconds)

Reading speed:

777 words ÷ _____ (total time in seconds) x 60 = _____ words per minute

Comprehension Check

A. Circle the letter of the correct answer to complete each sentence.

1. Betty, a New Caledonian crow, was able to _____.
   a. escape from a cage
   b. bend a piece of wire and use it to get food
   c. teach another crow how to make tools

2. Crows surprised people in Tokyo when they began to drop nuts _____.
   a. onto people in the streets and crosswalks
   b. in the street to crack them
   c. on crosswalks so cars would crack them

3. Scientists' observations of crows showed that crows _____.
   a. always behave instinctively
   b. copy other animals' behavior
   c. can solve problems and learn

4. When they find food, older crows _____.
   a. make a lot of noise to attract friends
   b. dig a hole and bury the food
   c. eat quietly so other animals will not bother them

5. A raven named Hugin surprised researchers when he _____.
   a. learned how to open specially designed containers
   b. stole breadcrumbs from a larger bird
   c. tricked another bird into thinking that food was in a place where it was not

6. By building a vending machine for crows, Joshua Klein showed that _____.

   a. crows can be trained
   b. crows imitate people
   c. crows are a problem in cities because they are messy and noisy

B. Answer the questions. Try not to look back at the reading.

1. What are three ways in which crows demonstrate intelligence?

   _____

   _____

   _____

2. In your opinion, are crows as intelligent as dogs? Write one sentence to explain why or why not.

   _____

   _____

C. Check your answers for the comprehension questions in the Answer Key on page 250. Then calculate your score and write it in the progress chart on page 249.

   _____ (my number correct) ÷ 8 x 100 = _____%

> READING 2

Before You Read

What can lizards such as geckos do that many animals cannot?

_____

_____

_____

Read

A. Read "Building a Better Robot." Time yourself. Write your start and end times and your total reading time. Then calculate your reading speed (words per minute) and write it in the progress chart on page 249.

Start time: _____ **End time:** _____ **Total time:** _____ (in seconds)

Reading speed:

697 words ÷ _____ (total time in seconds) x 60 = _____ words per minute

Building a Better Robot

1   Robert Full, a biologist at the University of California, Berkley, watches as a small lizard called a gecko walks up a vertical wall with ease. Although the wall is very smooth, the
5 small spotted creature does not slip or even strain as it runs to the ceiling. It might as well be walking on flat ground.

    Squirrels and birds can climb the trunks of trees but only by digging sharp claws
10 into the rough exterior of the tree. Similarly, humans can climb walls by using ladders and ropes, but until the right person thought to take a closer look at the gecko, no one had even come close to understanding how to go
15 straight up a smooth surface.

    Research on the gecko began when engineers trying to build robots took their questions to biologists to see if their colleagues in the natural sciences could provide answers from
20 nature. The collaboration between the two, called biomutualism, led to a partnership in which both biologists and engineers would set out to create a machine that could climb walls.

    The search for a climbing robot began with
25 the foot. Biologists used microscopes to look closely at what it was that made geckos stick. They discovered that the lizard's feet were covered with very fine hairs, and those hairs split into finer hairs, and those hairs split into even
30 finer hairs. In fact, what attached the gecko to the wall was not suction or a sticky substance; it was a phenomenon that occurred at the molecular level. The hairs were so small and fine that they followed a different natural law.

35   Dr. Full now picks up an artificial gecko, a mechanical creature complete with a head and tail. He sets down his laboratory-made gecko, and with a slight jerk it begins to propel itself up the very same wall. Except for the hum of
40 its motor, the room is silent as the mechanized robot gecko makes steady progress toward the ceiling. This robot can be used to go where humans cannot. It can find victims trapped in buildings or gather information in places
45 where there are chemicals, explosives, or other substances that are dangerous for humans.

    The cockroach provided another model that helped robot designers. They wanted a robot that could climb over rough terrain without
50 falling. Such a robot would be useful in search and rescue efforts after an earthquake or flood. Biologists decided to study cockroaches because they can climb over, into, onto, and out of a variety of spaces. These normally offensive
55 creatures actually have amazing legs and feet. Because they have six legs, not two as humans do, cockroaches are more stable. In addition, each leg has strong hairs called spines that help the insect right itself before it falls and get out
60 of small spaces. The result of the research led to Rhex. Rhex is about the size of a small dog, and with its six spiny legs it can climb over objects that are bigger than itself, even smooth objects that would be too slippery for most
65 small animals. Another version of Rhex can swim in the water, and still another version can be used to travel along a coastline looking for explosives.

It is only recently that nature's designs have
70 entered researchers' field of vision. Robots are
just one area. Now there are more fuel-efficient
cars that look like fish and hoses like writhing
robot snakes that work their way into burning
buildings to fight fires. Dr. Full believes that
75 partnerships like these between biology and
other fields will become even more common
in the future, not just for creating robots but for
inspiring breakthroughs in medicine, energy
efficiency, or agriculture.

80 By taking their questions to nature, engineers
and researchers have made many of their design
dreams come true. Climbing a glass building
is not just for superheroes in comic books
anymore. A robot can ascend a smooth wall
85 using a dry adhesive technology based on the
characteristics of the gecko's feet. At the same
time, Full notes that such partnerships will only
work if the human side recognizes its obligation
to protect the environment of lizards, birds, and
90 other creatures that share the planet.

B. Read "Building a Better Robot" again, a little faster this time. Write your start and end times and your total reading speed (words per minute) and write it in the progress chart on page 249.

Start time: _____   **End time:** _____   **Total time:** _____ (in seconds)

Reading speed:

697 words ÷ _____ (total time in seconds) x 60 = _____ words per minute

Comprehension Check

A. Read the statements about the reading. Write *T* if the statement is true and *F* if the statement is false.

_____ **1.** Geckos are able to climb up a smooth surface without falling.

_____ **2.** Robot geckos are able to climb up a smooth surface without falling.

_____ **3.** Geckos stick to the wall because of a special sticky substance on the bottom of their feet.

_____ **4.** Rhex is the same size as a normal cockroach.

_____ **5.** Rhex has six legs.

_____ **6.** One day people may be able to climb smooth walls using technology based on the characteristics of the gecko.

B. Create a complete sentence by writing the letter of the best match in the blank.

_____ **1.** Biomutualism is

_____ **2.** A gecko robot can

_____ **3.** Rhex can

_____ **4.** There is now a fire hose that

_____ **5.** Dr. Full believes

a. climb smooth walls.

b. looks like a snake.

c. a partnership between biology and other disciplines.

d. humans should take care of the planet.

e. climb over objects larger than itself.

C. Check your answers for the comprehension questions in the Answer Key on page 250. Then calculate your score and write it in the progress chart on page 249.

_____ (my number correct) ÷ 11 x 100 = _____%

Tall Trees

> THINK BEFORE YOU READ

A. Work with a partner. Look at the pictures. Ask and answer the questions. If you don't know a word in English, ask your partner or look in your dictionary. Then write your new words on page 235.

   1. How are the trees different from one another? Describe the details.

   2. Which tree in the picture is the most gorgeous, in your opinion?

   3. What types of trees can you see in the area where you live?

B. Work in small groups. Ask and answer the questions.

   1. Do humans need trees? Explain.

   2. Why are some people fascinated by trees?

The Biggest Trees on Earth

Hyperion: the World's Tallest Tree

> PREPARE TO READ

A. Look at the words (and phrases) in the list. Write the number(s) next to each word to show what you know. You may be able to write more than one number next to some of the words. You will study all of these words in this chapter.

1. I can use the word in a sentence.

2. I know <u>one meaning</u> of the word.

3. I know <u>more than one meaning</u> of the word.

4. I know how to pronounce the word.

B. Work with a partner. Look at the picture and guess the answers to the questions. You will check your answers later. If you don't know a word in English, ask your partner or look in your dictionary. Then write your new words on page 235.

1. How tall do you think Hyperion is? _____

2. How long can trees live? _____

3. Where are most of the world's trees located? _____

_____ assume

_____ diameter

_____ ecosystem

_____ emerge

_____ frontier

_____ giant

_____ limb

_____ manage to

_____ penetrate

_____ rot

C. Scan the textbook reading "The Biggest Trees on Earth" and write the correct answers to the questions in Exercise B.

> READ

Read "The Biggest Trees on Earth." Note the important details in the text.

ഔ The Biggest Trees on Earth ര

1   The redwood forests of Northern California are all that remain of a great forest that covered the earth in prehistoric[1] times. Also known as sequoias, the redwoods are among the largest, tallest, oldest, and most gorgeous trees on earth. Ancient survivors in a world in which change can happen suddenly, these tall trees survived
5   the fall of a **giant** meteor[2] that left a hole that was miles wide in **diameter** and may have killed the last of the dinosaurs. Because a single tree can live to be more than 2,000 years old, some of the redwoods that are alive today were already tall trees when the Chinese were building the Great Wall and when Columbus first sailed to the Americas. Scientists are just beginning to understand why these
10   remarkable trees have **managed to** survive for so long and grow so tall.
       The giant sequoia, a type of redwood that grows in the Sierra Mountains,[3] is the largest species of living tree on Earth. It is closely related to the coastal redwood, but there are differences. The sequoia loves sunshine and gets water from melting snow. Therefore, it is never found in the same forest as a coastal
15   redwood, which has adapted to the damp and cloudy climate of the coast.
       Currently, the world's largest living tree is a giant sequoia named General Sherman, a 275-foot-tall giant that measures 36.5 feet around the base of its huge trunk. While General Sherman is more than 100 feet shorter than the tallest redwood, it is considered the world's largest tree because of its overall

(continued on next page)

---

[1] **prehistoric:** the time in history before anything was written down

[2] **meteor:** a piece of rock or metal that floats in space

[3] **Sierra Mountains:** a mountain range in the U.S. state of California

20 size. According to the writer and tree climber Richard Preston, if the wood in General Sherman were cut into foot-wide boards[4] an inch thick, and the boards were laid down end to end, they would cover a distance of 125 miles (660,000 feet, or 201 kilometers).

The coastal redwoods may not be as large as sequoias overall, but they are taller.
25 In a coastal redwood's first twenty years of life, it can grow from a seed into a tree that is 50 feet tall. In its next 1,000 years of life, it continues to grow rapidly, and if conditions are right, it can easily reach heights of 200 feet or more. At 300 feet, a redwood can be as tall as a 30-story building.

The tallest living tree on record is a coastal redwood that was co-discovered in
30 2006 by naturalists[5] Michael Taylor and Chris Atkins. Named Hyperion after the Ancient Greek god of light, their discovery took the title of world's tallest tree from a redwood named The Tall Tree, which had previously held the record at 367.8 feet. Hyperion has been recorded at 379.3 feet and is still growing. Biologists and tree experts keep its exact location a secret in order to protect the **ecosystem** around
35 the tree.

For many years, scientists were curious about what grew in the top of a redwood, but no one had ever been able to climb up into the crown. Redwood branches begin 100 feet or more above the ground in an adult tree. The area where they start, called the crown, is a new **frontier** for scientists. Researchers used to believe
40 that the crown was a fairly empty place. In fact, before the 1980s, researchers had to wait for a tree to fall to study it. Now, mountain climbing techniques and tools allow them to climb into the trees to study the various species of plant and animal life that make their homes on the trees' **limbs**. Since a redwood lives for centuries, we know that many of these ecosystems have been around for thousands of years.
45 However, very little was known about them until recently.

One of the main scientific questions about these enormous trees concerns water. How does a tree like Hyperion manage to send water to branches that are 250 feet above the ground? Under normal conditions, it can take two weeks for water to travel from the roots to the highest parts of the crown. However, coastal
50 redwoods have another way to get water; they pull it directly from the air into their branches. In this way, the upper branches of the tree get the water they need to support a variety of plant and animal life.

Biologists have observed that other plants grow in the dead parts of the tree. When a large branch dies, the tree simply redirects its energy to new growth in
55 other areas. The dead branch is still part of the tree, but as it **rots**, insects and other plants **penetrate** the dead wood and complete the process of creating a soil-like environment full of minerals. The dead places become gardens where new plants **emerge**.

No one knows how tall a redwood can actually grow or how long it can live.
60 The redwood forests of California are smaller than they formerly were. Scientists **assume** that at one time a redwood giant reached 400 feet and lived for 4,000 years, but they have yet to find one. Perhaps such a tree still exists and is just waiting to be discovered.

---

[4] **board:** a long flat piece of wood used for making fences, floors, or walls
[5] **naturalist:** someone who studies plants or animals, especially outdoors

Vocabulary Check

Circle the letter of the correct answer to complete each sentence. The boldfaced words are the target words.

1. The tops of redwood trees are a new **frontier** in science. Scientists _____ them.
   - **a.** have always studied
   - **b.** are beginning to study
   - **c.** used to study

2. When a plant **emerges**, it _____.
   - **a.** dies
   - **b.** produces a flower
   - **c.** appears

3. When insects **penetrate** a tree, they _____.
   - **a.** live on it
   - **b.** go inside it
   - **c.** live underneath it

4. A tree's **limbs** are also called _____.
   - **a.** branches
   - **b.** leaves
   - **c.** trunks

5. When part of a tree **rots**, it _____.
   - **a.** gets water from the roots
   - **b.** produces flowers
   - **c.** is dead

6. The **diameter** of a hole tells you _____.
   - **a.** how deep the hole is
   - **b.** how wide the hole is
   - **c.** the shape of the hole

7. It was difficult; in the end, the climbers **managed to** _____.
   - **a.** reach the top
   - **b.** fall out
   - **c.** give up trying

8. Scientists are trained not to **assume**, but to _____.
   - **a.** look for facts
   - **b.** guess
   - **c.** work together

9. If you hear someone talk about a **giant** tree, the tree is probably _____.
   - **a.** young
   - **b.** beautiful
   - **c.** tall

10. You cannot have an **ecosystem** without _____.
    - **a.** minerals
    - **b.** life
    - **c.** scientists

READ AGAIN

Read "The Tallest Trees on Earth" again and complete the comprehension exercises. As you work, keep the reading goal in mind.

> 📖 **READING GOAL:** To write a travel journal about the places described

Comprehension Check

A. Scan the reading for the missing information about General Sherman.

General Sherman

Name: _General Sherman_

Type of tree: _____

Location: _____

Height: _____

Trunk Base: _____

Water source: _____

Quantity of wood in tree: _____

B. Answer the questions in your own words.

1. How are sequoias and coastal redwoods different? Give two or three examples.

_____

_____

_____

2. During which stage of life do redwoods grow the fastest?

_____

_____

_____

3. Why is it easier for researchers to study trees now than in the past?

_____

_____

_____

4. How is redwoods' water usage different from that of other trees?

_____

_____

_____

5. In what ways is the crown of a tree its own ecosystem?

_____

_____

_____

6. What information is still unknown about coastal redwoods?

_____

_____

_____

C. You have just returned from a two-week trip to the forests of coastal California. On a separate sheet of paper, write a two-paragraph travel journal entry about your experiences. Be sure to mention specific details about the impressive trees you saw during your trip.

D. Read a classmate's travel journal entry. Did he or she mention the same details as you?

> DISCUSS

Work in small groups. Ask and answer the questions.

1. What are the advantages of vacationing in a natural setting instead of a big city?

2. What things do you not like about vacationing in natural settings?

3. Would you like to visit the Sierras in northern California? Which other natural places in the world would you like to visit?

4. What animals are part of the ecosystem where you live?

Up a Tree

> PREPARE TO READ

A. Look at the words (and phrases) in the list. Write the number(s) next to each word to show what you know. You may be able to write more than one number next to some of the words. You will study all of these words in this chapter.

1. I can use the word in a sentence.

2. I know <u>one meaning</u> of the word.

3. I know <u>more than one meaning</u> of the word.

4. I know how to pronounce the word.

B. Work with a partner. Look at the picture. Ask and answer the questions. If you don't know a word in English, ask your partner or look in your dictionary. Then write your new words on page 235.

1. What do you see in the picture? Describe the details.

2. Why do you think the girl is climbing a tree?

3. Have you ever done something adventurous in nature, like climb a tree? Explain.

_____ alert

_____ bush

_____ cylinder

_____ desperately

_____ foliage

_____ gap

_____ grab

_____ gravity

_____ layer

_____ lean

_____ leap

_____ shrug

_____ swing

_____ tangle

_____ work (one's) way

C. Read the first two paragraphs of the story "Up a Tree." Underline three words or phrases that help you visualize the story.

❯ READ

Read "Up a Tree." Find the paragraph that goes with the picture on page 68.

ೞ Up a Tree ೞ

1   We left Los Angeles on a bright winter morning and started our new life in the small Northern California town of Sweetwater. It was near the Redwood Forests and Dad's new job, but the beaches were cold and the days full of a grey wet mist. It was pretty, but I hated it.

5   School was my biggest challenge. There were only two sixth grade classrooms, and from what I could tell, all the other students had known each other forever. I was a new urban kid, and I didn't get this strange new species. These country people with their muddy[1] boots and plaid[2] shirts were very different from my beach friends in Santa Monica. For the first few weeks, I spent all my free time

10   reading library books in the hallway.

       Aside from books, my only consolation[3] was a small horse named Gunther. Gunther had come with the property we lived on, along with a few chickens and a tired yellow cat. I decided to learn to ride Gunther to please Dad. The little horse was white with brown spots and was good-natured. He was fast, too, when he

15   wanted to be, which was usually when we turned to come home. I knew how he felt. I wanted to turn around and go home, too, but not to the house in Sweetwater.

       And then I met Rhonda. I was reading a book on the front porch one unusually sunny Saturday when she called. We had never spoken, but I knew her name. She

20   had blonde hair and always wore sweatshirts and mud-caked tennis shoes. She was tall and fierce, so I had put her on my "people to avoid" list.

       Rhonda did not waste time or words. She told me she had a horse too and asked if I wanted go horseback riding. I had the feeling that her mother had

(continued on next page)

---

[1] **muddy:** covered with wet, sticky dirt

[2] **plaid:** a pattern of squares and crossed colored lines, used mainly on cloth

[3] **consolation:** someone or something that makes you feel better when you are sad or disappointed

forced her to make the call and was probably standing right behind her, but I
25 didn't care.

I got Gunther and rode to a corner where she had suggested we meet. She
looked down at me from a giant of a horse. Dark with a white blaze on its nose,
Rhonda's horse looked as scary as she did. Looking up at her, I suggested she lead
the way.

30 "Where do you want to go?"

"I don't know. Where do you want to go?"

"Follow me."

I assumed we would go along the highway as I usually did, but Rhonda led
me into some trees and down a steep slope.[4] I **leaned** way back on Gunther and
35 managed not to slide off. Branches were hitting me in the face leaving bits of
foliage in my hair. I was beginning to wish I had stayed home with my book
when a **gap** opened up between some **bushes**. We came out onto a dirt road,
and without stopping to wait, Rhonda kicked her horse and took off. Gunther
followed, and suddenly he was galloping at full speed, faster than he'd ever run
40 before. Sunlight danced through the leaves, and the wind made my eyes water as
we raced through the forest, leaning into curves and **leaping** over rotting logs.[5]
For the first time since the move, I felt alive, **alert** to the forest around me and
the movements of the horse.

Suddenly, we rounded a corner and emerged from the cool shadowy road into
45 bright hot sunlight. We were in a clearing surrounded by green hills. Rhonda
jumped off her horse, threw herself under the nearest tree, and pulled out some
gum. Offering me a piece, she said she had taken her sister's horse without
asking.

"Won't you get in trouble?" I asked lamely.[6]
50 "I don't care."

I accepted the gum, and we sat in the shade, listening to the buzz of cicadas[7]
and the swish of the horses' tails. A train whistle sounded high in the hills. I felt
dusty and warm and was just starting to relax when Rhonda broke the silence.

"I want to climb that tree."

55 I turned and followed her gaze to a giant white birch tree. The trunk was a
thick **cylinder** that grew straight up for about 20 feet and then sent out broad
limbs that reached to the edge of the clearing. When I pointed out that we
couldn't get to the branches, she **shrugged**. (not sure)

"Watch me," she said.

60 Walking to a pine tree that was growing very close to the white birch, she
turned and motioned me to follow. The pine was smaller, but it had **layers**
of branches radiating out from the trunk. Rhonda **grabbed** one of the lower
branches and **swung** herself into the tree. Nervously I followed. If this was some
sort of test, I was not going to fail. I took hold of a branch. It was rough and sticky
65 with sap.[8] I managed to find places for my hands and feet, and soon we were two
stories up in the top part of the pine, which had seemed much closer to the giant
white birch when we were on the ground.

---

[4] **slope:** a piece of ground or a surface that is higher at one end than the other

[5] **logs:** thick pieces of wood cut from trees

[6] **lamely:** (asked) without confidence

[7] **cicadas:** insects that live in hot areas, have large wings, and make high singing noises

[8] **sap:** the watery substance that carries food through a plant

"Come on," said Rhonda.

"I'm not going over there."

70 "Chicken!⁹"

She turned and **worked her way** down the branch toward the white birch. Then pushing her hair behind her ears, she eased her foot over one of the outstretched limbs of the white birch, carefully shifting her weight onto it so that her legs were around the limb of the white birch. Cautiously she lifted one hand

75 and waved at me.

"Are you crazy? I called.

Suddenly there was a snap. The branch Rhonda had been holding had broken. Barely connected to the trunk by a small strip of bark, it slowly separated from the tree. **Desperately**, I grabbed at it and tried to hang on, but her weight ripped it

80 out of my hand. A foolish grin flashed across Rhonda's face. Then she disappeared in a **tangle** of branches. There was a crash and then another as **gravity** pulled her to Earth, her blonde head bouncing as her body hit tree limb after tree limb on the way down.

My mouth fell open. The gum I had been chewing fell straight down and

85 bounced off her shoulder. Had I killed her by letting go of the branch? For a moment or two there was silence, and then I heard a sharp intake of breath. I let out a sigh of relief. She was alive. Then she moved. I watched in disbelief as she rolled over onto her side and got to her hands and knees.

"Rhonda?" I screamed. "Are you OK?"

90 She didn't answer for a minute, and then I realized why. She was laughing too hard to speak.

---

⁹ **chicken:** not brave enough to do something

Vocabulary Check

A. Complete the sentences with the boldfaced words from the reading.
Use the correct form of the word.

1. Don't plant a big tree close to your home; plant something small like a(n)

   _____ bush _____.

2. In the fall, some trees' _____ foliage _____ changes color.

3. She saw a(n) _____ gap _____ where the bushes seemed to separate

   and thought there might be a road.

4. We had to dig through many _____ layers _____ of dry leaves, soil, and

   rocks to get to the roots.

5. We went off the trail, so we had to push through a(n)

   _____ tangle _____ of different kinds of plants to get to the road.

(continued on next page)

6. The kids like to hang from the branches and _____ back and forth.

7. I saw a frog _____ from one rock to another.

B. Write the letter of the correct definition next to the word. Be careful. There is one extra definition.

_____ **1.** alert

_____ **2.** cylinder

_____ **3.** shrug

_____ **4.** grab

_____ **5.** gravity

_____ **6.** desperately

_____ **7.** work one's way

_____ **8.** lean

a. a shape, object, or container with circular ends and straight sides

b. a large amount or quantity of something

c. able to think clearly and quickly

d. to go somewhere slowly and with great effort

e. in a way that shows you realize the situation is serious

f. to raise and then lower your shoulders in order to show that you do not know something or do not care about something

g. the force that causes something to fall to the ground

h. to move or bend in a particular direction

i. to take hold of something with sudden movement

> READ AGAIN

Read "Up a Tree" again and complete the comprehension exercises. As you work, keep the reading goal in mind.

> 📖 **READING GOAL:** To use visualization to help you remember details about the reading

Comprehension Check

A. Circle the letter of the correct answer to each question.

1. Why did the author's family move to Sweetwater?
   a. to be closer to nature
   b. because her father's job was there
   c. to raise horses

2. Why does the author spend so much time in the library at first?

    a. She feels lonely and out of place.

    b. She wants to learn about the town of Sweetwater.

    c. She is behind the other students in her class.

3. What word best describes Rhonda's personality?

    a. fearless

    b. warm

    c. cautious

4. Why is riding horses with Rhonda an important experience for the author?

    a. She learns to overcome her fear of riding at full speed.

    b. She is able to please her father by training Gunther.

    c. She feels happy for the first time since coming to Sweetwater.

5. What makes climbing the white birch tree difficult?

    a. The branches are covered in sticky sap.

    b. The branches are too high up to reach.

    c. The branches keep hitting the author in the face.

6. What causes Rhonda to fall at the end of the story?

    a. She tries to jump onto the white birch tree, but it is too far away.

    b. A pine branch she is holding onto snaps and breaks off.

    c. The author accidentally lets go of Rhonda's hand while helping her.

B. Work in small groups. Each student will choose a different part of the story below. Study the details in your part of the story very carefully. Then, on a separate sheet of paper, draw a picture showing the events in your part of the story. Include as many details as possible.

Parts of the story:

1. Rhonda and the author ride their horses through the forest.

2. Rhonda and the author sit together in the clearing.

3. Rhonda and the author try to climb up the white birch tree.

C. Work in the same group. Look at each other's pictures and answer the questions. Do not look back at the reading.

1. Is the path Rhonda and the author took through the forest straight or curved?

    _____

2. What do Rhonda and the author jump over while riding through the forest?

    _____

(continued on next page)

3. What is the weather like while Rhonda and the author are sitting in the clearing?

_____

4. What can Rhonda and the author hear while they are sitting in the clearing?

_____

5. How is the shape of the pine tree different from the shape of the white birch tree?

_____

6. Which tree is Rhonda in when she falls?

_____

D. Look back at the reading and check your answers to Exercise B.

▶ DISCUSS

Work in small groups. Ask and answer the questions.

1. Which is more dangerous: riding a horse or climbing a tree? Explain.

2. Would you like to live in a place like Sweetwater? Why or why not?

3. Which character are you more similar to—the author or Rhonda? Explain.

4. How do you think the author's life will change after meeting Rhonda?

▶ VOCABULARY SKILL BUILDING

Vocabulary Skill: Nouns as Adjectives and Verbs

Nouns often go together with other nouns to make compound nouns. In a compound noun, the first noun is used as an adjective. It describes the following noun. Compound nouns may appear as one word, such as _sunlight_, or as two words, such as _tree expert_. If you are not sure about how to create a compound word, check a dictionary.

Some nouns are also used as verbs.

EXAMPLE:

tangle: (v.) to become twisted together; (n.) a twisted mass of something

They always **tangle** the two ropes together.

A **tangle** of limbs emerged just overhead.

In order to tell the part of speech, look at the way the word is used in a sentence.
- If it directly follows _be_ or precedes a noun, it is probably being used as an adjective.
- If it follows an article or other determiner, such as _this_ or _my_, it is a noun.
- If it directly follows the subject, it is a verb.

A. Read the sentences. Notice the underlined words. Write *A* for adjective, *N* for noun, and *V* verb.

_____ 1. With a <u>shrug</u>, she jumped into the lake.

_____ 2. When she asks me if I am nervous, I <u>shrug</u> because I really don't know.

_____ 3. There were small <u>branches</u> that supported insects as well as other plants.

_____ 4. We <u>branched</u> off on a side path that was narrower and more overgrown.

_____ 5. They <u>swing</u> in the trees like monkeys.

_____ 6. When I was a child, I loved to play on the <u>swing</u> in my schoolyard.

_____ 7. <u>Tree</u> climbers who take care of people's backyard trees are called arborists.

_____ 8. The dogs would <u>tree</u> the cat at night, and she would not come back down until morning.

_____ 9. We cut through the deeply <u>layered</u> foliage.

_____ 10. She <u>layered</u> the vest over her sweater before she went out in the snow.

B. Combine the words in the list to create as many compound nouns as you can. You may use a word more than once. You may check your dictionary.

adult	cloud	life	storm	view
animal	expert	noise	sun	winter
climate	forest	ocean	track	

1. _storm cloud_____

2. _____

3. _____

4. _____

5. _____

6. _____

7. _____

8. _____

Learn the Vocabulary

A. Read the sentences. Guess the meaning of the boldfaced words based on context. Then write the definition below. Write the letter of the context clue that helped you next to the sentence.

Context Clues

a. an example

b. a definition

c. a simile or comparison to something similar

d. contrasting meaning

e. a restatement of the word or phrase

f. a familiar situation or image created from surrounding words and phrases

_____ 1. The **foliage** grew on the dead parts of the tree like a little garden in the sky.

      foliage: _____

_____ 2. He made a running **leap** just as the boat was leaving the dock and landed on the deck just in time.

      leap: _____

_____ 3. We found a metal **cylinder**; it was about the size and shape of a soda can.

      cylinder: _____

_____ 4. We need to look for a new **frontier** in biology; for instance, we have not yet fully explored the world's oceans.

frontier: _____

_____ 5. There was a two-foot **gap** between one rock and the next, and he leaped across the empty space.

gap: _____

_____ 6. Joe didn't research the issue; he just **assumed** he was correct.

assumed: _____

_____ 7. They dug through **layers** of dirt and sand until they finally came to hard rock.

layers: _____

_____ 8. She was quite **alert**, a state in which she felt neither sleepy nor hungry but aware of everything happening all around her.

alert: _____

B. Look up the meanings of the words from Exercise A in your dictionary. Copy the definition that fits the context. Compare the dictionary definitions to the definitions you wrote. Are they similar?

1. foliage: _____

2. leap: _____

3. cylinder: _____

4. frontier: _____

5. gap: _____

6. assumed: _____

7. layers: _____

8. alert: _____

C. Make cards for the new words in this unit. Include the words from Exercise B.

D. Go back to the vocabulary list at the beginning of each chapter. What did you learn about the target words? Add your numbers to the lists.

Vocabulary Practice 4, see page 240

> ## THINK BEFORE YOU READ

A. Work with a partner. Look at the pictures. Ask and answer the questions. If you don't know a word in English, ask your partner or look in your dictionary. Then write your new words on page 235.

　1. What do you see in the pictures? Describe the details.

　2. Which four stages of life are shown in the pictures?

　3. What do people enjoy and not enjoy about each stage?

B. Work in small groups. Rank the stages from 1 (best time of life) to 4 (worst time of life). Explain your ideas to your partners.

C. Listen to other groups talk about their rankings. Do they have the same ideas as you?

On Turning Ten

> PREPARE TO READ

A. Look at the words (and phrases) in the list. Write the number(s) next to each word to show what you know. You may be able to write more than one number next to some of the words. You will study all of these words in this chapter.

1. I can use the word in a sentence.

2. I know <u>one meaning</u> of the word.

3. I know <u>more than one meaning</u> of the word.

4. I know how to pronounce the word.

B. Work with a partner. Look at the picture. Ask and answer the questions. If you don't know a word in English, ask your partner or look in your dictionary. Then write your new words on page 235.

1. What do you see in the picture? Describe the details.

2. How is the boy feeling?

3. When you were ten years old, what things interested you most? What things bothered you?

_____ come down with

_____ digit

_____ disfiguring

_____ drain

_____ insight

_____ look back

_____ psyche

_____ simplicity

_____ skin

_____ solemnly

_____ soul

_____ turn (ten)

_____ wizard

Reading Skill: Understanding Figurative Language— Multiple Levels of Meaning

In Unit 2, you learned that words are sometimes used *figuratively*, or in a different way from their usual meaning. In English, many words have multiple levels of meaning, beyond their usual and figurative uses. Take the word *limb*, for example.

EXAMPLES:

*If you fall, you might break a **limb**.* (usual meaning: **limb** = an arm or a leg)

*If you climb a tree, hold on to a **limb**.* (secondary meaning: **limb** = tree branch)

*The police officer went **out on a limb** to save us.* (figurative meaning: **out on a limb** = in a risky situation)

When words have multiple levels of meaning, it is important to look for the shared basic meaning, or core meaning, among the levels. For example, the limb of a human and the limb of a tree are similar in that they are long and thin and extend from the base of a living thing. Because tree limbs are long and thin, they are risky to stand on, which explains the expression *out on a limb*. If you understand the core meaning, you will understand any new forms and uses of the word you see.

C. Read the first paragraph of the poem "On Turning Ten" on the next page. Answer the questions.

1. Which meaning of *come down* is expressed in the paragraph?

_____ **a.** get lower, as in *Prices are coming down*.

_____ **b.** reach a particular place, as in *Her hair comes down to her waist*.

_____ **c.** become sick with something, as in *He's coming down with a cold*.

2. What is the core meaning that connects all the uses of *come down*?

_____

_____

READ

Read "On Turning Ten." As you read, look for words that express a meaning different from their most common usage.

On Turning Ten

BILLY COLLINS

Billy Collins is an American poet who provides readers with **insights** into ordinary life experiences.

1   The whole idea of it makes me feel
    like I'm **coming down with** something,
    something worse than any stomachache
    or the headaches I get from reading in bad light—
5   a kind of measles[1] of the spirit,
    a mumps[2] of the **psyche**,
    a **disfiguring** chicken pox[3] of the **soul**.

    You tell me it is too early to be **looking back**,
    but that is because you have forgotten
10 the perfect **simplicity** of being one
    and the beautiful complexity introduced by two.
    But I can lie on my bed and remember every **digit**.
    At four I was an Arabian **wizard**.
    I could make myself invisible
15 by drinking a glass of milk a certain way.
    At seven I was a soldier, at nine a prince.

    But now I am mostly at the window
    watching the late afternoon light.
    Back then it never fell so **solemnly**
20 against the side of my tree house,[4]
    and my bicycle never leaned against the garage
    as it does today,
    all the dark blue speed **drained** out of it.

    This is the beginning of sadness, I say to myself,
25 as I walk through the universe in my sneakers.
    It is time to say good-bye to my imaginary friends,
    time to **turn** the first big number.

    It seems only yesterday I used to believe
    there was nothing under my skin but light.
30 If you cut me I would shine.
    But now when I fall upon the sidewalks of life,
    I **skin** my knees. I bleed.

---

[1] **measles:** an illness in which you have a fever and small red spots on your face and body; the disease, mainly affecting children, can be prevented by vaccination

[2] **mumps:** an illness in which your throat swells and becomes painful; the disease, mainly affecting children, can be prevented by vaccination

[3] **chicken pox:** an illness that causes itchy spots on the skin and a slight fever; the disease, mainly affecting children, can be prevented by vaccination

[4] **tree house:** a wooden structure for children to play in, built in the branches of a tree

"On Turning Ten" from The Art of Drowning by Billy Collins, 1995. All rights controlled by the University of Pittsburgh Press, Pittsburgh, PA 15260. Used by permission of the University of Pittsburgh Press.

Vocabulary Check

Complete the text with the boldfaced words from the reading. Use the correct form of the word.

Sometimes I watch my son play in the yard and it makes me (1)_____ on my childhood. I remember the simple activities that I enjoyed. Those years were a time of (2)_____, when people were less busy and children had freedom. I would wave a stick and pretend that I was a(n) (3)_____ with wild white hair and frighten the neighbor's cat. I would go riding with a friend to buy ice cream. We could leave our bikes outside the ice cream shop, and no one would steal them.

I remember how much I enjoyed the day I (4)_____ the chicken pox. My mother looked at the red spots on my face with serious eyes. Then she (5)_____ told me not to scratch. She said the pox were temporary but that I would have (6)_____ marks forever if I didn't leave them alone. Knowing my mother was nearby was good for me, for my (7)_____.

When I finally returned to the complexity of school, I had to deal with friends and fights and really tough math problems. I would struggle with my math worksheets, trying to add rows of (8)_____ without making a mistake. It seemed so important at the time, but now all I remember is the smell of my eraser as I rubbed out wrong numbers.

Now that I am thirty-nine and about to (9)_____ forty, my body is getting old, but I also feel a weight on my heart and (10)_____. My life often feels (11)_____ of energy and magic. I worry about the bills and my health. If I fall and (12)_____ my knee today, I'll probably feel pain for a week. But then I spend time with my son. I begin to feel his feelings, and I am young again. I hope these (13)_____ into his world will help me to be a better father.

READ AGAIN

Read "On Turning Ten" again and complete the comprehension exercises. As you work, keep the reading goal in mind.

> 📖 **READING GOAL:** To understand the usage of words with multiple levels of meaning

Comprehension Check

A. Work in small groups. Write a one-sentence summary of the reading. Explain the implied main idea of the reading.

_____

_____

B. Listen to other groups read their summary sentences. Do they express the same main idea?

C. Study the sentences. Then write the shared basic meaning of the boldfaced words.

1. The old man **looked back** on his life and his many happy moments.
I **looked back** at the car behind me; it was very close.

basic meaning of **look back:** _____

2. Sometimes I miss the **simplicity** of childhood: no work, no bills, no stress.
Because of the **simplicity** of the test, every student got a perfect score.

basic meaning of **simplicity:** _____

3. To be good at math, you must be able to add **digits** quickly.
Humans can move all ten **digits** on their hands, which allows them to make tools.

basic meaning of **digit:** _____

4. When they heard the bad news, their faces suddenly grew **solemn**.
Harold made a **solemn** promise to love his wife forever.

basic meaning of **solemn:** _____

5. The water slowly **drained** from the bathtub.
Caring for children and going to work really **drains** your energy.
What a long day of work! I'm totally **drained**!

basic meaning of **drain:** _____

(continued on next page)

6. Some teenagers have **skin** problems.
The boy cried when he **skinned** his knee.
I stepped on a banana **skin** and fell.

basic meaning of **skin**: _____

7. I was tired of standing, so I **leaned** against the wall.
Joe hasn't decided what to do yet, but he is **leaning** towards retiring.
When Luisa needed financial help, she knew she could **lean** on her family.

basic meaning of **lean**: _____

8. Next week I **turn** twenty-one. I am so excited!
When you finish reading this page, please **turn** to the next page in the book.
The car **turned** the corner and went down Fifth Street.

basic meaning of **turn**: _____

D. Work with a partner. Compare your answers from Exercise C. Are your answers similar?

> DISCUSS

A. Write a short poem, titled "On Turning (Age)." Decide what age you want to write about. In your poem, be sure to express how you feel about turning that age. Try to use vocabulary from this unit in your poem.

B. Read your poem for a group of students. Don't say which age you are writing about. For example, you might say, "This is my poem, titled 'On Turning (blank).'"

C. Listen to other students read their poems. Which ages do you think they are talking about? Do they have positive or negative attitudes about turning that age?

A New Take on the Golden Years

> PREPARE TO READ

A. Look at the words (and phrases) in the list. Write the number(s) next to each word to show what you know. You may be able to write more than one number next to some of the words. You will study all of these words in this chapter.

1. I can use the word in a sentence.

2. I know <u>one meaning</u> of the word.

3. I know <u>more than one meaning</u> of the word.

4. I know how to pronounce the word.

B. Work with a partner. Look at the picture. Ask and answer the questions. If you don't know a word in English, ask your partner or look in your dictionary. Then write your new words on page 235.

1. What do you see in the picture? Describe the details.

2. Are the people in the picture behaving typically for their age? Explain.

3. Why do some people live longer than others? Make a list of reasons.

_____ anticipate

_____ breakthrough

_____ flexibility

_____ in sum

_____ likelihood

_____ one thing leads to another

_____ pursue

_____ spare

_____ strenuous

_____ take up

_____ volunteer

Reading Skill: Understanding Examples

Because main ideas are often abstract and general in nature, authors give specific examples of people, places, and things to help you form a picture in your mind as you read. If you can clearly picture the examples, it will help you to understand the author's main ideas as you read. Later, the examples will help you to remember the main ideas.

C. Read the first two paragraphs of "A New Take on the Golden Years" on the next page. Check (✓) the examples that are mentioned.

_____ **1.** Fern and Benny are in poor health.

_____ **2.** Fern volunteers at a library.

_____ **3.** Fern and Benny worry about money sometimes.

_____ **4.** Benny has a second career as an actor.

_____ **5.** Fern and Benny live far away from their family.

_____ **6.** Benny travels around the world.

D. Study the examples you checked for Exercise C. Check (✓) the main idea that the examples explain.

_____ **1.** Because of the high cost of living in today's world, many retired people are going back to work.

_____ **2.** People are living longer these days and finding new ways to enjoy their time.

_____ **3.** Old age has pros and cons.

E. Now read paragraphs 3 and 4 of "A New Take on the Golden Years." Compare your answer from Exercise D with the ideas expressed in the paragraphs. Are they similar?

READ

Read "A New Take on the Golden Years." Are your answers from Exercise B, question 3, mentioned in the reading?

A New Take on the Golden Years

1   In many ways, Benny Wasserman was like many sixty-year-old men. He lived with his wife, Fern, in Los Angeles, California. He had raised three boys (a doctor and two lawyers),
5   retired from a successful career in business, and was now enjoying his "golden years." There were grandchildren to play with. Fern was **volunteering** at the local library and hospital, and they both had many books to
10   read. Then one day one of his son's coworkers observed that Wasserman looked a lot like Albert Einstein. This being Los Angeles, he suggested that Wasserman have some professional photos taken to send to a talent
15   agent. **One thing led to another**, and today Wasserman has a second career as an actor.

       With his flyaway white hair, Wasserman always plays the same character, Albert Einstein, who also happens to be one of his
20   heroes. These days, Wasserman flies around the world appearing in television commercials in countries from Spain to South Korea. In Hollywood, he often plays the inspirational Einstein in children's movies. He has his own
25   agent, and even his grandchildren think he's cool.

       Although it was unexpected, Wasserman's experience is not that unusual. Old age is just not what it used to be. Many healthy older
30   people are discovering a new stage of life that did not exist a hundred years ago, when the average lifespan was between forty and fifty years. Today people can expect to live nearly twice that long, and for some the possibility
35   of living to 100 is not as unlikely as it used to be. In fact, the number of centenarians[1] is expected to double in the next fifteen years.

       So, one might ask, what should people do to make sure they'll be around and healthy
40   for nine or ten decades? And a second perhaps equally important question might be what people will do with those extra years. According to Dan Buettner, the author of *Blue Zones*, a book about the areas of the world
45   where people are most likely to live long and healthy lives, there are four factors that seem to contribute to the **likelihood** that someone will celebrate a triple-digit birthday.

       The first two are physical: a healthy diet
50   and regular exercise. People who garden, for example, increase their chances of living longer. For one thing, they are out in the sunshine getting plenty of vitamin D, which is good for their bones. And if they are
55   growing fresh vegetables, it is likely that they are eating them, too, and fresh vegetables are full of life-preserving antioxidants[2] and vitamins. According to Buettner, tomatoes, green leafy vegetables, squashes, and beans
60   are all part of the longevity[3] diet. Another benefit to cultivating food at home is that home gardeners get regular, yet not overly **strenuous**, exercise. There is a lot of scientific evidence to support the importance of regular,
65   non-strenuous activity for maintaining body strength and **flexibility** as one ages.

(continued on next page)

---

[1] **centenarian:** someone who is 100 years old or older

[2] **antioxidant:** a substance in some foods that cleans the body and protects it from cancer

[3] **longevity:** long life/the length of a person or animal's life

The third and fourth factors are associated with the psyche. One important psychological factor is having strong personal relationships. The research is clear. People who are lucky enough to live among a community of close friends and family simply live longer. A great-grandfather who still lives with his family, jokes with his great-grandchildren, and carves the turkey at Thanksgiving enjoys better mental health than a man of the same age living alone or in a rest home[4] among strangers. In Sardinia, Italy, a small town of 1,700 people where five of the world's forty oldest people live and 135 people per million live to see their 100th birthday, it is not uncommon for a ninety-year-old man to chop wood in the morning, eat lunch with his family in the afternoon, and then visit with friends at a café in the evening.

The fourth factor that contributes to a long life is having a strong sense of purpose. For some, that sense of purpose might be helping with the grandchildren; for others, like Fern Wasserman, it might also include volunteer work at a hospital. When people know that someone is counting on them, they have a reason to get up in the morning. They report having energy all day and doing their work with ease, whereas those without a similar sense of purpose say they feel drained at the end of a busy day.

In sum, it seems that the lifestyle that leads to a long life is one that is full of pleasurable and meaningful activities. People who can **anticipate** two or three bonus decades, free from the stresses of raising children and paying the bills, will find themselves with the time to **pursue** activities that feed the soul. Whether continuing to make **breakthroughs** in nuclear physics or just playing the role of a nuclear physicist on television, older people are already changing the rules of aging.

Benny and Fern Wasserman are just one example of this trend. They jump out of bed each morning looking forward to a day full of meaningful activities. Fern continues to volunteer, while Benny has **taken up** writing. In fact, in addition to having a busy acting career, he published his first book at age seventy-three. In his **spare** time, he plays basketball and ping-pong,[5] and he has recently begun learning how to play the guitar. Who knows? It might be time for Benny to leave Einstein behind and try for a role as a superhero!

---

[4] **rest home:** a place where old or sick people can live and be taken care of

[5] **ping-pong:** an indoor game played on a tabletop by two people with a small light plastic ball and two paddles

Vocabulary Check

Write C (correct) or X (incorrect) for the way the boldfaced target word is used in each statement. Then correct the incorrect statements to make them true.

_____ 1. Taking a short walk is **strenuous** exercise.

_____ 2. A medical student who studies and works eighty hours a week has a lot of **spare** time.

_____ 3. When a person has a **breakthrough**, that person finds a solution to a problem he or she has been working on for a long time.

_____ 4. Children do not have as much physical **flexibility** as old people.

_____ 5. Jack met Susan at a dance. **One thing led to another**, and two years later they got married.

_____ 6. When both parents have brown eyes, there is a **likelihood** that the children will also have brown eyes.

_____ 7. Ben still travels, acts, writes, and exercises. **In sum**, he has stayed active.

_____ 8. People are paid when they are **volunteering** at hospitals.

_____ 9. If you have **taken up** golf, you won't need equipment.

_____ 10. When you **anticipate** hot weather, you leave your jacket at home.

_____ 11. If you **pursue** a hobby, you can learn new skills.

READ AGAIN

Read "A New Take on the Golden Years" again and complete the comprehension exercises. As you work, keep the reading goal in mind.

> 📖 **READING GOAL:** To use the examples to figure out the main ideas

Comprehension Check

A. These examples are not in the reading, but they could be added. Write the number of the paragraph where you could add each example.

_____ **a.** In the areas Buettner studied, he noticed most people ate little meat, fat, and sugar.

_____ **b.** Two hundred years ago, life expectancy was only thirty-five years in most parts of the world.

_____ **c.** For Benny Wasserman, it means knowing that his agent is depending on him to arrive on time for his next acting job.

_____ **d.** In Loma Linda, a community in California with many centenarians, residents frequently socialize with neighbors.

_____ **e.** Buettner says that many of the centenarians he's studied get daily exercise by walking or doing simple farm work.

B. Read the examples. Then write the main idea that the examples support. Don't look back at the reading.

1. *Paragraph 3:*

A hundred years ago, the average lifespan was between forty and fifty years.

The possibility of living to 100 is not as unlikely as it used to be.

The number of centenarians is expected to double in the next fifteen years.

Main idea of paragraph 3: _____

2. *Paragraph 5:*

People who garden increase their chances of living longer.

Tomatoes, green leafy vegetables, squashes, and beans are all part of the longevity diet.

Regular activity is important to maintain body strength and flexibility as one ages.

Main idea of paragraph 5: _____

3. *Paragraph 6:*

A great-grandfather who still lives with his family enjoys better mental health than a man of the same age living among strangers.

In Sardinia, Italy, a small town with many centenarians, it is not uncommon for a ninety-year-old man to eat lunch with his family in the afternoon and then visit with friends at a café in the evening.

Main idea of paragraph 6: _____

4. *Paragraph 7:*

For Fern Wasserman, it includes volunteer work at a hospital.

When people know that someone is counting on them, they have a reason to get up in the morning.

Main idea of paragraph 7: _____

C. Now compare your answers from Exercise B with the first sentence of each paragraph in the reading. Are they similar?

D. Read about another factor that contributes to longevity. The main idea sentence is missing. Study the examples, then write a main idea sentence.

There may be another factor in longevity besides eating well, exercising regularly, and having a healthy psyche. _____

_____. For example, studies of centenarians show that longevity tends to run in families. It has also been pointed out that many of the "blue zone" areas Buettner has identified are islands or isolated communities where people tend to have a similar genetic makeup. Scientists have also found a connection between longevity and race. Studies show, for example, that Japanese women enjoy the longest life expectancy in the world at 85.62 years. In sum, there may be a factor to longevity that is beyond individuals' control.

DISCUSS

Work in small groups. Ask and answer the questions.

1. Of the longevity factors mentioned in the reading, which do you apply to your life?

2. Which of the longevity factors is the most important, in your opinion? Which is the least important? Explain.

3. Which of the longevity factors is the easiest to apply to your life? Which is the most difficult? Explain.

4. What other things can people do if they want to have a long life?

VOCABULARY SKILL BUILDING

Vocabulary Skill: Numerical Prefixes

Numerical prefixes form the basis of many words. Here is a list of common numerical prefixes and the numbers they represent.

EXAMPLE WORD	PREFIX	NUMBER
unicycle (a one-wheeled cycle)	*uni-*	one
monorail (a train that travels on one rail)	*mono-*	one
biennial (happening every two years)	*bi-*	two
triathlon (a three-sport competition)	*tri-*	three
decade (a ten-year period)	*dec(a)-*	ten
centenarian (a 100-year-old person)	*centi-*	one hundred
millimeter (one-thousandth of a meter)	*milli-*	one thousand

A. Write the letter of the correct word next to the definition.

_____ **1.** a vehicle with three wheels that you ride by pushing the pedals with your feet

_____ **2.** when something (e.g., a magazine) comes every other month

_____ **3.** a period of 100 years

_____ **4.** a period of 1,000 years

_____ **5.** only one color

_____ **6.** one type of clothing that everyone wears, usually at work or school

_____ **7.** an event that involves ten sports

a. uniform

b. decathlon

c. monochrome

d. bimonthly ·

e. tricycle ·

f. century

g. millennium

B. Complete the sentences using your knowledge of numerical prefixes.

1. A pentagon has five sides, so a decagon has _____.

2. A centimeter is a meter divided into _____ sections.

3. Most cattle and deer have two horns, but a unicorn is a magical horse that has _____.

4. One-thousandth of a second is a _____.

5. If a polytheistic religion has many gods, a religion based on a belief in one god is _____.

6. A shape that has three sides and three angles is called a _____.

7. A 100-year-old country celebrates its centennial, so a country that celebrates its bicentennial is _____.

Learn the Vocabulary

> ## Strategy
>
> ### Using Word Cards: Different Types of Cards for Different Types of Learning
>
> There are many different things involved in knowing a word. For example, you might understand the meaning of a word but not know the correct pronunciation. When you make a word card, it is important to think about your purpose in making the card. Your purpose will depend on how much you already know about the word and, of course, what you don't know and would like to learn. Once you know what your purpose is, you can choose the best type of card to make.

A. Read the explanations. Write the target words in this unit and any words that you wrote on page 235 in the space after the explanation that best fits your purpose for learning each word.

Learning the meaning
Purpose: You want to learn the meaning of a word that is new to you.

How to make the card

1. Write the word or expression on one side of the card.

2. Write the translation, write a simple English definition, and/or draw a picture of the word on the other side of the card.

3. If it helps you to understand the meaning of the word, include an example sentence under the translation, definition, or picture. However, leave a blank space for the word so that you can mentally complete the sentence with the missing word when you are reviewing your cards.

Words from this unit:

Learning other words in the same word family as a known word
Purpose: You know one form of the word pretty well and want to learn other word forms in the same family.

How to make the card

1. Write the known form of the word on one side of the card.

2. Write the other forms of the word on the other side of the card, with their parts of speech written next to them.

Words from this unit:

Learning the pronunciation of a known word

Purpose: You know the meaning of the word but have trouble pronouncing it or recognizing it when other people say it.

How to make the card

1. Write the word on one side of the card.

2. Write the pronunciation on the other side of the card. Use the pronunciation symbols from the dictionary or your own system for remembering the correct pronunciation.

3. If the word has more than one syllable, clearly mark the stressed syllable.

Words from this unit:

_____

Learning the grammar of the word

Purpose: You know the meaning of the word but have trouble using it correctly in writing.

How to make the card

1. Write the word on one side of the card.

2. On the back of the card, write an example sentence from the dictionary or other authentic source. Write one sentence for each word form if using several word forms.

3. Identify specific patterns or rules that govern the word. For nouns, check whether it is count or noncount or has special spelling issues; for verbs, use a dictionary to look up the different forms of the verb. Decide whether it is transitive and takes an object or intransitive and does not.

4. For adjectives and adverbs, check their form and placement in a sentence by looking at examples.

Words from this unit:

_____

B. Make cards for the words you wrote under each explanation. Follow the instructions for how to make each type of card.

C. Go back to the vocabulary list at the beginning of each chapter. What did you learn about the target words? Add your numbers to the lists.

_____

Vocabulary Practice 5, see page 241.

Food for Thought

▷ THINK BEFORE YOU READ

A. Work with a partner. Look at the pictures. Ask and answer the questions. If you don't know a word in English, ask your partner or look in your dictionary. Then write your new words on page 235.

1. What do you see in the pictures? Describe the details.

2. How are the meals in the pictures different from each other? Think of as many differences as you can.

3. Which meal would you rather eat? Explain.

B. Write a question about food to ask five of your classmates. For example, you might ask, "What do you think about people who don't eat meat?" or "How much do you worry about what you eat? A lot, a little, or not at all?" Write your classmates' answers on a separate sheet of paper.

My question: _____

C. Tell the class one interesting thing you learned about your classmates.

Feeding the Children Well

▶ PREPARE TO READ

A. Look at the words (and phrases) in the list. Write the number(s) next to each word to show what you know. You may be able to write more than one number next to some of the words. You will study all of these words in this chapter.

1. I can use the word in a sentence.

2. I know <u>one meaning</u> of the word.

3. I know <u>more than one meaning</u> of the word.

4. I know how to pronounce the word.

B. Work with a partner. Look at the picture. Ask and answer the questions. If you don't know a word in English, ask your partner or look in your dictionary. Then write your new words on page 235.

1. What do you see in the picture? Describe the details.

2. Did you like eating healthy food when you were a child?

3. What can adults do to make sure children eat well?

_____ curriculum

_____ dedicated

_____ defrost

_____ exhort

_____ follow suit

_____ fossil fuel

_____ made from scratch

_____ organic

_____ overhaul

_____ produce

_____ remodel

_____ spacious

_____ stock

C. Read the first three paragraphs of the magazine article "Feeding the Children Well." Check (✓) the examples that are mentioned.

_____ **1.** School chefs in Berkeley work harder than they did in the past.

_____ **2.** Berkeley schools serve only frozen pizza and Tater Tots®.

_____ **3.** The schools serve celery, kale, and broccoli.

_____ **4.** Students in Berkeley can have soup and salad for lunch.

_____ **5.** The schools can afford to serve fresh vegetables only for breakfast but not for lunch.

_____ **6.** Children at the schools learn about healthy eating.

D. Study the examples you checked in Exercise C. Check (✓) the main idea.

_____ **1.** Berkeley schools are making a breakthrough in the effort to get children to eat well.

_____ **2.** It is difficult for many schools to afford healthy food for students.

_____ **3.** Health problems are increasing because children are not eating healthy meals at school.

▶ READ

Read "Feeding the Children Well." Check your answer from Exercise D.

Feeding the Children Well

1   At 5 A.M., when the sun is just beginning to rise over Martin Luther King Jr. Middle School in Berkeley, California, the district's cooks are already preparing thousands of meals. They
5 have to start work hours before the students even hit the snooze button[1] because these days—unlike the last several decades in the history of school lunches—the cooks do a whole lot more than **defrost** Tater Tots®[2] and
10 cheese pizza.
    One staffer pushes fresh celery into a chipper, while another leafs kale.[3] Around the **spacious**, newly **remodeled** kitchen, others chop broccoli. . . . The heads will go out to
15 various Berkeley schools for salad, while the stems will be made into soup. A child's drawing of a friendly octopus,[4] posted on the door, **exhorts** "Eat Natural Healthy Food!" And so it is done.
20   Every day, this staff makes 7,100 breakfasts and lunches for students at each of Berkeley's sixteen public schools.
    As in most cities nationwide, Berkeley's students were once fed processed food that
25 was precooked and frozen for easy distribution. Today, nearly everything is **made from scratch.** Berkeley schools have spent three years reshaping the menu and becoming **dedicated** to serving food that is healthy, fresh, local,
30 and delicious. Although other Bay Area school

---

[1] **snooze button:** part of an alarm clock you push to turn off the alarm for a short period of time, allowing you to sleep a little longer

[2] **Tater Tots®:** a frozen potato product

[3] **kale:** dark green vegetable with curled leaves

[4] **octopus:** an animal with eight tentacles (arms) that lives in the ocean

districts are starting to **follow suit**—San Francisco lets students choose fresh fruit and low-fat vegetable side dishes . . . and Oakland is offering salad bars[5]—Berkeley is
35 still the only district of its size in the nation to completely **overhaul** its food program. Now everyone is wondering: Is it working? Can this level of fresh, **organic**, and local food for so many students be sustained?
40 At the center of this revolution—not just for Berkeley but for the nation—is. . . Ann Cooper. Cooper, Berkeley's director of nutrition, has a wide smile and short-trimmed brownish hair and is dressed in neatly pressed chef's
45 whites. She never rests, from the moment the kitchen's staff begins cooking at 5 A.M. until they finally close at 4:00 or 5:00 in the afternoon.
"When I started, there wasn't a stove in a
50 Berkeley kitchen," she says as she chops. "I had sixty employees and none of them actually knew how to cook. They just knew how to operate box cutters and can crushers. That's all we needed, because everything either came in
55 a can or frozen in a cardboard box."
Today, the new King kitchen—opened in August 2008 after an $8.7 million renovation—is fully **stocked**, with pots and pans, ladles and whisks.
60 Besides freshness, Berkeley's menu also stresses organic, locally grown food. Thirty percent of the food served in the district's cafeterias is local, and all **produce** is regionally grown, mostly in California. Cooper says that
65 the food's origin is just as important as its quality because when foods travel a shorter

distance to end up on your plate, they use less **fossil fuel** in their transportation. Food has to be sustainable, both for the health of kids and
70 the health of the economy and environment, she says.
"I really started focusing on what we teach kids," said Cooper. "The first thing we try to teach them is about regional usage. We need
75 to start thinking about whether we need to move food 100 miles before we eat it. Then we started talking to kids about organic food. Most school districts can't afford organic, but we as a nation need to start thinking about
80 this. We can't keep feeding our kids pesticides[6] and antibiotics[7] and hormones."[8]
"I'm in charge of all cooking and gardening classes in our district," said Cooper. "They serve this good food in the cafeteria. They learn these
85 recipes for these meals in classes, and they grow these foods in the gardens. It's hands-on experience and academic **curriculum** to tie it together. We have to make kids understand that their food choices make a big difference."
90 "If we continue to feed kids bad food, if we don't teach them what good food is, what we're going to have are kids with a life less long than our own," she said. Cooper explains that the Centers for Disease Control (CDC)
95 estimates that one of every three Caucasian[9] children and half of all African-American and Latino[10] kids will be insulin dependent[11] within a decade. "The CDC says that kids born after 2000 could be the first generation to
100 have shorter lives than their parents," Cooper adds. "Things need to change."

[5] **salad bar:** a place in a restaurant where you can make your own salad

[6] **pesticide:** a chemical substance used to kill insects and small animals

[7] **antibiotics:** drugs that are used to kill bacteria

[8] **hormone:** a chemical substance produced in one part of the body that causes a change or activity in another part of the body

[9] **Caucasian:** someone who belongs to the race with pale skin

[10] **Latino:** someone who comes from a country in Latin America

[11] **insulin dependent:** someone (usually with diabetes) who needs injections of insulin, a substance in the body that allows sugar to be used for energy, to survive

Vocabulary Check

A. Complete the sentences with the boldfaced words from the reading. Use the correct form of the word.

1. The store was _____ with everything we might need for a picnic lunch at the beach.

2. People will pay more for _____ vegetables because they are grown without chemicals.

3. I like to go to the market to buy fresh _____, such as broccoli, carrots, and apples.

4. The school's _____ requires two years of English and four years of math.

5. Coal and oil are examples of _____.

6. This classroom is used for only one purpose; it is _____ to nutrition classes.

7. I don't like the shape or design of this classroom. Can we _____ it?

B. Circle the letter of the correct answer to each question.

1. What do you call the food that you make at home with fresh ingredients?
   a. stay-at-home   **b.** organic   **c.** made from scratch

2. What can you do to frozen fish that you cannot do to a kitchen?
   a. remodel   **b.** defrost   **c.** sustain

3. Which word means to try hard to persuade someone to do something?
   a. exhort   **b.** dedicate   **c.** overhaul

4. If someone else does the same thing that you just did, then what can you say that person does?
   a. remodel   **b.** follow suit   **c.** overhaul

5. I have a lot of cooking equipment, so what kind of kitchen do I need?
   a. a dedicated kitchen   **b.** an organic kitchen   **c.** a spacious kitchen

6. When you change something a lot, what do you do?
   a. sustain it   **b.** exhort it   **c.** overhaul it

READ AGAIN

Read "Feeding the Children Well" again and complete the comprehension exercises. As you work, keep the reading goal in mind.

> 📖 **READING GOAL:** To identify and then summarize the implied main ideas

Comprehension Check

A. Check (✓) the statements Ann Cooper would agree with.

_____ **1.** Anyone could be a chef at a Berkeley school.

_____ **2.** Not much has changed in the last three years at Berkeley schools.

_____ **3.** Other schools should watch what Berkeley is doing and follow suit.

_____ **4.** Children in Berkeley schools should eat the highest quality food from around the world.

_____ **5.** Schools should teach children to make wise food choices in order to help them develop lifelong healthy eating habits.

_____ **6.** Organic food is worth the high price.

_____ **7.** The best way for children to learn about healthy eating is through technology such as computers and video games.

_____ **8.** The problem of unhealthy eating in the United States is an emergency.

B. Look at the reading again. Study the examples in each paragraph. Then circle the letter of the sentence that best expresses the paragraph's main idea.

1. *Paragraph 4*:
  a. Processed food has a few advantages, such as being easier to distribute.
  b. Berkeley is making a greater effort than other schools to serve healthy food.
  c. No one thinks that healthy eating in schools can be sustained.

2. *Paragraph 5*:
  a. Chefs at Berkeley schools work long hours each day.
  b. Berkeley is leading the nation in serving healthy food to children.
  c. Ann Cooper is the energetic force behind the change at Berkeley.

(continued on next page)

3. *Paragraphs 6/7*:

   a. Berkeley schools now have better trained chefs and better cooking equipment.

   b. It costs schools like Berkeley a lot of money to remodel their food programs.

   c. Chefs in Berkeley schools have to be able not only to cook but also to operate box cutters and can crushers.

4. *Paragraph 8*:

   a. Berkeley schools hope to reduce their use of fossil fuels.

   b. Berkeley schools serve only locally grown, organic food.

   c. Berkeley schools try to avoid transporting food from far away because it is not sustainable.

5. *Paragraphs 9/10*:

   a. Cooper believes that education is an important part of getting children to eat right.

   b. Cooper believes that Berkeley schools are not doing enough to teach children about healthy eating.

   c. Cooper has many responsibilities; she is not only a chef, but also a teacher in the Berkeley school system.

6. *Paragraph 11*:

   a. In the future, Cooper hopes more and more schools will follow the Berkeley schools' food program.

   b. There will be serious consequences in the near future if American children don't start eating better.

   c. Research has shown that there is a connection between race and medical conditions such as insulin dependence.

C. Write a one-paragraph summary of the reading. Use your answers from Exercise B and *Prepare to Read*, Exercise D, on page 98 to help you.

_____

_____

_____

_____

_____

_____

_____

_____

_____

_____

> ## DISCUSS

Work with a partner. Tell your partner why you agree or disagree with the following statements.

1. Being a chef is a great job.

2. The children in my city eat healthy food.

3. I can buy fresh local produce at my market.

4. It is important to eat food that is grown locally.

Meat Under Fire

> PREPARE TO READ

A. Look at the words (and phrases) in the list. Write the number(s) next to each word to show what you know. You may be able to write more than one number next to some of the words. You will study all of these words in this chapter.

1. I can use the word in a sentence.

2. I know <u>one meaning</u> of the word.

3. I know <u>more than one meaning</u> of the word.

4. I know how to pronounce the word.

B. Work with a partner. Look at the picture. Ask and answer the questions. If you don't know a word in English, ask your partner or look in your dictionary. Then write your new words on page 235.

1. What do you see in the picture?

2. How does the girl feel? Why?

3. Have you ever had this problem? Explain.

_39_	acre
_61_	advocate
_25_	cite
_27_	consumption
_23_	digest
_78_	grain
_65_	objection
_107_	on the defensive
_60_	reluctantly
_58_	texture
_76_	willing

Reading Skill: Distinguishing Fact from Opinion

When you read, it is important to distinguish *facts*, statements that are known to be true, from *opinions*, statements that may or may not be true. Pay careful attention to how authors present ideas in a text. They often use signal words to help you understand if a statement is a fact or an opinion.

Common fact signal words:

establish, point out, know, show, admit, reveal

Common opinion signal words:

say, believe, think, view, argue, may

C. Read the first paragraph of the Internet article "Meat Under Fire." Check (✓) the statement that tells an opinion.

_____ **1.** In the United States, meat eating has become a controversial issue.

_____ **2.** More and more people are against eating meat.

_____ **3.** Meat eating is a bad habit.

> READ

Read "Meat Under Fire." Pay attention to the fact and opinion signal words.

http://www.meatunderfire.com

MEAT UNDER FIRE

1 Some people look at a juicy steak and say "Yum!" However, others look at that same piece of beef in horror. They view meat eating as a bad habit at best and a crime at worst.
5 The anti-meat crowd is exhorting people to stop eating meat altogether, but meat lovers are not giving up easily. Meat is now at the center of a culture war over what to eat and how to feed children. Who would have
10 thought that meat eating would become such a controversial issue in the United States?

Vegetarianism is not new. The people of ancient India and Greece, for example, had a great respect for animals and did not eat
15 them. Similarly, many of today's vegetarians refuse to eat meat out of consideration for animals. They believe that animals raised for food suffer. For example, in the United States, most cattle are kept in extremely
20 small spaces where they cannot eat grass or lie down. These cattle are fed corn, which they cannot **digest**. The cattle get sick as a result.

Another reason for the rise in vegetarianism is
25 a concern for human health. Vegetarians **cite** medical studies that establish a connection between a high **consumption** of red meat and many diseases, such as cancer and heart disease. Most commercial meat is also full of
30 antibiotics and hormones. These drugs are

(continued on next page)

given to animals in order to prevent sickness and make the animals fatter, but they may also be harmful to humans over time.

Sustainability is a third reason for the attack on meat. Environmentally minded vegetarians argue that raising cattle for meat is an extremely inefficient use of land, water, and fossil fuels. Studies have shown that an **acre** of land dedicated to growing plants can produce more than twice as much food as an acre used for raising animals. They say that efficient use of land is good for the ecosystem.

Many environmentalists also connect meat consumption and global warming. They point out that in order to provide space for raising cattle, oxygen-producing forests must be cut down. The animals that take their place produce harmful gases such as carbon[1] and methane.[2] These gases are known to contribute to rising temperatures and global warming.

But isn't eating meat part of what makes us human? Centuries ago, ancient people made cave paintings showing people celebrating hunting animals. These paintings reveal that throughout history people have enjoyed the smell, taste, and **texture** of a roasted chicken or a lamb stew. Still, many meat eaters **reluctantly** admit that there are problems with the meat industry. They **advocate** solutions that do not involve giving up meat altogether, such as creating farming practices that are more humane to animals.

To deal with the **objections** about the poor treatment of animals raised for food, many supermarkets now offer antibiotic and hormone-free beef from grass-fed cattle and free-range chickens that were given the freedom to wander around. Consumers who buy this meat know that the animals they are consuming ate a healthy, natural diet and lived as nature intended, in spacious outdoor environments.

To protect their health and the environment, some meat eaters are **willing** to reduce their consumption of animals. By combining meat with beans, vegetables, and **grains**, people can easily decrease the amount of meat that they eat. This will benefit not only human health but the health of the entire planet.

But what if meat could be produced in a way that did not harm animals or the environment? Scientists are attempting to develop a type of meat that comes from a laboratory rather than an animal. Current experiments have produced an unpleasant substance that even the scientists do not want to eat, but supporters of the project are hopeful. They believe that someday we will be able to buy animal-free meat products that will satisfy both vegetarians and non-vegetarians alike.

In the meantime, look for changes in society to see which side is winning. Airlines, hotels, and other large institutions now offer vegetarian meals as well as traditional meat-based dishes. Grocery stores stock many non-meat alternatives made of beans or rice. Restaurant owners and cookbook authors are following suit with meatless menu options. Many people now think it is good manners to provide meat-free dishes at parties. Vegetables with their crunch and color are now taking up more and more space in the refrigerator and on the dinner plate. Meat is still on the menu, but it is definitely **on the defensive**.

---

[1] **carbon:** one of the elements; in an impure form it appears as coal, gasoline, etc.

[2] **methane:** a colorless gas with no smell

Vocabulary Check

A. Circle the letter of the correct answer to complete each sentence. The boldfaced words are the target words.

1. The students **cited** _____ when they wrote their report.

   a. research   **b.** stock   **c.** consumption

2. Some people who want to protect animals' lives **advocate** _____.

   a. sustainability   **b.** meat-eating   **c.** vegetarianism

3. When a person is **on the defensive**, he or she is in a situation where other people _____.

   a. disagree   **b.** follow suit   **c.** help

4. An **acre** is a _____.

   a. measurement of land   **b.** type of farm   **c.** group of workers

5. When you are **willing** to do something, you _____.

   a. do not do it   **b.** feel angry about it   **c.** do not mind it

6. People eat **grains** when they eat _____.

   a. bread and cereal   **b.** meat and fish   **c.** cheese and eggs

7. The **texture** of steak is _____.

   a. flat   **b.** salty   **c.** chewy

B. Write the boldfaced word from the reading next to the correct definition. Use the correct form of the word.

1. _____ = the amount of food or drink that is eaten or used

2. _____ = to change food in the stomach into a form that the body can use

3. _____ = a reason against doing something

4. _____ = done in a way that is slow or unwilling

READ AGAIN

Read "Meat Under Fire" again and complete the comprehension exercises. As you work, keep the reading goal in mind.

> 📖 **READING GOAL:** To evaluate different perspectives on an issue and take a position

Comprehension Check

A. Are the statements facts or opinions? Write *F* (fact) or *O* (opinion).

_____O_____ **1.** Animals raised for food suffer.

_____ **2.** There is a connection between eating lots of red meat and getting heart disease.

_____ **3.** Raising cattle for food is an inefficient use of land.

_____ **4.** Land used to grow plants can produce more food than land used to raise animals.

_____ **5.** To make new space for raising cattle, forests must be cut down.

_____ **6.** Methane gas contributes to global warming.

_____ **7.** Throughout history people have eaten meat.

_____ **8.** Cave paintings showing ancient people celebrating hunting animals are beautiful.

_____ **9.** Free-range chickens eat a healthy, natural diet.

_____**10.** Someday we will prefer animal-free meat products.

_____**11.** It is good manners to provide meat-free dishes at parties.

_____**12.** If people stop eating meat, the planet's environmental problems will be solved.

B. Work with a partner. Compare your answers from Exercise A. Underline the places in the text where you find the answer to each question.

C. Complete the chart on the next page with information from the reading. Then add your own opinion in the third column.

Argument/Problem	Solution	Your opinion
1. In the meat industry, animals are not treated humanely.	*Raise animals humanely. Consumers can choose to pay more.*	
2. Meat contributes to disease.	*Eat less meat.*	
3. Raising cattle for meat is an inefficient use of land, water, and fossil fuels.		
4. Meat consumption contributes to global warming.		

D. Write a short paragraph summarizing the opinions in the article. What do you agree with? What do you disagree with? Explain.

_____

_____

_____

_____

_____

_____

_____

_____

> ## DISCUSS

Work in groups of four. One of you will be the talk show host. Three of you will be guests, each choosing and playing the role of one of the guests in the list. (One of the guest roles will not be chosen.) The person who is the talk show host should ask the guests questions related to the reading (e.g., "How do you feel when you see someone eating meat?")

Guests: chicken farmer, vegetarian, environmentalist, chef

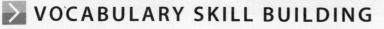

VOCABULARY SKILL BUILDING

Vocabulary Skill: The Prefixes *anti-*, *de-*, and *re-*

A prefix is a word part that is added to the beginning of some words. Prefixes change the meaning of a word but not the form.

- *Anti-* means against. It can be added to nouns and adjectives.

- *De-* shows that something is the opposite, taken away, or made smaller. It can be added to verbs.

- *Re-* means to do again in a better way or to bring something back to the way it was before.

EXAMPLE	MEANING
antibacterial	something that fights against/kills harmful bacteria
defrost	to warm something so that it is no longer frozen
restock	to bring in more supplies to replace those that have been used

A. Write the letter of the correct definition next to the word. Be careful. There are **four** extra definitions.

_____ **1.** reheat

_____ **2.** anti-meat

_____ **3.** debone

_____ **4.** redo

_____ **5.** antiwar

_____ **6.** reshape

_____ **7.** reopen

_____ **8.** restart

_____ **9.** devalue

_____ **10.** debug

a. to remove a problem from a system

b. to stop a project before it is complete

c. to form, shape, or organize again or in a different way

d. to make a meal or drink hot again

e. to remove the shape from something

f. to do something again

g. to begin something, such as a project or machine, again

h. to kill bugs

i. to remove the heat from something

j. to open something a second time after it has been closed

k. to be against war

l. to take the bones out of a fish or a piece of meat

m. to be against eating meat

n. to change something so that it is not worth as much

B. Complete the sentences with the words from Exercise A. Use the correct form of the word.

1. A person who does not eat meat and wants others to stop eating meat is
   anti-meat.

2. A restaurant closes after lunch for a few hours but then
   reopen for dinner.

3. The new president does not like the organizational structure and is going
   to _reshape_ the company.

4. The car stopped suddenly, and we could not get it to
   restart, so we called for help.

5. The soup is cold, but you can _reheat_ it, and it will warm
   you up.

6. I made too many mistakes when I wrote this report, so now I have to
   redo it.

C. Complete each sentence by adding the correct prefix to the word.

1. A person who thinks that computers are bad for society is
   _anti_technology.

2. If you take a machine apart, you _de_construct it.

3. A person who wants to make a house look the way it did when it was first
   built wants to _re_store it.

4. A teacher who does not believe that children need to practice at home is
   _anti_homework.

Learn the Vocabulary

A. Write *Yes* if it is OK to learn the two words together. Write *No* if the two words fall into one of the categories above. If you write *No*, write the number of the rule that applies.

_No, 1_	**1.** digest	digress
_____	**2.** texture	sauce
_____	**3.** objection	agreement
_____	**4.** reluctantly	slowly
_____	**5.** defrost	freeze
_____	**6.** fossil fuel	truck
_____	**7.** dedicate	delicate
_____	**8.** overhaul	make over
_____	**9.** spacious	roomy
_____	**10.** broccoli	kale
_____	**11.** willing	tasks
_____	**12.** substance	instance

B. Make cards for the words from Unit 6 that were new to you when you started the unit. Include target words and words you wrote on page 235. Review them with a partner.

C. Add your new cards to your old cards. Now put your cards into groups of thirty to forty cards each. Look through each group of cards carefully to make sure it doesn't have similar words. If you find two similar words in the same group, put one of those words into a different group of cards.

D. Review each group of cards separately for the next week.

E. Go back to the vocabulary list at the beginning of each chapter. What did you learn about the target words? Add your numbers to the lists.

Vocabulary Practice 6, see page 242.

FLUENCY PRACTICE 2

Fluency Strategy

To read more fluently, you need to take in groups of words rather than one word at a time. This allows you to notice compound words, phrasal verbs, idioms, and collocations. Many of these phrases have a new meaning when they are combined. Try these strategies to stop yourself from reading word by word:

- Read with your eyes, not with your hands or your mouth. Try to move your eyes down the page rather than from side to side.

- Do not try to translate every word you read into your native language. Instead, keep reading to get the main idea. Stopping to look up a word may cause you to lose your train of thought. You can always go back and reread and look up words later.

> READING 1

Before You Read

Preview "Running Around the World" on the next page. What do you think it is about? Circle the letter of the correct answer.

a. runners from different countries

b. someone who is trying to travel around the world on foot

c. people whose work causes them to travel a great deal

Read

A. Read "Running Around the World" on the next page. Time yourself. Write your start and end times and your total reading time. Then calculate your reading speed (words per minute) and write it in the progress chart on page 249.

Start time: _____ **End time:** _____ **Total time:** _____ (in seconds)

Reading speed:

826 words ÷ _____ (total time in seconds) x 60 = _____ words per minute

Running Around the World

1   If a cheetah, a wolf, and a well-trained human all entered a marathon, who would win? The cheetah would take an early lead, and the wolf might pass the cheetah after a

5 few miles. At the end of the 26 miles, however, the human would be the first to cross the finish line. In fact, the human species has the best design for long-distance running. Despite having just two legs, humans have an

10 incredible capacity for running. Our powerful lungs give us the strength needed to run great distances. And because of our skin's ability to sweat, we can control our body temperature while we run. The ability to run helped early

15 humans survive. While we don't often need to run for survival these days, running still plays an important role in human cultures all over the world.

    Marathon running is perhaps the best-known

20 example of human running culture. That is because it is big business. The best runners compete for millions of dollars in races that are watched by millions on television. To join this group of top runners, many experts say

25 that you need to choose your parents well. Ideally, your parents were born and raised in high mountains where the air has less oxygen. This means that they have a more efficient lung capacity than people who live closer to

30 sea level, and you can assume that you will too. The legendary runners of Kenya, who have won many of the top marathons, have this advantage.

    Seven of the world's top ten marathon

35 winners have emerged from the small farming town of Iten in Kenya's western highlands. Most of them are members of the Kalenjin tribe. The Kalenjini live a life of simplicity. They consume organic vegetables, and many of

40 the families are dedicated to running, taking it up early in life and running in groups several times daily.

    The Kalenjini also have ideal bodies for running. Their slim bodies and long legs are

45 perfect for concentrating power where a runner needs it most—the legs. And because Iten is 8,000 feet above sea level, the Kalenjini develop an enormous lung capacity. They need it to get oxygen out of the thin air. This gives

50 the Kalenjini an important edge when they compete in races at lower altitudes.

    Thousands of miles away from Iten, in the mountains in western Mexico, live the Tarahumara. They call themselves the running

55 people because they love to run long distances through the mountains. Although they have little contact with the outside world, they are admired for their skill and the pleasure they take in the sport. They often run in homemade

60 shoes, traveling for several days through bushes and across dry areas where there is very little water, yet they manage to outperform runners who have the benefit of expensive running equipment. For the Tarahumara,

65 running seems to be its own reward.

    Some monks high in the mountains near Kyoto, Japan, run for a different reason. They run to pursue a sort of spiritual insight called enlightenment. The 1,000-day challenge of

70 the monks of Hiei involves intense periods of running, as well as a period of strenuous physical difficulty. Only 46 monks have finished the challenge since 1885. Only six men have attempted the race since World War II. The

75 motivation to succeed is high, and monks solemnly promise to finish or kill themselves.

    A monk who volunteers for the challenge begins by running about 25 miles (40 kilometers) every day for 100 days. The

80 distance is similar to that of a marathon. The monk must be willing to complete three 100-day cycles, with periods of rest between the cycles. Next, the monk must run about 25 miles a day for 200 days without a single

85 day of rest. Then comes a different type of

(continued on next page)

challenge. For nine days, the monk cannot eat, drink, or sleep. At the end of the nine-day period, he is often near death. If he survives, he will go on to complete the final year of the

90 challenge. There are two 100-day cycles in the final year. During each cycle, the monk runs about 52 miles (84 kilometers) every day. He must complete the strenuous run within 18 hours and then repeat it again the next day.

95 That means that in each 100-day cycle, he is running two marathons a day.

The few monks who have pursued enlightenment by completing the rigorous

100 1,000-day challenge say that they now see the world in a new way. They report that they are more alert; they can see, hear, taste, and smell much better than before. They also say that they have a much greater appreciation for life.

These three running cultures are very

105 different from one another, yet they all remind us that running is a part of all human cultures. We may not need to run as a means of transportation anymore, but running is still important—for sport, for fun, for

110 enlightenment.

B. Read "Running Around the World" again, a little faster this time. Write your start and end times and your total reading time. Then calculate your reading speed (words per minute) and write it in the progress chart on page 249.

Start time: _____   **End time:** _____   **Total time:** _____ (in seconds)

Reading speed:

826 words ÷ _____ (total time in seconds) x 60 = _____ words per minute

Comprehension Check

A. Circle the letter of the correct answer.

1. Why are humans better at long distance running than animals?
   a. They can sweat, and they have big lungs.
   b. They are faster.
   c. They have long powerful legs.

2. What three areas of the world are discussed in this reading?
   a. Kenya, Australia, and France
   b. Australia, Mexico, and the United States
   c. Kenya, Mexico, and Japan

3. What are two advantages that the Kalenjini runners have?
   a. large lungs and the ability to sweat
   b. large lungs and bodies that are suited for running
   c. a special diet and a love of running

4. What do the Tarahumara call themselves?
   a. the mountain people
   b. the running people
   c. the enlightened people

5. What is special about the Tarahumara?
   a. They run for fun.
   b. They win large amounts of money.
   c. They drink large amounts of water when they run.

6. Why do the monks of Hiei run?
   a. because they love running
   b. to become more powerful
   c. for spiritual enlightenment

7. What happens if a monk does not finish his challenge?
   a. He can no longer be a monk.
   b. He must start again.
   c. He must kill himself.

B. Circle the correct answers to complete the summary of "Running Around the World." Try not to look back at the reading.

Humans have long had an incredible capacity for long-distance running.

Because of their (1) *long / short* legs and ability to sweat, humans can outrun

most animals. People from many cultures run. Marathon competitions are

(2) *big business / a new concept*.

Many of the top-performing marathon winners come from a tribe in Kenya,

where people have the advantage of training (3) *at sea level / in high mountains*.

Others, such as the Tarahumara of Mexico, run for fun. The monks of Hiei,

meanwhile, run in order to become (4) *physically strong / spiritually enlightened*.

They follow a program that gets increasingly more difficult over the course of

several years, and when they finish, they feel that they are more alert and alive.

C. Check your answers for the comprehension questions in the Answer Key on page 250. Then calculate your score and write it in the progress chart on page 249.

_____ (my number correct) ÷ 11 x 100 _____%

→ READING 2

Before You Read

Preview "Trends in Tourism." Answer the questions.

1. What is the format of the reading?
   a. a magazine article from a tourist industry magazine
   b. a website for travel professionals
   c. a textbook for students of travel and tourism

2. What types of tourism will you read about? Circle the words that best describe the topics.

   artistic   environmental   food-related   musical
   dangerous   exciting   historic   ocean-related

Read

Read "Trends in Tourism." Time yourself. Write your start and end times and your total reading time. Then calculate your reading speed (words per minute) and write it in the progress chart on page 249.

Start time: _____   **End time:** _____   **Total time:** _____ (in seconds)

Reading speed:

802 words ÷ _____ (total time in seconds) x 60 = _____ words per minute

---

http://www.trendsintourism.com

TRENDS IN TOURISM

1　Today, tourism is a huge industry worldwide. With so many people spending money on travel, the industry has become highly competitive. To stay ahead of the competition,
5　travel professionals need foresight. That is where we at *Trends in Tourism* can help.

Trends in Tourism helps travel professionals get to the top and stay there. How? Our highly skilled researchers identify the latest
10　trends in tourism and find opportunities. They then make predictions about future growth areas. For a small fee, we will share that valuable information with you, our colleagues in the industry.

15　Here are just a few examples of trends that our researchers were among the first to identify.

Storm chasing
The 1996 movie *Twister*, about tornado-
20　chasing scientists, captivated audiences. After the movie came out, there was a sudden increase in travel to destinations where violent storms are common. These storm-chasing tourists do not hesitate to pay
25　thousands of dollars to experience a violent storm firsthand.

Opportunities: Right now, there are only a few tour operators in the storm-chasing market. Most are located in the United States. Look for opportunities in other extreme weather destinations, such as Australia and South East Asia. The time is right to get in on this trend. A word of caution, however: There are real dangers associated with storm chasing. Learn about the legal risks before trying to penetrate the storm-chasing market.

Dark tourism

Dark tourism is another growing trend. "Dark tourists" travel to the scene of natural disasters, such as the terrible flooding after Hurricane Katrina in New Orleans. They travel to the scene of manmade disasters, such as the Chernobyl nuclear power plant in Russia. They visit former prisons, such as Alcatraz in San Francisco Bay. Alcatraz was built on an island, and as people tour, they hear stories and imagine the daring escapes of the famous prisoners who chose to leap into the icy ocean rather than stay in prison. They tour "haunted" houses or castles in lonely places in England and Scotland. They visit crime scenes on tours such as the Jack the Ripper walking tour of London. Apparently, some people have no objection to paying good money to be engulfed in scenes of violence, suffering, and death.

Opportunities: The number of dark tourists has grown significantly over the past few years. While some might find this trend disturbing, it will likely continue.

Ecotourism

Many people combine a love of nature with their vacations. Ecotourism is a new type of travel adventure that takes people into endangered ecosystems around the world. They might catch a glimpse of a rare species in Vietnam or swing from a cage high above the tropical rain forest in Peru.

Opportunities: We expect ecotourism to take off in scenic areas where there are spacious landscapes and gorgeous views but also in forested areas like Costa Rica, where canopy tours take people up into the delicate foliage at the top of the cloud forest. While some people say that ecotourism may damage natural areas, others believe that it protects these places. Because ecotourism helps the local economy, people do not clear the land for other uses.

Culinary tourism

Fewer people are eating and cooking at home. At the same time, culinary tourism is on the rise. People whose idea of cooking is to defrost a frozen dinner are now traveling to distant lands to learn how to cook the local food and prepare creations made from scratch. Popular destinations include Italy, Thailand, and France. Culinary tourists happily pay thousands of dollars for the privilege of sweating over a hot stove and then eating their own creations.

Opportunities: We expect that culinary tourism will become more widespread. As experts advocate healthier international cooking, look for growth in travel to destinations such as Vietnam, West Africa, and the Middle East.

Extreme tourism

Extreme tourists risk their lives in exchange for an unforgettable adventure. These people love the thrill of danger and are willing to take a chance in anticipation of having a good story to tell their grandchildren. Perhaps the most famous extreme tourist is Hungarian billionaire Charles Simonyi. For $25 million, Simonyi became the world's first space tourist, visiting the International Space Station for the first time in 2007, and then again in 2009 at a cost of $35 million. Another example of extreme tourism is mountain-climbing tours to destinations such as Mt. Everest. Clients on such tours pay tens of thousands of dollars for the experience of exploring a new frontier.

Opportunities: Despite some recent accidents involving extreme tourists, interest remains high. There is a lot of room for growth in this market. However, we advise caution, as there are many legal risks associated with such extreme tours.

Do you want to learn more about the latest trends in tourism? Click here to subscribe to *Trends in Tourism*.

trends → recent changes

B. Read "Trends in Tourism" again, a little faster this time. Write your start and end times and your total reading time. Then calculate your reading speed (words per minute) and write it in the progress chart on page 249.

Start time: _____ End time: _____ Total time: _~330~_ (in seconds)

Reading speed:

802 words ÷ _____ (total time in seconds) x 60 = _____ words per minute

Comprehension Check

A. Complete the chart with information from the reading.

Type of tourism	Pros	Cons
1. *Culinary*	People can learn about culture through cooking.	To cook, people have to sweat over a hot stove.
2. *Dark Tourism*	Natural disasters and crime scenes are interesting to many tourists.	The situations could be disturbing.
3. *Extreme Tourism*	People enjoy the thrill of doing something dangerous but exciting.	People are risking their lives.
4. *Storm Chasing*	It's exciting to see big storms.	There may be legal risks if someone gets hurt.
5. *Ecotourism*	Tourists can see rare animals and plants in their natural setting.	It may damage wild areas.

B. Write the type of tourism that you think would be best for the tourists described below.

1. Marcus is a young man in his 20s. He likes to jump out of airplanes and ride motorcycles, but he is always looking for new adventures that allow him to face fear and test his physical strength.

   Type of Tourism: _~Extreme Tourism~_

2. Gretchen and her husband, Bunyat, are history teachers. They like to read mysteries and watch scary movies.

   Type of Tourism: _~Dark Tourism~_

3. Hilda is a retired police officer. She likes excitement and used to be quite a risk taker, but she can no longer move quickly, so she is looking for other types of thrills.

   Type of Tourism: _~Storm Chasing~_

4. The Chin family is interested in nature. Mr. Chin is a biologist, and he wants to teach his children more about the wonders of the natural world.

Type of Tourism: _____ *Ecotourism* _____

5. Patricia and Elena are friends. They want a vacation that will help them get to know the local culture, the markets, and the food.

Type of Tourism: _____ *Culinary Tourism* _____

C. Check your answers for the comprehension questions in the Answer Key on page 250. Then calculate your score and write it in the progress chart on page 249.

_____ (my number correct) ÷ 10 x 100 = _____%

Astronomy:
Is Anybody Out There?

▶ THINK BEFORE YOU READ

A. Work with a partner. Look at the picture. Ask and answer the questions. If you don't know a word in English, ask your partner or look in your dictionary. Then write your new words on page 236.

  1. What do you see in the picture? Describe the details.

  2. Is this place on Earth? How do you know?

  3. Would you like to visit this place? Why or why not?

B. Survey your classmates. Write the number of students who answer *Yes*, *No*, and *Not sure* in the chart.

	Yes	No	Not sure
1. Do you believe intelligent life exists on other planets?			
2. Do you think aliens have visited Earth before?			
3. Do you know someone who has seen a UFO[1]?			
4. Have you ever seen a UFO?			

C. Tell your class one interesting thing you learned about your classmates.

---

[1] **UFO (unidentified flying object):** a strange object in the sky that may be a spaceship from another planet

CHAPTER 13 — Another Earth

> PREPARE TO READ

A. Look at the words in the list. Write the number(s) next to each word to show what you know. You may be able to write more than one number next to some of the words. You will learn all of these words in this chapter.

1. I can use the word in a sentence.

2. I know <u>one meaning</u> of the word.

3. I know <u>more than one meaning</u> of the word.

4. I know how to pronounce the word.

B. Work with a partner. Look at the pictures. Ask and answer the questions. If you don't know a word in English, ask your partner or look in your dictionary. Then write your new words on page 236.

1. What do you see in the pictures? Describe the details.

2. Have you ever looked through a telescope?

3. Why are some people fascinated by astronomy?

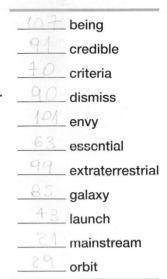

107	being
91	credible
70	criteria
90	dismiss
101	envy
63	essential
99	extraterrestrial
85	galaxy
43	launch
21	mainstream
29	orbit

When you talk about the ideas in a reading, it is important to be able to *paraphrase*. You paraphrase when you explain an author's idea in your own words, without changing the original meaning.

To paraphrase, you have to change not only the words in a sentence but the structure as well. One strategy is to reverse the order of the sentence, so the last phrase of the original sentence becomes the subject of the new one. Study the example below:

Original sentence in reading:

Many stars and planets that are far away from Earth can be seen <u>through a telescope</u>.

Paraphrase:

<u>Using a telescope</u>, a person can observe many distant stars and planets.

C. Read the first paragraph of the blog entry "Another Earth" on the next page. Underline the two sentences in the paragraph that tell the main idea of the reading.

D. Read the sentences. They are possible paraphrases of the sentences you underlined for Exercise C. Mark each as *I* (inaccurate), *S* (too similar), or *B* (best paraphrase).

_____ **1.** Astronomers have already discovered some planets similar to Earth, and if you think about how many stars there are, it is likely that we are not alone in the universe.

_____ **2.** We know we are not the only intelligent life in the universe because astronomers have already discovered planets like Earth, and many more are waiting to be discovered.

_____ **3.** Intelligent life is likely to exist in the universe, given the large number of stars out there and the fact that scientists are discovering planets like our own.

READ

Read "Another Earth." Note the examples used to support the main idea.

○○○

http://www.anotherearth.com

ANOTHER EARTH

1 My son Kaveh is ten years old, and like his father, he is fascinated by outer space. The walls of his room are decorated with posters of *Star Trek,*[1] rocket ships, and photos of
5 Saturn's rings. We both grew up looking through telescopes and dreaming of the aliens that might live on other planets. The difference is this—he is sure that aliens exist. I know I'm going out on a limb here, but now
10 I agree with him. Astronomers have already discovered a handful of Earthlike planets, and when you consider the number of stars out there, it's pretty likely that there are more. These scientific findings indicate that we are
15 not alone in the universe.

Back in the 1970s when I was ten, most people thought that outer space was a cold, empty place. It is true there were movies about aliens, but there was no scientific proof
20 of life, or even the conditions for life. The **mainstream** belief was that humans would need to travel long distances to find out whether there were planets outside our own solar system. However, all that has changed.
25 Scientists can now look for and identify planets from right here at home.

The basic idea is that to find planets, we have to begin by observing stars. Planets are big, and their weight affects the stars they **orbit**.
30 Planets, especially big Jupiter-sized planets, have a gravitational pull. This pull causes the stars they orbit to wobble.[2] By studying how a star moves and whether it wobbles, we can determine whether it has a planetary system.
35 To be sure, we have to study a single star for many years. Even so, astronomers have already discovered over 150 planets using this "wobble" technique. In fact, about 6.5 percent of the stars they have studied have planets.

40 Another method of identifying planets is being used by NASA's[3] Kepler mission, which was **launched** in March 2009. This method also relies on observation of stars. The Kepler spacecraft contains a special telescope that
45 can measure small decreases in a star's brightness. These events can be caused by a planet passing in front of a star, what NASA astronomers call a "transit." Transits are very difficult to observe. Kepler project manager
50 James Fanson compared it to "measuring a flea[4] as it creeps[5] across the headlight of an automobile at night." Despite the complexity of the process, Kepler discovered several planets in its first months of operation, and
55 NASA hopes to discover as many as 1,000 more in the years to come.

One of Kaveh's favorites is a warm and rocky planet called Gliese 581c that orbits a star called Gliese 581, which is about twenty light
60 years[6] away. Astronomers believe that the planet has the perfect conditions for water, which is **essential** for life as we know it. Gliese 581c is bigger than our Earth by half, but it has a year that lasts only thirteen days.

(continued on next page)

---

[1] *Star Trek:* a popular science fiction television series about a group of people exploring space

[2] **wobble:** to move in an unsteady way from side to side

[3] **NASA:** National Aeronautics and Space Administration; a U.S. government organization that controls space travel and the scientific study of space

[4] **flea:** a very small insect with wings that jumps and bites

[5] **creep:** to move in a quiet, careful way, especially to avoid attracting attention

[6] **light year:** the distance that light travels in one year

At first, astronomers thought that Gliese 581c was in what's called the habitable zone, a place where life could survive. In our solar system, the habitable zone includes our sister planets, Mars and Venus. Along with Earth, these planets meet the main **criteria** for supporting life. They are close enough to the sun for solar energy to drive the chemistry of life—but not so close as to boil off water or break down the organic molecules[7] on which life depends. However, now astronomers believe that Gliese 581c is not in a habitable zone. They say that although water may exist on the planet, it is probably in the form of gas, not liquid.

Gliese 581c may not have life forms, but there are plenty more possibilities farther out. What will astronomers find when they search beyond this planet? There are over 100 billion stars in our **galaxy**, known as the Milky Way. From Earth we can see over 3,000 other galaxies. That's a lot of stars, a lot of potential solar systems with planets in habitable zones. The probability that one of these planets is actually sustaining life seems too high to **dismiss**.

I find it **credible** that *every* star with a planetary system has at least one Earth-like planet. Of course, just because a planet is Earth-like doesn't mean it has an intelligent civilization living on it. But out of the billions of planets out there, it is almost certain that some do; the numbers are just too big. The universe is most likely filled with **extraterrestrial** life, just waiting to be discovered.

I **envy** Kaveh and the world he is growing up in. Maybe in my lifetime, but certainly his, astronomy will have advanced to the point where scientists will be able to identify a planet where a person could breathe the air, go for a swim, pick flowers, or make contact with another **being**. When that happens, the question will not be *should* we but *how* will we get **to that planet?**

---

[7] **molecule:** the smallest unit into which any substance can be divided without losing its own chemical nature

Vocabulary Check

Complete the passage with the boldfaced words from the reading.
Use the correct form of the word.

Recent research suggests that there is a possibility that Earth is not

the only planet that has life. While this belief is being discussed in

magazines, newspapers, and other (1)_____ media, it seems

that scientists and governments are also taking the possibility of

(2)_____ life seriously.

Technology has allowed scientists to (3)_____ spacecraft

that have sent back useful information about other planets and solar

systems. In our own solar system, astronomers are studying the moons that

(4)_____ Jupiter. On a moon named Europa, they have found oxygen, one of the (5)_____ elements for life.

Here on Earth, scientists have found bacteria that can survive in ice for long periods of time. This finding makes the idea of biological life in space more (6)_____. Of course, bacteria are not as interesting as movie aliens with four eyes and green skin, but it does meet the (7)_____, or basic requirements, for biological life.

Statistics also suggest that conditions for life probably exist outside of our planet. Earth is a lonely planet in a giant collection of stars called the Milky Way (8)_____. There is a lot that scientists have to discover as they explore the distant center of the universe. It is true that researchers don't know if intelligent alien (9)_____ exist. But it is not possible to (10)_____ the fact that rocky planets with water and oxygen are out there, and if we can distinguish the planets that can support life from those that cannot, we can narrow our search.

Scientists who have opportunities to explore the universe are the (11)_____ of small children who are willing to believe that someday they will travel to another planet.

READ AGAIN

Read "Another Earth" again and complete the comprehension exercises on the next page. As you work, keep the reading goal in mind.

> 📖 **READING GOAL:** To paraphrase important sentences

Comprehension Check

A. Do the statements from the reading tell main ideas or details?
Write *M* (main idea) or *D* (detail).

_____ **1.** Scientific findings indicate that we are not alone in the universe.

_____ **2.** Planets are big, and their weight affects the stars they orbit.

_____ **3.** Scientists can now look for and identify planets from right here at home.

_____ **4.** The basic idea is that to find planets, we have to begin by observing stars.

_____ **5.** About 6.5 percent of the stars astronomers have studied have planets.

_____ **6.** In our solar system the habitable zone includes our sister planets, Mars and Venus.

_____ **7.** From Earth we can see over 3,000 other galaxies.

_____ **8.** The universe is most likely filled with extraterrestrial life, just waiting to be discovered.

B. Paraphrase the sentences from Exercise A in your notebook. Be sure to change the words and structures but keep the original meaning.

C. Work with a partner. Listen to your partner read his or her paraphrases. Say which original sentence is being paraphrased. Then switch roles.

D. Answer the questions in your own words.

1. In what ways is the author similar to his son?

2. Why does the author envy his son?

3. How does the "wobble technique" of detecting planets work?

4. How does the "transit technique" of detecting planets work?

5. What types of planets can sustain life?

6. What are the differences between Earth and the planet Gliese 581c?

7. Why does the author believe that the probability of extraterrestrial life is "too high to dismiss"?

> DISCUSS

Work in small groups. Ask and answer the questions.

1. Is being an astronomer a good job? Explain.

2. Would you like to visit Gliese 581c? Why or why not?

3. What is your reaction to the reading? Did anything surprise you?

Seeing Is Believing

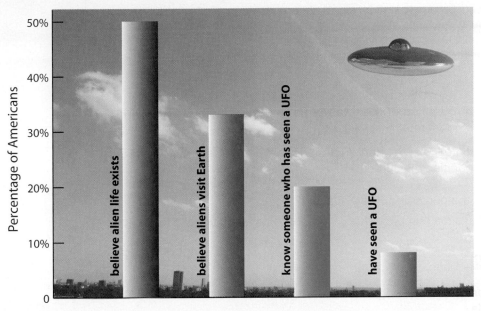

Figure 1: Americans' Opinions about UFOs

(bar graph, y-axis: Percentage of Americans, 0 to 50%)

Bars labeled: believe alien life exists; believe aliens visit Earth; know someone who has seen a UFO; have seen a UFO

> PREPARE TO READ

A. Look at the words in the list. Write the number(s) next to each word to show what you know. You may be able to write more than one number next to some of the words. You will learn all of these words in this chapter.

  1. I can use the word in a sentence.

  2. I know <u>one meaning</u> of the word.

  3. I know <u>more than one meaning</u> of the word.

  4. I know how to pronounce the word.

B. Work with a partner. Look at the graph. Ask and answer the questions. If you don't know a word in English, ask your partner or look in your dictionary. Then write your new words on page 236.

  1. What do you see in the graph?

  2. Compare the information in the graph with the survey you did on page 122. Are your classmates' opinions similar to or different from Americans' opinions?

  3. Why do most people doubt that aliens visit Earth?

_____ account

_____ fabric

_____ fundamental

_____ literally

_____ overestimate

_____ planetarium

_____ probe

_____ prompt

_____ punch

_____ shortcut

_____ skepticism

_____ vast

_____ worthy

Reading Skill: Understanding Visual Aids

Authors often include visual aids alongside their readings. Some visual aids help explain complex ideas in the reading. Others give additional information that the author didn't have space to put in the reading. If you study the visual aids in a reading, you will have better comprehension of the author's main ideas.

When you read, be sure to look for signal phrases that refer you to visual aids. For example, you might notice a signal phrase such as "See Fig. 1." In this phrase, *Fig* is an abbreviation for *Figure*, another way to say *visual aid*. This is the author's signal that you should stop to study a visual aid before continuing with the reading.

C. Read the introduction of the Internet news story "Seeing Is Believing." Answer the questions.

1. Which sentence in the introduction does the visual aid on page 129 go with? Underline the sentence.

2. What is the purpose of the visual aid?

   a. to explain a complex idea   **b.** to give additional information

> READ

Read "Seeing Is Believing." Look for any signal words that reference visual aids.

http://www.news/aliens.com/

SEEING IS BELIEVING

1 *Popular culture is full of stories about aliens. They are a common theme in movies, television shows, illustrated books, and video games. They are also an important part*
5 *of many people's belief system. Research has shown that close to 33 percent of Americans and millions more people around the world believe that aliens visit the Earth in "unidentified flying objects" or UFOs (see*
10 *Fig. 1, p. 129). Despite the popularity and interest in space travel, little serious research has been done on it. The mainstream media* *consider the topic somewhat ridiculous, and most discussions of aliens traveling to Earth*
15 *are limited to the Internet. This made it all the more surprising when journalist Peter Jennings, a well-respected reporter for ABC News, decided to do a serious investigation of the UFO phenomenon. "As a journalist,"*
20 *says Jennings, "I began this project with a healthy dose of **skepticism** and as open a mind as possible." In researching the UFO phenomenon, Jennings spoke with dozens of credible witnesses who claimed*

to have seen the mysterious objects. These witnesses included political leaders, such as former U.S. President Jimmy Carter, police officers from towns and cities across the United States, and a number of experienced military pilots. He also spoke with a variety of astronomers and physicists. In speaking with these scientists, Jennings always began the discussion with a simple question: Is it even possible for aliens to visit Earth in the first place? This debate is the focus of the following excerpt from Jennings's final report on the UFO phenomenon, which he titled "Seeing Is Believing."

SEEING IS BELIEVING:

If Aliens Can Visit, How Did They Get Here?
by Peter Jennings

There have been countless **accounts** of alien visitations around the world, but one of the things that **prompts** skepticism is how they would get here in the first place. If aliens are from another world, they must have some extraordinary means of travel—nothing like what is available anywhere on Earth. It is hard to [**overestimate**] the difficulty of going from star to star. "The distances are so **vast**, the energy requirements are so extreme, it would be very, very difficult to travel between the stars," said James McGaha, a retired Air Force pilot and amateur astronomer.

A law of science, determined by Albert Einstein, says nothing can travel faster than the speed of light—186,000 miles per second. The fastest object made by man, the scientific **probe** Helios 2, traveled at 2,500 miles per second. At that rate, Helios 2, launched in 1976, would take 19,000 years to reach the nearest star (see Fig. 2). As a result, some scientists think that sort of space travel is a waste of time. "Scientifically, we have a rule: You want to be alive at the end of your experiment, not dead," said Dr. Neil deGrasse Tyson, director of the Rose Center's Hayden **Planetarium** at the American Museum of Natural History in New York.

Einstein's Wormhole[1] Loophole
If humans can't travel to the stars, many scientists say extraterrestrial life can't come here either. However, Michio Kaku, one of the leading theoretical physicists in the world, says many scientists are too quick to dismiss the idea of other civilizations visiting Earth. Einstein may have said nothing can go faster than the speed of light, but he also left a loophole,[2] said Kaku, a professor at the City University of New York. In Einstein's theory, space and time is a **fabric**.

Kaku explained: "In school we learned that a straight line is the shortest distance between two points. But actually that's not true. You see, if you fold the sheet of paper and **punch**

Vehicle / Object	Top speed, miles per hour (kph)	Distance to nearest star in years
Helios 2 spacecraft	150,000 (241,402)	19,000
Voyager spacecraft	39,600 (63,756)	73,000
NASA space shuttle	17,500 (28,157)	165,189
X-43 jet plane	6,958 (11,199.6)	414,464
NHRA dragster car	333 (539)	8,681,081

Figure 2: Fastest Objects Made by Humans

(continued on next page)

---

[1] **wormhole:** a theoretical distortion of space time in a region of the universe that would link one location or time with another, through a path that is shorter in distance than would otherwise be expected

[2] **loophole:** a small mistake in the law

a hole through it, you begin to realize that a wormhole is the shortest distance between two points." (See Fig. 3.)

A civilization that could harness[3] the power
90 of stars might be able to use that **shortcut** through space and time, and perhaps bridge

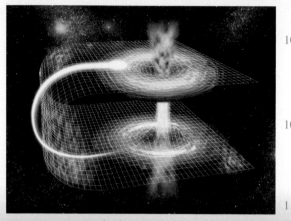

Figure 3: Wormhole

the vast distances of space to reach Earth, he said.

"The **fundamental** mistake people make
95 when thinking about extraterrestrial intelligence is to assume that they're just like us except a few hundred years more advanced. I say open your mind, open your consciousness to the possibility that they are
100 a million years ahead," he said.

Kaku believes that only this type of civilization—millions of years more advanced than ours and capable of using wormholes as shortcuts—could reach Earth and might be
105 one explanation for UFOs. "When you look at this handful of [UFO] cases that cannot be easily dismissed, this is **worthy** of scientific investigation," he said. "Maybe there's nothing there. However, on that off chance[4]
110 that there is something there, that could **literally** change the course of human history. So I say let this investigation begin."

---

[3] **harness:** control and use the natural force or power of something

[4] **off chance:** hoping that something will happen although it is unlikely

Vocabulary Check

A. Write C (correct) or X (incorrect) for the way the target word is used in each statement. Then correct the incorrect statements to make them true.

_____ **1.** When I find it hard to believe something, I show **skepticism**.

_____ **2.** If I say that person is as big as a house, I mean it **literally**.

_____ **3.** We are in a hurry, so we should not take the **shortcut**.

_____ **4.** Scientists are getting information from a **probe** that is traveling in space.

_____ **5.** **Fabric** is difficult to bend and fold because it breaks easily.

_____ **6.** We can learn about space at a **planetarium**.

_____ **7.** Some people take reports of alien sightings very seriously because these **accounts** often come from experienced pilots and other military personnel.

B. Complete the sentences with the boldfaced words from the reading. Use the correct form of the words.

1. Often one person's claim to have seen an alien will _____ others to come forward with their stories.

2. The astronomer did not read the report about aliens landing in New York because he said it was not _____ of his time.

3. Many people _____ the amount of time they will have and plan more activities than they can finish.

4. Life as we know it needs oxygen and water. This is a _____ truth.

5. He used a knife to _____ another hole in the belt so he could make it smaller.

6. The universe is so _____ that we have difficulty imagining its size.

> READ AGAIN

Read "Seeing Is Believing" again and complete the comprehension exercises. As you work, keep the reading goal in mind.

> 📖 **READING GOAL:** To use the visual aids to help you summarize the main ideas

Comprehension Check

A. Answer the questions about the visual aids in the reading.

Figure 1:
1. Which paragraph does it go with? *the introduction* _____
2. What is its purpose? *to give extra information* _____

Figure 2:
1. Which paragraph does it go with? _____
2. What is its purpose? _____

Figure 3:
1. Which paragraph does it go with? _____
2. What is its purpose? _____

B. Work with a partner. Study the visual aids. Answer the questions without looking back at the reading.

1. Do many Americans believe intelligent life exists on other planets?
2. Do most Americans believe aliens are visiting Earth?
3. What is the fastest object made by man?
4. Why do many people think it is not possible for living things to visit other planets?
5. What is a possible shortcut to other planets?
6. In what way is space like a fabric?
7. What type of civilization could travel between the stars?

C. Write a short summary of the main ideas of the reading. Use the visual aids and your answers from Exercise B to help you. Do not look back at the reading.

_____

_____

_____

_____

_____

_____

_____

_____

_____

D. Work with a partner. Compare your summaries. Did you mention the same main ideas?

DISCUSS

Work in small groups. Ask and answer the questions.

1. Did you change your belief about the possibility of extraterrestrial life as a result of reading this? Explain.

2. Which of the following people would you be most likely to believe if they told you they had seen a UFO? Explain.

   a. a seventy-year-old farmer

   b. a military pilot

   c. an astronomer

   d. a close friend

3. If Einstein's wormhole theory is true, do you think humans should try to develop the technology to explore space and look for other life? Explain.

4. What do you expect the first human-alien encounter would be like? Friendly or unfriendly? Why?

VOCABULARY SKILL BUILDING

Vocabulary Skill: The Prefixes *inter-* and *extra-*

In Unit 6 you learned that adding a prefix to a word can change its meaning. Here are two more prefixes that appear in this unit.

- *inter–*: between or involving two or more different things, places, or people. It is used with adjectives.
- *extra–*: outside or beyond. It is used with adjectives.

EXAMPLE	MEANING
international	something that occurs between nations
extraterrestrial	something that is not on our Earth (*terrestrial* means Earth)

A. Work with a partner. Answer the questions in your own words.

1. What is an example of **international** travel?

2. Have you ever met an **extraordinary** person? What made the person special?

3. Why is it a good idea to do **extra-credit** work?

4. If humans were capable of **interplanetary** space travel, which planet would you visit and why?

5. What countries could belong to an **inter-American** observatory?

6. What is an **extracurricular** activity that you would like to participate in outside of your regular studies?

7. What is an example of an **interpersonal** skill?

8. What do you think an **extraterrestrial** being would look like?

B. Complete the sentences with the boldfaced words from Exercise A.

1. There is a(n) _____ soccer league that includes countries from Canada to Mexico to Brazil.

2. In addition to academics, the college offers sports and drama in _____ clubs.

3. He is a good salesperson because of his _____ awareness.

4. She will write a(n) _____ report in order to raise her grade in the class.

5. He has a(n) _____ memory. He can read an article and then repeat it back to you word for word.

6. Scientists still do not have any proof of _____ life.

Learn the Vocabulary

A. Make word cards for all the words that were new to you in this unit. Then add example sentences to the back of the word cards. Put a blank in place of the word.

B. Draw or paste a picture on the same side of the word card.

C. Look at your classmates' pictures. Say which word you think is on the other side of the card.

D. Go back to the vocabulary list at the beginning of each chapter. What did you learn about the target words? Add your numbers to the lists.

Vocabulary Practice 7, see page 243

> THINK BEFORE YOU READ

A. Work with a partner. Look at the picture. Ask and answer the questions. If you don't know a word in English, ask your partner or look in your dictionary. Then write your new words on page 236.

1. What do you see in the picture? Describe the details.

2. Is it better to live in a house or an apartment? List the advantages and disadvantages of each in the spaces below.

	Houses	Apartments
Advantages		
Disadvantages		

B. Work in small groups. Look at the picture and the unit title. Ask and answer the questions.

1. What do you think the readings in this unit will be about?

2. What is your idea of an ideal home? Describe it.

The Small House Movement

> PREPARE TO READ

A. Look at the words in the list. Write the number(s) next to each word to show what you know. You may be able to write more than one number next to some of the words. You will learn all of these words in this chapter.

1. I can use the word in a sentence.

2. I know <u>one meaning</u> of the word.

3. I know <u>more than one meaning</u> of the word.

4. I know how to pronounce the word.

B. Work with a partner. Look at the pictures. Ask and answer the questions. If you don't know a word in English, ask your partner or look in your dictionary. Then write your new words on page 236.

1. What do you see in the pictures? Describe the details.

2. Would you like to live in the house in the pictures? Why or why not?

3. Why do some people choose to live in small houses?

_____ displace

_____ domestic

_____ layout

_____ maintenance

_____ movement

_____ partition

_____ practical

_____ prior

_____ storage

When authors give many details related to a particular main idea, it is important to distinguish which details are the *key details*, or the most important details, and which details are less important.

A key detail clearly shows a writer's main idea to be true. If you are able to identify key details, it shows you understand the main idea. It is also important to cite key details when summarizing a reading. These key details will make your summary clear and easy to understand.

C. Read the first two paragraphs of the newspaper feature "The Small House Movement" on the next page. Answer the questions.

1. What is true about average home size in the United States?

   a. It is increasing.

   b. It has not changed.

   c. It is decreasing.

2. What key detail supports the answer to question 1?

   a. The average home size was 2,479 square feet in 2007, up from 983 square feet in 1950.

   b. A 10,000-square-foot home has always represented the American dream.

   c. More and more people have started to question the need for large domestic spaces.

Read "The Small House Movement." Pay attention to the key details in each paragraph.

The Small House Movement

1 In the United States, the average family size continues to decrease. At the same time, the average home size has grown. According to the most recent U.S. Census,[1] the average home
5 size in the United States was 2,479 square feet in 2007, up from 983 square feet in 1950. In communities across the United States, it is possible to see homes that are larger than 10,000 square feet. For their owners, these
10 vast homes represent a piece of the American dream. However, a growing number of people, including artists, architects, city planners, and environmentalists, have started to question the need for such large **domestic** spaces. They
15 point out that despite their simplicity, small homes offer a number of benefits, not just to their owners, but to the world.

"I have been living in houses smaller than some people's closets," says California architect
20 Jay Shafer. Shafer currently lives with his wife in a 70-square-foot home that he built himself outside San Francisco. The narrow wooden home has a small working fireplace, a kitchen, and a table that folds up to reveal a computer.
25 Beyond the main room is a bathroom with a shower; upstairs is a tiny loft[2] with a bed and **storage** for clothing. "It sleeps two really comfortably," Shafer says with a smile.

Shafer is one of the original members of the
30 Small House **Movement**, a collection of artists and architects who promote small living spaces. The group's goal is to help people create a balanced and enjoyable lifestyle, something that can be achieved, Shafer says, by living

35 simply and **practically**. The group has grown in popularity as more and more people have discovered the benefits of small living spaces.

One obvious motivation to live in smaller homes is their low price. Whereas prices in
40 downtown New York City easily reach $1,200 per square foot or more, costs of construction company Jot House's small homes are as little as $100 per square foot, depending on location. Jot House founder Bryant Yeh says he was
45 inspired to create low-cost homes that featured modern designs. The Los Angeles-based company's one-story homes have a simple **layout** with a kitchen and bath. This allows for an open plan with large rooms that can work as
50 spaces for artists, or which can be **partitioned** into smaller enclosed spaces to fit the needs of multiple residents. The simple design of the houses means that they can be built in as little as three weeks, compared to the typical year-
55 long building process for many homes.

The low price of smaller homes makes them especially useful in times of great need. After Hurricane Katrina flooded much of the city of New Orleans in 2005, thousands of **displaced**
60 residents found themselves with no place to live. Among them were Julie Martin and her family. "**Prior** to Katrina we specialized in **restoring** beautiful historic homes," she says. In fact, the Martins restored and lived in the oldest
65 house on the Gulf Coast[3] before Hurricane Katrina destroyed it. Since then, Martin has worked with Shafer to create the Martin House Company, which sells small homes. Martin now

(continued on next page)

---

[1] **census:** an official account of all the people in a country

[2] **loft:** a raised area above the main part of a room, usually used for sleeping

[3] **Gulf Coast:** the part of the Atlantic Coast that is south of the United States, east of Mexico, and west of Cuba

lives in one herself. Many hurricane victims like Martin have been able to rebuild their lives by moving to small homes. The U.S. government has spent millions to assist in their construction. The low price of the houses makes them an attractive alternative to keeping hurricane victims in hotels or government buildings.

For Small House Movement founding member Sarah Susanka, owning a small house is not just about saving money. It is also about saving the environment. In her book *The Not So Big House*, the North Carolina-based architect points out that half of the energy use in the United States is for buildings. Reducing the size of homes is an easy way to limit energy use and the pollution that goes with it. Susanka says the idea to build smaller homes came to her while she was visiting friends. "People walked [me] through their house to get to the space they actually lived in . . . the dining room and the living room." By focusing on detail and making maximum use of available space, Susanka says residents can have a better overall living experience, without wasting natural resources.

Perhaps the greatest advantage of small houses is the flexibility they offer to their residents. Shafer's and Martin's houses, while small, have a special feature—a set of wheels. The small size and weight of each architect's home means it can be transported by truck. This allows the tenants/residents to live in a variety of places without the inconvenience of having to pack up and move their possessions. The small homes also require little **maintenance,** allowing their owners more free time to do the things they truly love. "The reason I've [lived in small homes] is mostly because I don't like vacuuming, and dusting,[4] and taking care of a lot of stuff that I'm not really using," says Shafer.

In many ways, the Small House Movement represents a return to the past and a time of simplicity. People who choose a small house point to a past when people had fewer possessions and children played outside. For these homeowners, bigger is not better after all.

---

[4] **dust:** clean dirt from a surface by moving something such as a soft cloth across it

Vocabulary Check

A. Circle the letter of the correct answer to complete each sentence. The boldfaced words are the target words.

1. After they got married, they were very **domestic** and spent their time _____.

   a. in the city   **b.** at home   **c.** in nature

2. The apartment building has several **layouts** that give you a choice of _____.

   a. size and shape   **b.** appliances and furniture   **c.** services

3. That house requires a lot of **maintenance** because it is _____.

   a. big and has a yard   **b.** modern   **c.** not used very often

4. The Riveras need a lot of **storage** for their _____.

   a. cat   **b.** windows   **c.** sports equipment

B. Write the letter of the correct definition next to the word. Be careful. There are two extra definitions.

_____ **1.** displace

_____ **2.** partition

_____ **3.** practical

_____ **4.** movement

_____ **5.** prior

a. to help something develop and be successful

b. useful; suitable for an appropriate purpose

c. very large in area

d. to divide a room into two or more parts

e. to make a group of people or animals leave the place where they normally live

f. before; arranged or happening before the present situation

g. a group of people who share the same ideas or beliefs and work together to achieve a particular aim

READ AGAIN

Read "The Small House Movement" again and complete the comprehension exercises on the next page. As you work, keep the reading goal in mind.

📖 **READING GOAL:** To write a summary that includes key details

Comprehension Check

A. Complete the chart with the missing details from the reading.

Person in the reading	Location	Job title	Why s/he designs small houses
Jay Shafer			
	Los Angeles		
		owner of the Martin House Company	
			to save the environment

B. Read the statements. Write *T* (true) or *F* (false). Under each statement, write a key detail from the reading that shows why it is true or false.

_____ **1.** Really spacious homes are found throughout the United States.

     key detail: _____

_____ **2.** Jay Shafer's house is small.

     key detail: _____

_____ **3.** People like architects and writers can't do their work in a small house.

     key detail: _____

_____ **4.** Julie Martin lost everything in Hurricane Katrina.

     key detail: _____

_____ **5.** The U.S. government is not dedicated to the idea of building more small houses.

key detail: _____

_____ **6.** Big houses are usually environmentally friendly.

key detail: _____

_____ **7.** Small houses are convenient for people who travel.

key detail: _____

_____ **8.** Jay Shafer enjoys cleaning his house.

key detail: _____

C. Write a summary of the reading. Explain the basic topic and the author's main ideas about the basic topic. Include one key detail to support each main idea.

_____

_____

_____

_____

_____

_____

_____

_____

_____

D. Work with a partner. Compare your summaries. Did you mention the same basic topic and the same main ideas? Did you include the same key details?

> ## DISCUSS

Design a floor plan[1] for your dream house. Label each room. Add details such as windows and fireplaces. Then share your design with a partner. Ask and answer the questions.

1. Does your house face north, south, east, or west? Why?

2. What is the room you want to be the most comfortable?

3. In what ways is your kitchen efficient?

4. Are there closets in convenient locations?

5. Is your house practical? Explain.

_____
[1] **floor plan:** a drawing that shows the shapes and locations of the rooms in a building

Twenty-four Rooms in One

PREPARE TO READ

A. Look at the words (and phrases) in the list. Write the number(s) next to each word to show what you know. You may be able to write more than one number next to some of the words. You will learn all of these words in this chapter.

1. I can use the word in a sentence.

2. I know <u>one meaning</u> of the word.

3. I know <u>more than one meaning</u> of the word.

4. I know how to pronounce the word.

B. Work with a partner. Look at the picture. Ask and answer the questions. If you don't know a word in English, ask your partner or look in your dictionary. Then write your new words on page 236.

1. What do you see in the picture? Describe the details.

2. How big do you think the apartment in the picture is?

3. Would you like to live in this apartment? Why or why not?

_____ float

_____ impose on

_____ mount

_____ ongoing

_____ radiance

_____ replicate

_____ shift

_____ shortage

_____ suspend

_____ tear down

_____ transformation

C. Scan the newspaper feature story "Twenty-four Rooms in One." Find and underline the answer from Exercise B, question 2.

> READ

Read "Twenty-four Rooms in One." Pay attention to the key details in each paragraph.

Twenty-four Rooms in One

1   GARY CHANG stood in the middle of his Hong Kong apartment on a recent Saturday morning, looking at a wall-size screen. He stepped on the balance board of his Nintendo
5 Wii game system for a second run of downhill skiing and began to **shift** from side to side, moving in time with a computer-generated figure across the room from him.

    Soon enough, having worked up an appetite,
10 he was ready to move on. He used a remote control[1] to raise the screen, revealing a large yellow-tinted window behind it, filling the room with **radiance.** "Like sunshine," Mr. Chang said, though the colorized gray daylight made
15 the view—a forest of apartment towers in Hong Kong's . . . Sai Wan Ho district—look like an old sepia print.[2]

    He grabbed a handle near the wall-**mounted** television, pulling a section of the wall itself
20 toward the center of the room. Behind it, a small countertop with [a two-burner stove], a sink and a spice rack[3] appeared. Opposite the countertop, on the back of the now-displaced wall, he lowered a hinged[4] worktop. Suddenly,
25 he was standing in a kitchen.

    This room . . . and the "video game room" he was sitting in minutes before are just two

of at least twenty-four different layouts that Mr. Chang, an architect, can **impose on** his
30 344-square-foot apartment. What appears to be an open-plan studio actually contains many rooms, because of sliding wall units, fold-down tables, and chairs.

    Mr. Chang, forty-six, has lived in this
35 seventh-floor apartment since he was fourteen, when he moved in with his parents and three younger sisters; they rented it from a woman who owned so much property that she often forgot to collect payment.

40   Like most of the 370 units in the 17-story building, which dates to the 1960s, the small space was partitioned into several tiny rooms—in this case, three bedrooms, a kitchen, a bathroom and a hallway. Mr. Chang's parents
45 shared the master bedroom (though when they first moved in, his father lived in the United States, where he worked as a waiter at Chinese restaurants in various cities). His sisters shared a second bedroom, and the third, almost
50 incredibly—although not unusually for Hong Kong—was occupied by a tenant, a woman in her twenties, whom Mr. Chang remembers only for the space she took up. Mr. Chang slept in the hallway, on a sofa bed.

(continued on next page)

---

[1] **remote control:** a thing you use for controlling a piece of electrical or electronic equipment without having to touch it

[2] **sepia print:** an old photograph that is a dark reddish-brown color

[3] **spice rack:** a place to store the powders and seeds used to flavor food

[4] **hinge:** a metal part used to fasten a door to its frame

55　　These days, he uses a . . . Murphy bed[5] of his own design, hidden behind a sofa during the day. "That old routine of folding out the bed is similar in spirit to what I do today," he said. "But the reasons are different. Then, it was just
60　necessary. Now, it's all about **transformation**, flexibility, and maximizing space."

　　Mr. Chang's experiment in flexible living began in 1988, when his family moved into a bigger apartment a few blocks away, with
65　his grandparents and uncles. His mother suggested that he take over the lease on their old apartment "because the rent was unusually low," he said. Instead he bought it, for about $45,000. He had been wanting to **tear down** the
70　walls since his teenage years. In the last [twenty years], he has remodeled four times. His latest effort took a year and cost just over $218,000.

　　Mr. Chang hopes that some of his home's innovations might be **replicated** to help
75　improve domestic life in Hong Kong, which has been troubled in recent years. The population grew by nearly a half-million in just the last ten years, and between 2003 and 2007, there has been an increase in reports of domestic
80　problems, at least partly caused by the city's **shortage** of space.

　　"It's a big problem," Mr. Chang said. "Killing each other is not uncommon.

　　"People feel trapped," he said. "We have to
85　find ways to live together in very small spaces."

　　In Mr. Chang's solution, a kind of human-size briefcase,[6] everything can be folded away so that the space feels expansive.

　　The wall units, which are **suspended** from . . .
90　the ceiling, seem to **float** an inch above the . . . floor. As they are shifted around, the apartment becomes all manner of spaces—kitchen, library, laundry room, dressing room, living room, an enclosed dining area, and a wet bar.[7]

95　　One can imagine three, possibly four people living here, using Mr. Chang's double bed and the guest bed that folds down over the bathtub—though six or seven, the number of residents when Mr. Chang was growing up,
100　would be another matter.

　　Buying a new apartment might have been a less expensive solution to his storage problem, he admits. "But why do that?" he asked as he stood in the kitchen making noodle soup. "I see
105　my place as an **ongoing** experiment."

---

[5] **Murphy bed:** a type of bed that can be stored upright when it is not being used

[6] **briefcase:** a flat suitcase with a handle usually used by business people for carrying papers or documents

[7] **wet bar:** a small bar with a sink

Vocabulary Check

A. Circle the letter of the correct answer to complete each sentence.

1. When a city does not have enough of something, there is a _____.
   a. radiance　　　**b.** shift　　　**c.** shortage

2. You can _____ in water.
   a. mount　　　**b.** suspend　　　**c.** float

3. In order to make an old building go away, people have to _____.
   a. replicate it　　　**b.** tear it down　　　**c.** impose on it

4. My work is not finished. It is _____.

    a. troubled   **b.** mounted   **c.** ongoing

5. I want to copy your design. I hope I can _____ it.

    a. innovate   **b.** impose on   **c.** replicate

B. Write *C* (correct) or *X* (incorrect) for the way the boldfaced target word is used in each statement. Then correct the incorrect statements to make them true.

_____ **1.** After the wedding, his new wife **imposed** a lot of changes **on** his apartment.

_____ **2.** After the sun disappeared, the room was filled with **radiance**.

_____ **3.** The architect's **transformation** of the old apartment kept it the same as it had been when he was growing up.

_____ **4.** I **shifted** the painting because it was leaning to one side.

_____ **5.** He plans to **suspend** a light from the floor.

_____ **6.** I'm going to **mount** the television on the wall so that I have more space on the floor.

▶ READ AGAIN

Read "Twenty-four Rooms in One" again and complete the comprehension exercises on the next page. As you work, keep the reading goal in mind.

> 📖 **READING GOAL:** To write a real estate advertisement for Gary Chang's apartment

Comprehension Check

A. Work with a partner. Check (✓) the main idea of the reading.

_____ **1.** Gary Chang shows that by renovating an old apartment so walls can be moved, a homeowner can save money and enjoy a more expansive space.

_____ **2.** Gary Chang's apartment is an example of how innovative design can transform a small space into one that feels expansive.

_____ **3.** Years of hard work and careful renovation have allowed Gary Chang to forget his memories of a troubled childhood in an overcrowded apartment.

_____ **4.** Hong Kong hopes to reduce domestic problems by replicating Gary Chang's success in transforming his small apartment.

B. Read the statements. Write *T* (true) or *F* (false). Under each statement, write a key detail from the reading that shows why it is true or false.

_____ **1.** There is enough space in his apartment for Gary Chang to exercise.

key detail: _____

_____ **2.** Chang can play video games while another person is cooking in his apartment.

key detail: _____

_____ **3.** The wall units in Chang's apartment are easy to shift.

key detail: _____

_____ **4.** The apartment has been in Chang's possession for more than twenty years.

key detail: _____

_____ **5.** Chang has invested a lot in his apartment.

key detail: _____

_____ **6.** There is not enough space in Chang's apartment for a guest to stay the night.

key detail: _____

_____ **7.** The population of Hong Kong is decreasing.

key detail: _____

_____ **8.** Shortage of space is a serious problem in Hong Kong.

key detail: _____

C. You are a real estate agent. Gary Chang asks you to help sell his apartment. Write an advertisement for Chang's apartment. Explain why people should buy it. Mention key details from the reading to support your ideas.

_____

_____

_____

_____

_____

_____

_____

_____

_____

_____

_____

_____

_____

D. Work with a partner. Compare your advertisements. Did you mention the same details?

> DISCUSS

Work in small groups. Ask and answer the questions.

1. Would you like to live in a small space alone or share a large space with roommates or family? Explain.

2. What sacrifices do people who live in small spaces have to make?

3. What are the benefits for people who live in small spaces?

4. What unusual homes would you be interested in living in? A tree house? A very old house? A small house? Other?

VOCABULARY SKILL BUILDING

Vocabulary Skill: Roots

Some words in English are built from a **root**, or Latin or Greek word part. The root combines with a prefix, a suffix, or both to become a word. Consequently, one root can form many different words. If you know the root, it is often possible to figure out the meaning of new words.

EXAMPLE:

Radius is a Latin root word that means "ray" or "spoke of a wheel."

Look at the illustrations and discuss the meaning of the boldfaced words.

*She looked beautiful in the **radiance** of the afternoon sun.*

*The hole was 40 feet across, so we knew the **radius** was 20 feet.*

*Heat **radiated** from the fire.*

A. The boldfaced words in the sentences share a root. Read the sentences and match the letter of the meaning to the root.

   a. bend   **c.** belief or trust

   b. hand   **d.** home, quality, or state

_____ **1.** *manus*

With the electricity out, we had to open the garage doors **manually**.

The **manuscript** for this book must be turned in by the end of the year.

My parents **manage** a small store in my hometown.

_____ **2.** *dom*

Do smaller families really need large **domestic** spaces?

Many people travel because they like to experience a sense of **freedom**.

After three hours of doing nothing, **boredom** set in.

_____ **3.** *flex/flect*

Gary Chang has created a **flexible** living space in a 344-square-foot apartment.

The apartment is a **reflection** of his desire to create architectural solutions that make the most of a small space.

Their goalie **deflected** the ball with his arm, and we were unable to score.

_____ **4.** *credo*

The idea that life may exist on other planets is **credible**.

You have to have good **credit** to buy a home.

Her ability to manage several tasks at once is **incredible**.

B. Circle the letter of the correct answer to complete each sentence.

1. Babies learn about the world by _____ their toys.
   a. reflecting   **b.** manipulating   **c.** radiating

2. We visited Bhutan, a _____ in South Asia.
   a. kingdom   **b.** replica   **c.** domicile

3. I could tell he didn't believe me by the _____ look on his face when I said that there is probably life on other planets.
   a. reflective   **b.** radiant   **c.** incredulous

4. Two companies _____ window frames specially designed for small houses.
   a. manufacture   **b.** radiate   **c.** master

5. The reporters wrote a story that _____ the construction company, which soon went out of business.
   a. manipulated   **b.** discredited   **c.** reflected

6. To be a great gymnast, one must have excellent _____.
   a. flexibility   **b.** reflexes   **c.** domicile

Learn the Vocabulary

Strategy

Using Word Parts to Guess Meaning

Words contain *parts*: roots, suffixes, and prefixes. The following are examples of words that you have learned so far. You have already studied some of the prefixes and suffixes, but not all. Look at the words and discuss their meanings:

Prefix	Meaning	Root	Meaning	Suffix	Meaning	Example Word
anti-	against	+ bio	life	+ ics	things having to do with	antibiotics
		astro	star	+ onomy	knowledge of	astronomy
dia-	through/across	+ meter	measure			diameter
man-	hand			+ age	action/process	manage
		pest	harmful insect	+ cide	killing	pesticide
extra-	beyond	+ terra	earth	+ al	relating to	extraterrestrial
trans-	across	+ form	form/shape	+ tion	action	transformation
ex-	out of/from	+ ceed	move/yield go			exceed

A. Use your knowledge of the word parts above to answer the questions. Underline the prefix, root, or suffix that helped you decide.

1. What kind of work does an astronaut do?

_____

_____

2. If someone is anti-city, where is he or she likely to live?

_____

_____

3. If you read the manual for a new appliance, what will you be able to do?

_____

_____

4. If an engineer makes machines, what kind of machine might a bioengineer make?

_____

_____

5. _Thermo-_ means heat, so what does a thermometer do?

_____

_____

6. How would you describe a transnational company?

_____

_____

7. When you extract the seeds from a fruit, what do you do?

_____

_____

8. Herbs are plants, so what does an herbicide do?

_____

_____

9. What makes a person extraordinary?

_____

_____

10. What should people do during a water shortage?

_____

_____

B. Now find the words from Exercise A in your dictionary and check your answers.

C. Make cards for the words that were new to you in this unit. Include target words and words that you wrote on page 236.

D. Go back to the vocabulary list at the beginning of each chapter. What did you learn about the target words? Add your numbers to the lists.

_____

Vocabulary Practice 8, see page 244

> THINK BEFORE YOU READ

A. Work with a partner. Look at the picture. Ask and answer the questions. If you don't know a word in English, ask your partner or look in your dictionary. Then write your new words on page 236.

1. What do you see in the picture? Describe the details.

2. What adjectives best describe the animal in the picture? Make a list.

B. Work in small groups. Ask and answer the questions.

1. Where can people go to see dangerous animals in the wild?

2. Why do some people like to see these dangerous animals close up?

3. Have you ever seen a dangerous animal in the wild? Explain.

How to Survive a Mountain Lion Attack

> PREPARE TO READ

A. Look at the words (and phrases) in the list. Write the number(s) next to each word to show what you know. You may be able to write more than one number next to some of the words. You will study all of these words in this chapter.

1. I can use the word in a sentence.

2. I know <u>one meaning</u> of the word.

3. I know <u>more than one meaning</u> of the word.

4. I know how to pronounce the word.

B. Work with a partner. Look at the picture. Ask and answer the questions. If you don't know a word in English, ask your partner or look in your dictionary. Then write your new words on page 236.

1. What do you see in the picture? Describe the details.

2. Do you enjoy hiking? If you've never gone hiking, would you like to?

3. What should hikers do if they see a mountain lion like the one on page 156?

_____ charge

_____ foe

_____ formidable

_____ frailty

_____ gaze

_____ grunt

_____ hold your ground

_____ majestic

_____ mating season

_____ menacing

_____ nostrils

_____ retreat

_____ sideways

_____ snarl

_____ spine-chilling

Reading Skill: Following Steps in a Process

When an author describes a *process*—the way to do a particular thing—pay attention to the *steps*, the things you must do in a particular order for the process to be successful. Look for numbers or signal words to help you follow each step. To remember the different steps, form a visual picture of each one in your mind. While focusing on each individual step, be sure to keep the final result, or goal of the process, in mind as well.

C. Preview the Internet article "How to Survive a Mountain Lion Attack." Answer the questions.

1. Is there a hook?

2. What is the final goal of the process?

3. Which paragraph explains the final goal of the process?

4. How many steps are in the process?

> READ

Read "How to Survive a Mountain Lion Attack." Pay attention to the numbers or signal words that indicate the steps in the process.

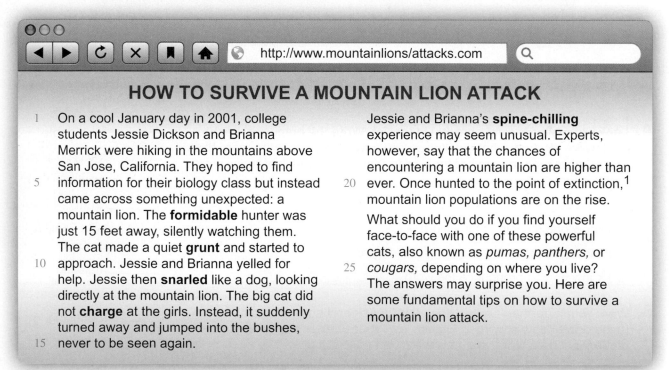

http://www.mountainlions/attacks.com

HOW TO SURVIVE A MOUNTAIN LION ATTACK

1   On a cool January day in 2001, college students Jessie Dickson and Brianna Merrick were hiking in the mountains above San Jose, California. They hoped to find
5   information for their biology class but instead came across something unexpected: a mountain lion. The **formidable** hunter was just 15 feet away, silently watching them. The cat made a quiet **grunt** and started to
10   approach. Jessie and Brianna yelled for help. Jessie then **snarled** like a dog, looking directly at the mountain lion. The big cat did not **charge** at the girls. Instead, it suddenly turned away and jumped into the bushes,
15   never to be seen again.

Jessie and Brianna's **spine-chilling** experience may seem unusual. Experts, however, say that the chances of encountering a mountain lion are higher than
20   ever. Once hunted to the point of extinction,[1] mountain lion populations are on the rise.

What should you do if you find yourself face-to-face with one of these powerful cats, also known as *pumas, panthers,* or
25   *cougars,* depending on where you live? The answers may surprise you. Here are some fundamental tips on how to survive a mountain lion attack.

---

[1] **extinction:** when a plant, animal, or language does not exist any more

TIP #1: KEEP YOURSELF OUT OF HARM'S WAY

30 Before entering the woods, find out if mountain lions have recently been seen in the area. Ask park rangers,[2] wildlife officials,
35 or the local police station if there have been any sightings. Avoid hiking, running, bicycling, or skiing when the sun is rising or setting, when mountain lions are most active. Keep in mind that attacks are most common
40 during **mating season**: late spring and early summer.

TIP #2: KEEP GOOD COMPANY

If you do plan on entering wilderness areas, do not go alone. Mountain lions are much
45 less likely to approach a group. Do not hike with dogs, as they are ideal prey for mountain lions and can increase the risk of attack. If you feel you must bring a dog, be sure to keep it on a leash.[3]

TIP #3: COME PREPARED

50 Bring a fully-charged GPS[4] device or cell phone with you that you can use to call for help in the event of an emergency. Notify friends and family about where you are going
55 and what time you plan to return. If you are hiking, bring a walking stick with you. It can serve as a weapon if needed.

TIP #4: KEEP AN EYE ON KIDS

Children are especially at risk of mountain
60 lion attacks. In fact, two-thirds of mountain lion victims are children. Before entering wilderness areas, talk to children about mountain lions and what to do if they see one.

TIP #5: STAY CALM AND DON'T RUN

65 There is a lot of irony in how people tend to respond to mountain lions. By running away, people actually prompt lions to chase and attack them. If you encounter a mountain lion, **hold your ground** and stay as calm as
70 possible. Make especially sure that children stay still and do not panic.

TIP #6: LOOK BIG AND TOUGH

Mountain lions prefer easy prey that won't put up a fight. For this reason, avoid any
75 signs of **frailty** when you come across one. Try to appear as large as possible. Stand up straight. Wave your arms over your head. If you are wearing a coat, stretch it out. Put children on your shoulders to increase your
80 height. Whatever you do, don't bend down, even to pick up children. Make direct eye contact with the mountain lion and appear as **menacing** as possible.

TIP #7: THREATEN FROM A DISTANCE

85 If a mountain lion starts to approach you, threaten it by throwing stones. If possible, keep a few stones ready in your pocket so you don't have to bend down to pick them up. Shout at the top of your lungs, or snarl like a
90 dog. Let it know that by attacking you, it risks injury as well.

TIP #8: PUT UP A GOOD FIGHT

If you are attacked, do not play dead. Stay on the defensive. There are a number of things
95 you can do to defend yourself. Use whatever means you have available to strike back[5]— your hands and feet, sticks, or sharp rocks. Aim for sensitive areas, such as the eyes and **nostrils**. Sometimes, a well-placed hit will be
100 enough to make a mountain lion **retreat**.

(continued on next page)

---

[2] **park ranger**: someone who is in charge of protecting a forest or area of countryside

[3] **leash**: a piece of rope, leather, etc., attached to a dog's collar in order to control it

[4] **GPS**: Global Positioning System: a system that uses radio signals from satellites to show your exact position on Earth on a special piece of equipment

[5] **strike back**: to attack someone or something that has attacked you first

TIP #9: UNDERSTAND YOUR FOE

In a fight, a mountain lion has two main weapons: its weight and its jaws. Whatever you do, remain standing. If the mountain lion drags you to the ground, it will lie on top
of you and use its jaws to break your neck. If you feel yourself being pulled down, roll **sideways** to shake the big cat off of you.

TIP #10: MAKE A CAREFUL RETREAT

At the first opportunity, begin slowly backing
away, one step at a time. Keep **gazing** directly at the mountain lion and threatening it by shouting and throwing stones. Be sure to give the mountain lion a way out—if it feels trapped, it may attack again.

TIP #11: TELL THE AUTHORITIES

Report any mountain lion sightings to wildlife authorities. Let them know the location, time of day, and circumstances under which the sighting occurred.

Experts say that Jessie and Brianna did exactly the right thing when they saw the mountain lion. If you see one of these **majestic** creatures in the wild, remember to stay calm, hold your ground, and act
threateningly if approached. Following these tips will greatly increase your odds of surviving.

Vocabulary Check

A. Work with a partner. Ask and answer the questions. The boldfaced words are target words.

1. What is the most **majestic** view you have ever seen?

2. Would you be able to **hold your ground** if you saw a mountain lion? Explain.

3. Which is more **menacing**—an angry cat or an angry dog?

4. What is a **formidable** challenge that you have faced?

5. If we meet creatures from other planets, do you expect them to be friends or **foes**? Why?

6. What would you do if a mountain lion **charged** at you?

7. Have you or has anyone you know ever had a **spine-chilling** encounter with an animal? Explain.

B. Complete the sentences with the target words from the reading. Use the correct form of the word.

1. For a long time, the big cat would _____ out over the land

   without moving.

2. To find out if she's angry, watch her nose. If her _____ are

   moving in and out, she is definitely mad.

3. The cat decided to _____; it stopped fighting and ran into the forest.

4. She _____ as she pushed the heavy couch to the other side of the room.

5. My dog is so sick and weak. I'm concerned about his _____.

6. A few months after the _____ the cats have babies.

7. Don't jump forward or backward; jump _____ to get out of the path of the creature.

8. If an animal _____, it may be getting ready to attack you.

❯ READ AGAIN

Read "How to Survive a Mountain Lion Attack" again and complete the comprehension exercises. As you work, keep the reading goal in mind.

> 📖 **READING GOAL:** To create an informative poster based on the reading

Comprehension Check

A. Work with a partner. Read the following scenarios. Check (✓) the situations where people did the right thing to escape from the mountain lion.

_____ **1.** Two young boys were hiking in the forest when they saw a mountain lion. They yelled and slowly walked backward until they reached their parents.

_____ **2.** A tall man was hiking alone with his dog when he saw a mountain lion. He got down on the ground and covered his head with his hands.

_____ **3.** A family of four was hiking in the woods when they saw a mountain lion next to a high wall. The father threw his water bottle at the animal and yelled at it.

_____ **4.** A young man was hiking with his dog when he saw a mountain lion. He bent over to pick up the dog so the big cat would not attack it.

B. Write the best response to each situation. Don't look back at the reading. Then compare answers with a partner.

1. You are hiking in the mountains when suddenly a mountain lion jumps on you.

   _____

   _____

2. You are hiking with a child, and suddenly you see a mountain lion.

   _____

   _____

3. You walk around a bend in the trail and see a mountain lion in front of you. There is a cliff behind the mountain lion.

   _____

   _____

4. You are walking with your dog when you see a mountain lion watching you from high up on a rock.

   _____

   _____

C. On a separate sheet of paper, write a short piece of advice for people in each of the situations.

1. You are hiking in the mountains when suddenly you come face-to-face with a mountain lion. Should you maintain eye contact?

2. You are walking through a rocky place when you see a mountain lion. There are rocks around your feet. Should you pick them up to throw at the lion?

3. You are hiking with children. What should you tell them to do if they see a mountain lion?

> DISCUSS

Work in small groups. Ask and answer the questions.

1. What would you do if you found out that a mountain lion or other dangerous animal was in your neighborhood?

2. Should people be allowed to go to places where they might be attacked by an animal?

3. Do you think that predators such as mountain lions, bears, and wolves should be saved from extinction? Explain.

Life of Pi

> PREPARE TO READ

A. Look at the words (and phrases) in the list. Write the number(s) next to each word to show what you know. You may be able to write more than one number next to some of the words. You will study all of these words in this chapter.

1. I can use the word in a sentence.

2. I know <u>one meaning</u> of the word.

3. I know <u>more than one meaning</u> of the word.

4. I know how to pronounce the word.

B. Work with a partner. Look at the pictures. Ask and answer the questions. If you don't know a word in English, ask your partner or look in your dictionary. Then write your new words on page 236.

1. What do you see in the pictures? Describe the details.

2. What do you think the story is about? How does the tiger come to be on the boat?

3. How does the man on the boat probably feel?

4. If you were in the man's situation, what would you do?

_____ come clean

_____ despair

_____ fury

_____ growl

_____ in the same boat

_____ intently

_____ outlast

_____ petrifying

_____ prick up (one's) ears

_____ rusty

_____ tame

_____ twitch

C. Read the first two paragraphs of the excerpt from *Life of Pi*. Answer the questions.

1. Who is Richard Parker?

2. Is the man in the boat in immediate danger? Explain.

> READ

Read the excerpt from *Life of Pi.* Pay attention to the descriptive details. Try to visualize the scene the author is describing.

ஒ *Life of Pi* ஐ

1   *After a shipwreck, the narrator, the son of a zookeeper, finds himself alone in a small life raft at sea. Soon he discovers that he is not alone. A tiger named Richard Parker is also on the life raft. The narrator is terrified and does not know what to do.*

    It was Richard Parker who calmed me down. It is the irony of this story that the
5 one who scared me [so much] to start with was the very same who brought me peace, purpose, even wholeness.

    He was looking at me **intently**. After a time I recognized the gaze. I had grown up with it. It was the gaze of a contented animal looking out from its cage the way you or I would look out from a restaurant table after a good meal, when the
10 time has come for conversation and people watching. Clearly Richard Parker had eaten his fill of hyena[1] and drunk all the rainwater he wanted. No lips were rising and falling, no teeth were showing, no **growling** or snarling was coming from him. He was simply taking me in, observing me, in a manner that was not menacing. He kept **twitching** his ears and varying the sideways turn of his head.
15 It was all so, well, catlike. He looked like a nice, big, fat domestic cat, a 450-pound tabby.[2]

    He made a sound, a snort[3] from his nostrils. I **pricked up my ears**. He did it a second time. I was astonished. Prusten?[4]

    Tigers make a variety of sounds. They include a number of growls, the
20 loudest usually made during the mating season. It's a cry that travels far and wide, and is absolutely **petrifying** when heard close up. Tigers go *woof* when they are [surprised], a short, sharp [explosion] of **fury** that would instantly make your legs jump up and run away if they weren't frozen to the spot. When they charge, tigers put out throaty, coughing roars. And tigers hiss[5] and snarl,
25 which, depending on the emotion behind it, sounds either like autumn leaves rustling[6] on the ground, or, when it's an infuriated snarl, like a giant door with

---

[1] **hyena:** a wild animal like a dog that makes a loud sound like a laugh

[2] **tabby:** a cat with orange, grey, or brown marks on its fur

[3] **snort:** a loud sound made by breathing through your nose

[4] **prusten:** a sound of friendliness made by a tiger

[5] **hiss:** make a noise that sounds like *sssssss*

[6] **rustle:** when leaves, papers, clothes make a soft noise as they rub against each other

rusty hinges slowly opening—in both cases, [completely] spine-chilling. Tigers make other sounds, too. They grunt and they moan. They purr,[7] though not as melodiously[8] or as frequently as small cats, and only as they breathe out.

30 (Only small cats purr breathing both ways. It is one of the characteristics that distinguishes big cats from small cats. Another is that only big cats can roar. A good thing that is. I'm afraid the popularity of the domestic cat would drop very quickly if [it] could roar its displeasure.) Tigers even go *meow* [like] domestic cats but louder and in a deeper range, not as encouraging to bend down and pick

35 them up. And tigers can be utterly, majestically silent, that too.

I had heard all these sounds growing up. Except for prusten. If I knew of it, it was because Father had told me about it. He had read descriptions of it. But he had heard it only once, while on a working visit to the Mysore Zoo, in their animal hospital, from a young male being treated for pneumonia.[9] Prusten is

40 the quietest of tiger calls, a puff[10] through the nose to express friendliness and harmless intentions.

Richard Parker did it again, this time with a rolling of the head. He looked exactly as if he were asking me a question.

I looked at him, full of fearful wonder. There being no immediate threat, my

45 breath slowed down, my heart stopped knocking about in my chest, and I began to regain my senses.

I had to **tame** him. It was at that moment that I realized this necessity. It was not a question of him or me, but of him and me. We were **in the same boat**. We would live—or we would die—together. He might be killed in an accident, or he

50 could die shortly of natural causes, but it would be foolish to count on [it]. More likely the worst would happen: the simple passage of time, in which his animal toughness would easily **outlast** my human frailty. Only if I tamed him could I possibly trick him into dying first, if we had to come to that.

But there's more to it. I will **come clean**. I will tell you a secret: A part of me

55 was glad about Richard Parker. A part of me did not want Richard Parker to die at all, because if he died I would be left alone with **despair**, a foe even more formidable than a tiger. If I still had the will to live, it was thanks to Richard Parker. He kept me from thinking too much about my family and my tragic circumstances. He pushed me to go on living.

---

[7] **purr:** a soft low sound a cat makes in its throat to show that it is pleased

[8] **melodiously:** having a pleasant tune or a pleasant sound

[9] **pneumonia:** a serious illness of the lungs that makes breathing difficult

[10] **puff:** the action of breathing in and out or blowing air out in short bursts

Vocabulary Check

A. Write C (correct) or X (incorrect) for the way the boldfaced target word is used in each statement. Then correct the incorrect statements to make them true.

_____ **1.** Farmers **tame** their produce.

_____ **2.** You may enjoy the **fury** of a mother cat.

_____ **3.** We faced similar problems, but it took us a long time to admit that we were **in the same boat**.

_____ **4.** Most cats and dogs live about twenty years, so they usually **outlast** their owners.

_____ **5.** They had a **petrifying** experience when they took the boat out on the ocean in beautiful weather.

_____ **6.** The dog **pricked up her ears** when she heard the key in the lock.

B. Circle the letter of the correct answer to complete each sentence. The boldfaced words are the target words.

1. The metal cage was **rusty** after a _____.
   a. hot dry summer   **b.** long wet spring   **c.** cold windy fall

2. The traveler was in **despair** after he _____.
   a. saw the cougar   **b.** met his friends   **c.** lost his money and documents

3. She would not **come clean** until we promised _____.
   a. she could take a hot shower   **b.** she could keep her secret   **c.** not to get angry

4. He stared **intently** at the speaker because he _____.
   a. was bored   **b.** wanted to learn the truth   **c.** needed glasses

5. Horses **twitch** their tails when they want to get rid of _____.
   a. flies   **b.** people   **c.** a cold wind

6. When the girl saw the lion and heard it **growl**, she _____.
   a. took pictures   **b.** picked it up and took it home   **c.** got scared and cried

READ AGAIN

Read the excerpt from *Life of Pi* again and complete the comprehension exercises. As you work, keep the reading goal in mind.

> **READING GOAL:** To write a one-sentence summary expressing the implied main idea

Comprehension Check

A. Circle the letter of the correct answer to each question.

1. Irony occurs when there is a contradiction of some sort. Which of the following best matches the irony of the narrator's story?
   a. It is ironic that the narrator knows a lot about tigers because he needs the knowledge to survive.
   b. It is ironic that the narrator needs the tiger to stay alive because the tiger is a dangerous threat.
   c. It is ironic that the tiger has already eaten the hyena because that gives the narrator time to think.

2. What unusual comparison does the narrator make when the tiger first looks at him?
   a. He compares the tiger to a house cat.
   b. He compares the tiger to a hyena, which is not a cat at all.
   c. He compares the tiger to a person who is interested in conversation and people watching.

3. What details does the narrator give that explain why he thinks he can handle a live tiger on a boat?
   a. He thinks the tiger is too weak to be a threat.
   b. The tiger reminds him of a big house cat.
   c. He knows a lot about tigers and how they communicate.

4. Which best describes what the narrator hopes to get from the tiger?
   a. He is hungry so he wants the tiger for food.
   b. He needs the tiger for companionship.
   c. He is lost and he thinks the animal may know how to find land.

5. What is the narrator most afraid of?
   a. being eaten by the tiger
   b. dying of hunger and thirst on the open ocean
   c. being alone

B. Answer the questions in your own words. Don't look back at the reading.

1. How does Pi (the main character and narrator) feel in the beginning of the story?

   _____

2. Why does Pi know so much about tigers?

   _____

3. How does Pi know Richard Parker isn't an immediate threat?

   _____

4. Why does Pi say he is "glad about Richard Parker"?

   _____

5. What does Pi think will happen to him and Richard Parker in the future?

   _____

C. Write a one-sentence summary of the reading. Express the implied main idea. Use your answers from Exercise B to help you.

   _____

   _____

   _____

D. Work with a partner. Compare your summary sentences. Are they similar?

> DISCUSS

Work in small groups. Ask and answer the questions.

1. How does the tiger feel about the narrator?

2. Do you think the narrator is making a good choice in wanting to tame the tiger? Explain.

3. What would you do if you were trapped in a boat with a dangerous animal?

4. What do you think will happen in the rest of the story?

> VOCABULARY SKILL BUILDING

Vocabulary Skill: Onomatopoeia

In poetry and literature, writers sometimes use *onomatopoeia*. They choose words with a meaning that imitates the sound. For example, the word *buzz* represents both the meaning and the sound that a bee or an electric saw makes.

Other common examples are the words that depict animal sounds.

Animal	Onomatopoeia
a horse	*neigh*
a dog	*woof*
a bird	*cheep*
a snake	*hiss*

A. Circle the letter of the correct onomatopoeic word for each situation.

1. A person shows disgust or disbelief.
   a. growl   **b.** grunt

2. A tire is slowly leaking air.
   a. hiss   **b.** roar

3. A smoker blows a smoke ring.
   a. snarl   **b.** puff

4. A seated dog makes a low quiet threatening sound.
   a. hiss   **b.** growl

5. Two house cats are fighting over territory.
   a. snarl   **b.** grunt

6. A male lion is showing his power.
   a. roar   **b.** puff

B. Answer the questions.

1. What makes a dog **growl**?

   _____

2. Besides a snake, what animals make a **hissing** sound?

   _____

3. What would you do if a house cat **snarled** at you?

   _____

4. Which is more frightening, the **howl** of a wolf or the **roar** or a lion? Explain.

   _____

Learn the Vocabulary

Strategy

The Keyword Technique

There are many ways to remember the meaning of a new word. Research on language learners shows that the keyword technique works well for many learners. Here's how it works:

1. Look at the new word, and choose a *keyword*. A keyword is a word in your native language that sounds similar to the beginning or all of the new word in English. Look at the example from a native speaker of Farsi.

EXAMPLE: New word = *rustle*
Keyword (Farsi word that sounds similar) = *rasoo* (*weasel,* a small wild animal that hunts)

2. Imagine a picture where the meaning of the new word and the meaning of the keyword are connected in some way. The connection can be strange. In fact, strange pictures are often easier to remember!

EXAMPLE:

3. To remember the word *rustle* in English, think of the image of the *rasoo* moving through the grass and making a rustling sound.

4. If you like to draw, you can draw the picture on the back side of your word card, with the English word on the front side.

rustle
/ˈrʌsəl/

A. Think of keywords for five of the target words from the unit, and write them below.

New word	Keyword
1. _____	_____
2. _____	_____
3. _____	_____
4. _____	_____
5. _____	_____

B. Now imagine a picture to connect the new word and the keyword for each of the new words in Exercise A. Write the new word on one side of a word card. Draw the picture on the other side of the card.

C. Show your cards to a classmate. Explain your pictures by pronouncing the keywords and telling your partner the meaning.

D. Add the cards to your other cards. Review all of your cards with a partner. (See page 18 for an explanation of how to review your cards with a partner.)

E. Go back to the vocabulary list at the beginning of each chapter. What did you learn about the target words? Add your numbers to the lists.

Vocabulary Practice 9, see page 245

FLUENCY PRACTICE 3

To increase your reading speed, don't focus on the meaning of every word. Divide sentences into groups of words, or *chunks*. For example, the following sentence can be broken into three chunks.

Students who want to practice fluency • should repeatedly read • the same materials.

The first chunk (*students who want to practice fluency*) is the subject, the thing that does the action. The next chunk (*should repeatedly read*) is the verb phrase, the description of the action. The third chunk (*the same materials*) is the object, the thing that receives the action.

If you think of the sentence as three chunks instead of twelve words, it is easier to understand.

> READING 1

Before You Read

> shy /ʃaɪ/ (adj.) : nervous and embarrassed about meeting and speaking to other people, especially people you do not know

A. Read the definition of *shy*. Then answer the questions on a separate sheet of paper.

   1. Do you think you are a shy person?

   2. What things are difficult for shy people?

   3. What causes people to be shy? Make a list of your ideas.

B. Preview "Why Are We Shy?" on the next page. Identify two possible causes of shyness mentioned in the reading.

Read

A. Read "Why Are We Shy?" Time yourself. Write your start and end times and your total reading time. Then calculate your reading speed (words per minute) and write it in the progress chart on page 249.

Start time: _____   **End time:** _____   **Total time:** _____ (in seconds)

Reading speed:

747 words ÷ _____ (total time in seconds) x 60 = _____ words per minute

Why Are We Shy?

1   Do you feel nervous when you meet new people? Does speaking in public send a chill up your spine? Is it sometimes difficult for you to express your true feelings to others? If
5 you answered "yes" to any of these questions, you may be a shy person. But if you are, don't despair. You are not alone. In fact, research shows that most people are shy. Almost 80 percent of people report feeling shy at some
10 point in their lives. And with each passing year, shyness becomes more common. With shyness being so widespread, scientists have long desired to know what causes it. Although they don't have any definite answers, they do
15 have some interesting ideas about why we are shy.

    A common belief is that people become shy during life as a result of troubling social experiences. But scientists now say there is
20 evidence that we are born shy. Studies show that 15 to 20 percent of babies behave shyly. These babies tend to be a little quieter and more reactive to unfamiliar sounds and images than other babies. Interestingly, these shy babies
25 usually have shy parents and grandparents. As a result, many scientists now believe that shyness is genetic.

    Family size might be a factor in shyness as well. A Harvard University study of shy children

30 found that 66 percent had older brothers and sisters. The Harvard researchers concluded that menacing behavior by the older siblings made the younger children become shy. Of course, children with no brothers and sisters may be shy
35 as well. Growing up alone, they are not able to develop the same social skills as children from big families. When they reach school, interacting with teachers and classmates can be difficult.

    People may even be shy simply because of
40 where they were born. A study of shyness in different countries found remarkable differences. In Japan, for example, most people said they were shy. But in Israel, only one in three people said so. The study's authors said the
45 difference can be explained by Japanese and Israeli opinions about failure. In Japan, say the researchers, people tend to blame themselves for their failures. In Israel, the opposite is true. Israelis often blame failure on external
50 factors: family, teachers, friends, or bad luck. In Israel, freedom of expression and risk taking are encouraged. This may be why Israelis worry less about failure and are less shy.

    Another cause of shyness might be
55 technology. Thanks to computers, face-to-face conversation is no longer essential in many situations. Activities such as buying groceries or filling up a car at the gas station once required

(continued on next page)

social interaction. Today, they can all be done
60 via machines. As a result, people are losing daily
practice in the fundamentals of conversation. As
technology continues to play a larger role in our
lives, scientists say shyness will likely increase
even further.
65   What, then, can shy people do? Scientists
agree that shyness can be overcome, but the
transformation cannot happen overnight. Often,
shyness is lost very slowly. Significant life steps
such as starting a career, getting married, or
70 buying a home instill shy people with a sense
of confidence. This new confidence then makes
it easier to interact with others. For some
people, however, shyness continues to be an
ongoing problem. Michael Jordan, for example,
75 has famously said that he is shy. This is despite
him being considered by many people to be the
greatest basketball player of all time.
    To overcome severe cases of shyness, scientists
say there are certain steps people can take.

80 First of all, it is important to be conscious
of negative thoughts. For example, people
who experience shyness when meeting others
should be honest with themselves about their
nervousness rather than trying to ignore it. They
85 should ask themselves why they feel nervous
and accept the answer. Once this is done, they
can try to shift their attention outward. As one
scientist says, "A big part of overcoming shyness
is getting in touch with how the people around
90 you are feeling and learning not to always focus
on yourself." Scientists say people can also
practice conversational strategies that they can
later replicate. For example, the skills that allow
someone to converse successfully with a family
95 member can also be applied when talking with
strangers. Finally, and perhaps most importantly,
shy people should remember that their condition
is widespread. In a world full of shy people, there
are a lot of other people who are in the same
95 boat.

B. Read "Why Are We Shy?" again, a little faster this time. Write your start
and end times and your total reading time. Then calculate your reading
speed (words per minute) and write it in the progress chart on page 249.

Start time: _____   **End time:** _____   **Total time:** _____ (in seconds)

Reading speed:

747 words ÷ _____ (total time in seconds) x 60 = _____ words per minute

Comprehension Check

A. Read the statements about shyness. Check (✓) the statements that are true according to the reading.

_____ **1.** There are fewer shy people now than there were in the past.

_____ **2.** Shy parents often have shy children.

_____ **3.** Most Israeli people are shy.

_____ **4.** Many shy people have older brothers and sisters.

_____ **5.** Children from big families often acquire social skills at home.

_____ **6.** Genetics, family size, and the place you are born all may cause shyness.

_____ **7.** Basketball player Michael Jordan is shy.

_____ **8.** If you are shy now, you will be shy forever.

B. Answer the questions in your own words on a separate sheet of paper.

1. How common is shyness?

2. What are four possible causes of shyness?

3. How can people overcome their shyness?

C. Check your answers for the comprehension questions in the Answer Key on page 250. Then calculate your score and write it in the progress chart on page 249.

_____ (my number correct) ÷ 11 x 100 = _____%

> READING 2

Before You Read

Work with a partner. Decide if you agree with the following statements. Explain your ideas.

1. Everyone wants the same things in life: a big house, a loving family, and a lot of money.

2. Most people know the secret to finding happiness.

Read

A. Read "Choosing to Be Different." Time yourself. Write your start and end times and your total reading time. Then calculate your reading speed (words per minute) and write it in the progress chart on page 249.

Start time: _____ **End time:** _____ **Total time:** _____ (in seconds)

Reading speed:

720 words ÷ _____ (total time in seconds) x 60 = _____ words per minute

Choosing to Be Different

1   In Northern Iran, nomads walk their goats through the desert to a summer home high in the majestic Zagros Mountains. In a small bedroom in Tokyo, a young man plays
5 computer games by night and sleeps by day. He has not left his bedroom in over a year. In the middle of a vast city, several families eat well but never go to a supermarket. They have cars and electricity but never need to go to a gas
10 station or pay an electric bill. In retirement communities throughout the United States, old people live a happy, child-free existence in gated neighborhoods sometimes referred to as "Disney for adults."

15   These people all come from very different backgrounds. The motivation for their behavior is also quite varied. Some are escaping from the present. Others are returning to the past. Still others are preparing for the future.

20   However, they all have one thing in common. They have chosen lifestyles that distinguish them from others.

Staying with traditions

   In many parts of the world, there are people
25 who know about modern life but are not interested in being a part of it. About a third of the Bakhtiari nomads of Iran have chosen not to go to cities, attend schools, or get jobs. During the 20th century, Iran's leader, the
30 Shah, tried to make the Bakhtiari give up their nomadic traditions. After the Shah was forced out of power, however, the Bakhtiari went back to their prior nomadic life. Every spring they

pack up their animal-hair tents and everything
35 that they own. They leave the desert on foot, traveling 200 miles to their summer home high in the mountains. In the fall, they pack everything up again and return to the desert.

Withdrawing

40   Rather than following traditions, some people reject them. The *hikikomori* of Japan are one example. Hikikomori are young people, usually young men, who do not follow the usual path of education, career, marriage, and family.

45   Unlike the Bakhtiari, they do not leave the cities physically. Instead, they retreat into their own enclosed worlds. They spend all of their time in their bedrooms. They never leave. They don't attend school or even share family
50 meals. They order take-out or someone leaves food for them, which they eat alone. Dirty dishes occupy more and more space, as the teenagers will not leave their rooms or allow anyone else to enter. The number of hikikomori
55 is not very large, but their existence troubles many people in Japan. What prompts this behavior? Are the hikikomori mentally ill? Or is their rejection of the mainstream Japanese lifestyle a sign of a wider social problem?

60 ## Searching for a better way

   Another group includes those who are concerned about the environment. They believe that the future of the planet depends on the creation of new ways of living. They belong
65 to the *urban homesteaders movement*. Urban

homesteaders live in the middle of large cities. However, they stay away from supermarkets, malls, and gas stations. They grow fruit and vegetables. They raise animals in their small
70 urban back yards. They use wind and solar power to produce their own electricity. They raise sheep and make cloth from the wool. They make their own fuel to power their cars and trucks. They collect rainwater for washing.
75 Any essentials that they cannot make or grow they get by trading with other homesteaders. Urban homesteaders aren't skeptical of all modern conveniences. Rather, they promote ways to enjoy life in the 21st century without
80 harming the environment.

Living the dream

The final group is larger than the others. It is made up of Americans 55 years of age and older living in retirement communities
85 in the southern United States. In these communities, the sun is always shining, the streets are safe and clean, the golf courses are always green, and the seniors' sleep is never imposed on by crying children or loud
90 teenagers. Children can visit, but only for a few days. This applies to anyone under the age of 18—even the residents' own grandchildren. To many residents, the "no-children" rule is the best thing about their new lives. Free
95 from the stress of work and raising children, these retirees choose to live their golden years in happy isolation. They spend their days enjoying their favorite activities in their own child-free "Disneyland."

B. Read "Choosing to Be Different" again, a little faster this time. Write your start and end times and your total reading time. Then calculate your reading speed (words per minute) and write it in the progress chart on page 249.

Start time: _____   **End time:** _____   **Total time:** (in seconds)

Reading speed:

720 words ÷ _____ (total time in seconds) x 60 = _____ words per minute

Comprehension Check

A. Circle the letter of the correct answer to complete each sentence.

1. About a third of the Bakhtiari people of Iran _____ to live a nomadic lifestyle.
   a. were forced
   b. choose to
   c. no longer want to

2. Each year the Bakhtiari travel from the desert to _____.
   a. vast cities
   b. gated communities
   c. the Zagros Mountains

(continued on next page)

3. Most hikikomori are _____.

    a. retired people

    b. parents

    c. teenagers

4. The author has a _____ view of hikikomori.

    a. positive

    b. neutral

    c. negative

5. Urban homesteaders create their own _____.

    a. cities

    b. electricity

    c. supermarkets

6. Most American retirement communities are in the _____ part of the country.

    a. northern

    b. eastern

    c. southern

7. Many retirement communities have a no-_____ rule.

    a. kids

    b. cars

    c. video games

B. Answer the questions in your own words on a separate sheet of paper.

1. What do all the people in the reading have in common?

2. How are the people in the reading different from each other?

C. Check your answers for the comprehension questions in the Answer Key on page 250. Then calculate your score and write it in the progress chart on page 249.

_____ (my number correct) ÷ 9 x 100 = _____%

▷ THINK BEFORE YOU READ

A. Work with a partner. Look at the pictures. Ask and answer the questions. If you don't know a word in English, ask your partner or look in your dictionary. Then write your new words on page 236.

1. What do you see in the pictures? Describe the details.

2. How are the two visions of the future different from each other?

B. Work in small groups. Discuss your ideas.

1. Which of the above visions of the future is more likely, in your opinion? Explain.

2. Look at the unit title and the titles of the readings in this unit. What do you think the readings in this unit are about?

CHAPTER 19

Reaching Our Limits: Welcome to 2100

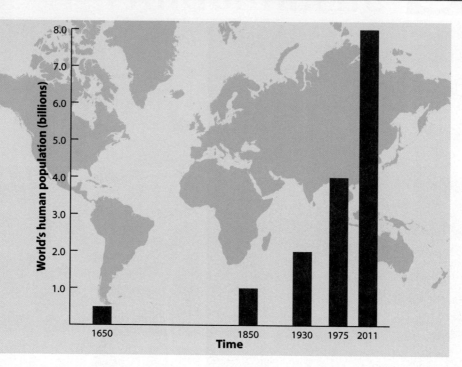

PREPARE TO READ

A. Look at the words (and phrases) in the list. Write the number(s) next to each word to show what you know. You may be able to write more than one number next to some of the words. You will study all of these words in this chapter.

1. I can use the word in a sentence.

2. I know <u>one meaning</u> of the word.

3. I know <u>more than one meaning</u> of the word.

4. I know how to pronounce the word.

B. Work with a partner. Look at the graph. Ask and answer the questions. If you don't know a word in English, ask your partner or look in your dictionary. Then write your new words on page 236.

1. What information does the graph show?

2. What are some possible explanations for the recent increase in the human population?

3. Is the increase in world population a positive thing? Explain.

_____ abandon

_____ abuse

_____ collapse

_____ drought

_____ harsh

_____ linked to

_____ out of the question

_____ resources

_____ settlement

_____ spray

_____ standard of living

_____ starvation

Reading Skill: Identifying Rhetorical Structure

It is important to be able to identify the rhetorical structure of a text. Rhetorical structure refers to the content and organization of a text as a whole. Some common rhetorical structures are

- description of a person, place, or thing
- classification of types of things into groups
- persuasion (trying to convince the reader to believe or do something)
- narrative (telling a story in chronological order)

To identify the rhetorical structure of a text, ask yourself the following:

1. How does the author organize his or her main ideas?
2. Which examples and details does the author choose to include?
3. What point of view does the author have: positive, negative, or neutral?
4. What is the author's purpose for writing?

If you can identify the rhetorical structure of a text, it will help you when you summarize it.

C. Read paragraphs 1 and 2 of the magazine article "Reaching Our Limits: Welcome to 2100" on the next page. Check (✓) the answer to each question.

1. Which paragraph gives the main idea of the reading?

_____ **a.** paragraph 1   _____ **b.** paragraph 2

2. Which examples does the author include?

_____ **a.** examples of future shortages of essential products   _____ **b.** examples of future technological innovations

3. What point of view does the author express?

_____ **a.** positive   _____ **b.** negative

4. What is the author's purpose in writing?

_____ **a.** to warn the reader   _____ **b.** to entertain the reader

> READ

Read "Reaching Our Limits: Welcome to 2100" on the next page. As you read, try to identify the rhetorical structure of the reading.

Reaching Our Limits: Welcome to 2100

1   Imagine that you live in a big city in the year 2100. You wake up in a small apartment, go into your kitchen, and check a series of electronic machines. They tell you that you

5   have about a half a gallon [2 liters] of water for the day—enough to drink, but not enough to take a shower. You'll use a chemical **spray** instead of showering. It's raining, which means little solar power is available. You have

10   enough electricity only to run your refrigerator and computer for a few hours. This is a big problem. You can't afford to lose all of the food in your refrigerator. Furthermore, you have to work on your computer, and going to

15   the office isn't an option. Driving is **out of the question** because of the high cost of fuel, and the subways are flooded because of rising sea levels. Of course, it could be worse. In other parts of the world, there is no water, food,

20   or electricity at all. Entire cities have been **abandoned**.

    This vision of the future isn't certain, but it is possible. Research is showing that our way of life—our use of water, soil, and energy—is

25   not sustainable. Scientists warn that if we don't limit our population growth and use of **resources**, our society will be deeply troubled in the future.

VICTIMS OF OUR OWN SUCCESS

30   In one sense, large populations are a sign of a successful civilization. In fact, most population growth is **linked to** increases in material wealth and technological innovations. The development of industry between 1650

35   and 1850 allowed the global population to double from about 500 million to 1 billion. Since then, further technological advances—in agriculture, medicine, and engineering—have enabled the population to grow to almost

40   7 billion. Over this time period, our **standards of living** have increased. Many of us travel more, live in bigger houses, and eat better than our ancestors ever did. History, however, shows that human populations can grow to the

45   point where they are no longer sustainable.

    As anthropologist[1] Joseph Tainter explains, "Every society that **collapsed** thought it couldn't happen to them. The Roman Empire thought it couldn't happen. The Maya[2]

50   civilization thought it couldn't happen . . . but it did." In the case of the Maya, environmental destruction and deforestation[3] led to a shortage of food, and **starvation** resulted. The Roman Empire grew to the point where it was

55   unable to financially support its population. When each society used up its resources, fighting broke out over the little that was left, and the civilizations collapsed.

RISING DEMAND, FALLING SUPPLY

60   Scientists now wonder if we are repeating the mistakes of these earlier civilizations. As the global population has grown over the last fifty years, consumption of resources has increased as well. In the United States alone,

65   use of petroleum and electricity has more than tripled since 1950. Water use has doubled to about 350 billion gallons (1.3 billion cubic meters) a day. Experts say that for each person added to the U.S. population, approximately

70   one acre of land is lost to urbanization. As a result, the amount of available farmland per person in the United States is expected to decrease from 1.8 acres today to 0.6 acres by 2050. At least 1.2 acres per person is

75   necessary to maintain current American dietary standards, however. These same trends in consumption can be seen worldwide.

---

[1] **anthropologist:** a social scientist who studies people, societies, and cultures

[2] **Maya:** one of the tribes of the Yucatan area in Central America

[3] **deforestation:** the cutting or burning down of all the trees in an area

As supplies of resources are dropping, prices are rising. Oil prices have gone from a few dollars a barrel[4] in the early 1970s to well over $100 in recent years. Food costs are expected to triple or even quintuple[5] by 2050. As Nobuo Tanaka, director of the International Energy Agency, says, "Current trends in energy supply and consumption are [clearly] unsustainable—environmentally, economically, and socially."

The environment, in fact, may be the resource we have **abused** most. At times, in attempting to repair our economies, we have further damaged the environment. About 80 percent of the world's original forests have been cut down to accommodate farmland and human **settlements**. Heavy use of fossil fuels has filled the atmosphere with carbon dioxide[6] and created a warming effect. **Droughts**, **harsh** storms, and rising sea levels have resulted. These environmental changes, in turn, create economic problems. Longer droughts mean less water for farming, resulting in less food. Rising sea levels flood subway systems and even wipe out communities.

LEARNING TO CHANGE OUR WAYS

The issue of sustainable living is complex, as it involves more than one problem. We must not only limit our population growth, we must also consume fewer resources. Meeting these challenges will not be easy.

Fortunately, however, many governments and individuals are starting to take action. A return to sustainable farming and energy use has begun around the world. More and more environmentally friendly products are being developed. Scientists, for example, are learning to make fuel from garbage and to use recycled plastics to make warm clothing. There are even plans for the construction of eco-cities, cities whose populations are able to survive without importing any food, water, or energy. The year 2100 may not be so bad after all. It may be a time of peace and stability, where humans have learned to live in harmony with nature. If that is to be the case, however, a lot of hard work has to be done between now and then.

---

[4] **barrel:** a large curved container with a flat top and bottom, usually made of wood or metal

[5] **quintuple:** multiply by five

[6] **carbon dioxide:** the gas produced when animals breathe out, when carbon is burned in air, or when animal or vegetable substances decay, which may make Earth warmer

Vocabulary Check

Complete the text with the boldfaced words from the reading. Use the correct form of the word.

There are environmental problems everywhere. In places where it hasn't

rained for months, (1) _____ are hurting farmers. If farmers

can't grow food, people will face (2) _____. In other places,

there is loss of other natural (3) _____, such as wood. People

cut down trees for firewood or for raising animals. This deforestation is

changing the climate.

(continued on next page)

It is true that humans have (4) _____ the environment and hurt the planet. However, there is hope that people will start solving the problems before human civilization begins to (5) _____.

One proposal is that humans find a new planet and create human (6) _____ in space. Such an idea is not (7) _____, but it will not happen in the near future.

A more practical solution that does not require us to (8) _____ Earth is for humans to use energy differently. Scientists are finding ways to pull energy from the sun and the wind. These natural sources of energy do not cause pollution and still allow people to have a high (9) _____: They can live comfortably, cleanly, and safely.

Finally, many people are willing to make changes. Some farmers have stopped using chemical (10) _____ on their plants. They use natural methods for controlling pests and create less pollution in the water.

In sum, humans are very closely (11) _____ nature. We cannot ignore the connection. While there are scary stories about what might happen, we do not have to accept a(n) (12) _____ future. We can understand the problem and then move on to the stories that discuss solutions.

> READ AGAIN

Read "Reaching Our Limits: Welcome to 2100" again and complete the comprehension exercises on the next page. As you work, keep the reading goal in mind.

> 📖 **READING GOAL:** To identify the rhetorical structure and write a summary

Comprehension Check

A. Check (✓) the sentence that best summarizes each paragraph.

1. *Paragraph 3:*

_____ **a.** Because our civilization has successfully developed industry and technology, we now enjoy high standards of living.

_____ **b.** Successful civilizations tend to have large populations, but if populations get too big, disaster can result.

_____ **c.** There are two signs that a civilization is succeeding: It has a sustainable population, and it has a lot of material wealth.

2. *Paragraph 4:*

_____ **a.** The ancient Romans and Mayans are examples of civilizations that overused their resources and collapsed as a result.

_____ **b.** The historical examples of the Roman and Mayan civilization show that every society will one day collapse.

_____ **c.** Joseph Tainter says most people do not understand the true reasons why the Roman and Mayan civilizations collapsed.

3. *Paragraph 5:*

_____ **a.** People in the U.S. use much more energy, water, and land than people in other parts of the world.

_____ **b.** The global population keeps growing because we are not using energy wisely.

_____ **c.** Like previous civilizations that collapsed, we risk using up our resources.

4. *Paragraph 7:*

_____ **a.** To help our economy, we often hurt the environment, which in turn creates new economic problems.

_____ **b.** Our environment has been greatly damaged by use of fossil fuels and the destruction of forests.

_____ **c.** Our mistreatment of the economy has led to serious environmental problems.

5. *Paragraph 9:*

_____ **a.** The year 2100 promises not to be so bad after all, thanks to the fact that people and governments are changing their ways.

_____ **b.** Around the world, people are making new efforts to live sustainably, but a lot more work has to be done.

_____ **c.** It is unclear what type of future we are heading toward: a time of peace and stability or a time of fighting over limited resources.

B. Work with a partner. Answer the questions about the reading.

1. Is there a hook?

2. What is the rhetorical structure of the text: description, classification, persuasion, or narrative?

3. Which main idea sentences in the reading help you identify the rhetorical structure? Underline two examples.

4. Which details in the reading help you identify the rhetorical structure? Underline three examples.

5. What does the author want the reader to do? Explain in your own words.

6. Does the information in the last two paragraphs support the author's main idea? Why do you think the author includes this information?

C. Write a summary of the reading. Include two to three detailed examples from the text. Use your answers from Exercises A and B to help you.

DISCUSS

Work in groups. Discuss the position of each of the city leaders about how to use tax dollars and decide which one you agree with. Share your positions with the class.

1. Mr. Brown: This city needs bigger freeways. We need to use tax dollars to reduce traffic. That will slow down pollution.

2. Ms. Chung: If we spend tax money on more and better public transportation, people won't have to drive as much and will use less energy.

3. Ms. White: The city needs more green space. Let's use tax dollars to create parks and plant trees to clean the air and provide shade.

4. Mr. García: The city should invest in sun and wind energy. It costs more, but it does less damage to the environment.

VOCABULARY SKILL BUILDING

Vocabulary Skill: Collocations

In English, certain words pair up with each other often to form *collocations*. Learning common collocations will help you use words the way native English speakers do. For example, English speakers say *take action*, not *do action*. Study these examples of collocation patterns from recent units.

EXAMPLES:

Noun + verb: *research shows*

Verb + noun: *waste time*

Adjective + noun: *outer space*

Adverb + verb: *locally grown*

Noun + noun: *belief system*

A. Circle the words that collocate with the words around them. Check your answers by looking in the reading.

1. It is important to (*do / take*) action before the pollution gets worse.

2. Research (*shows / tells*) that solar power technology works in many climates.

3. The products are advertised as environmentally (*positive / friendly*).

4. There is a (*building / rising*) demand for eco-cars.

5. People in the energy industry say (*typical / current*) trends favor the green energy industry.

6. Governments are starting to (*monetarily / financially*) support new research in alternative fuels.

7. A new generation is ready to (*meet / do*) the challenges of the 21st century's energy crisis.

8. It takes a lot of electricity to (*fuel / run*) a refrigerator.

9. The banks were (*deeply / highly*) troubled by the news about rising oil prices.

10. You use water when you (*take / have*) a shower.

B. Work with a partner. Ask and answer the questions using the collocations.

1. What academic **challenge** do you need to **meet**?

2. Were you ever **deeply troubled** by another student's behavior in class? Explain.

3. What is a **current trend** in fashion these days?

4. How long should parents **financially support** their children?

5. Would you believe **research** that **showed** that there is a planet that can support life?

6. What is a product that has experienced a **rise in demand** this season?

7. How much more would you spend for an **environmentally friendly** product?

8. What kind of **action** would you **take** if you wanted to reduce your energy use?

Desert State Puts Oil Wealth into World's First Sustainable City

> PREPARE TO READ

A. Look at the words (and phrases) in the list. Write the number(s) next to each word to show what you know. You may be able to write more than one number next to some of the words. You will study all of these words in this chapter.

1. I can use the word in a sentence.

2. I know <u>one meaning</u> of the word.

3. I know <u>more than one meaning</u> of the word.

4. I know how to pronounce the word.

B. Work with a partner. Look at the picture. Ask and answer the questions. If you don't know a word in English, ask your partner or look in your dictionary. Then write your new words on page 236.

1. What do you see in the picture? Describe the details.

2. What types of transportation do you see in the picture?

3. Where and when do you think this kind of city will be built?

_____ breeze

_____ dust

_____ flush out

_____ generate

_____ humid

_____ microclimate

_____ orient

_____ outskirts

_____ pedestrian

_____ promising

_____ put into perspective

_____ renewable

_____ self-sufficient

_____ take over

C. Read the first two paragraphs of the newspaper article "Desert State Puts Oil Wealth into World's First Sustainable City." Circle two references to the phrase "an expanse of grey rock and dust in one of the harshest environments on Earth."

> READ

Read "Desert State Puts Oil Wealth into World's First Sustainable City." Pay attention to the multiple text references.

Desert State Puts Oil Wealth into World's First Sustainable City

1   In an expanse of grey rock and **dust** in one of the harshest environments on Earth, the United Arab Emirates (UAE) is about to build the world's first sustainable city. It will be
5   designed by British architect Lord Foster.

The site is not **promising**. Miles from a polluted sea, a fierce sun raises temperatures to 50°C (120°F) in the summer. There is no fresh water, no soil, and no animals. But tens
10   of billions of petro-dollars[1] will be spent on these seven square kilometers of desert on the **outskirts** of Abu Dhabi, the capital of the UAE.

Called Masdar—"the source" in Arabic—the walled city is intended to house 50,000 people
15   and 1,500 businesses. It will have no cars and be **self-sufficient** in **renewable** energy. Masdar will get most of its power from the hot desert sun.

The formal introduction of the desert eco-
20   city will be made today at a meeting on future energy sources in Abu Dahbi. The United Kingdom's business secretary, John Hutton, and special representative for trade and investment Prince Andrew will attend.

(continued on next page)

---

[1] **petro-dollars:** money from the sale of oil

25   "It's certainly ambitious," said Gerard Evenden, senior partner in Lord Foster's architecture practice in London. "We were invited to design a zero-carbon[2] city. In this harsh place we needed to look back at history
30 and see how ancient settlements had adapted to their environments." The buildings will be grouped together as in a traditional desert village and will be cooled by wind towers that will collect the desert's **breezes** and **flush out**
35 hot air. No building will be more than five stories high; the city is to be **oriented** northeast to southwest to give a useful balance of sunlight and shade.

    It will feel a little like a city built in the age
40 of the cart and horse.[3] Most roads will be 10 feet (3 m) wide and just 223 feet (70 m) long to develop a **microclimate** and keep the air moving; roofs will allow in air and keep the sun out in the summer. No one will be more
45 than 656 feet (200 m) from public transport, and streets will end at community spaces with squares and fountains.

    "We are aiming to find a balance of light and heat," said Evenden. "It's only really hot for
50 three months of the year, but at other times it's **humid**."

    It is every architect's dream to build a new city, and Foster's team say they are starting at the beginning. Their plan is to reduce the
55 amount of energy needed to build and live in Masdar. Afterwards, they will let solar energy **take over**.

    "We will start with a large solar power station which will provide the energy to
60 construct the city. Some 80 percent of all the roof space will be used to **generate** solar power.

    . . . We could 'borrow' energy from outside, but we are trying to prove it can all be generated … [at] the site," said Evenden.

65   The architects are also planning some high-tech features. The residents and workers will move around on one of three levels. A light railway will take people to and from Masdar to Abu Dhabi; a second level is for **pedestrians**.
70 The third level is for "personalized rapid transport pods,"[4] which Evenden says are a little like driverless personal taxis. "They are in production in Holland, and used to move containers around in Rotterdam Port."

75   No one knows how much Masdar will finally cost or who will live there, but money is not a problem. Abu Dhabi, the capital of the Emirates, is competing with its neighbor Dubai to be the most famous Gulf city. The protection
80 of the environment is seen as a new way to show progress.

    Abu Dhabi is hoping to manufacture high-tech solar panels[5] to make Masdar a center of the global solar energy manufacturing industry.
85 "This will be the global capital of the renewable energy revolution. It's the first oil producing nation to have taken such a significant step towards sustainable living," said Jean-Paul Jeanrenaud, director of the World Wildlife
90 Fund's One Planet Living.

    "The numbers must be **put into perspective**. They are spending billions of dollars on renewables but trillions are still going into climate-changing oil economies. The future
95 is the sun and renewables, but there is no time to wait for this revolution," said Tony Juniper, director of Friends of the Earth.

---

[2] **zero-carbon:** something that does not create carbon (a pollutant)

[3] **cart and horse:** a time before the automobile when people used horses for transportation

[4] **pod:** a part of a vehicle or building that is separate from the main part

[5] **solar panel:** a piece of equipment, usually on the roof of a building, that uses the sun's energy to heat water or to make electricity

Vocabulary Check

A. Circle the letter of the correct answer to complete each sentence. The boldfaced words are the target words.

1. You are a **pedestrian** if you _____.
   a. drive your own car   b. walk on the street   c. take public transportation

2. On a hot day, a **breeze** can make you feel _____.
   a. more tired   b. cooler   c. hotter

3. When you are in the **outskirts** of a city, you are _____.
   a. downtown   b. in the county   c. outside of the downtown area

4. A **humid** climate makes you feel _____.
   a. hot and wet   b. hot and dry   c. cool and dry

5. When an idea looks **promising**, you think that it _____.
   a. won't work in reality   b. needs to be changed   c. is good to try

6. **Dust** is very similar to _____.
   a. sand   b. grass   c. water

7. An example of a **renewable** resource is _____.
   a. natural gas   b. energy from the sun   c. electricity

B. Write C (correct) or X (incorrect) for the way the boldfaced target word is used in each statement. Then correct the incorrect statements to make them true.

_____ 1. We can direct water from the river to **flush out** the streets and keep them clean.

_____ 2. One way to **put** a problem **into perspective** is to compare it to similar problems from history.

_____ 3. A **self-sufficient** person needs a lot of help from other people.

_____ 4. The expansive Sahara Desert is an example of a **microclimate**.

_____ 5. The house is **oriented** toward the west so we can watch the sunset.

_____ 6. The sun and the wind can **generate** clean energy.

_____ 7. If the king dies, the prince **takes over** the country.

READ AGAIN

Read "Desert State Puts Oil Wealth into World's First Sustainable City" again and complete the comprehension exercises. As you work, keep the reading goal in mind.

> **READING GOAL:** To describe a day in the life of a person living in Masdar

Comprehension Check

A. Study the reading closely. Circle all the text references to the "world's first sustainable city." Find at least five different references.

B. Work with a partner. Don't look back at the reading. Answer the questions with as much detail as possible. Then check your ideas by looking at the reading.

1. How will transportation within Masdar be organized?

2. How will Masdar residents travel back and forth from Abu Dhabi?

3. What will be Masdar's primary source of energy?

4. How will Masdar be kept cool?

5. How tall will buildings be?

6. How close will buildings be to each other?

7. How wide will the streets in Masdar be?

8. What things will there be in public spaces for Masdar residents to enjoy?

C. Imagine it is the year 2020 and you are a businessperson living in Masdar. Write a one-page diary entry. Describe a typical day in Masdar. Include details from the reading. Use your answers from Exercise B to help you.

D. Work with a partner. Read your diary entries to each other. Does your partner mention the same details as you?

 **DISCUSS**

Complete the activities.

1. Fill in the chart to decide whether Masdar would be a good place to live.

	A traditional city	Masdar
advantages		
disadvantages		

2. Work with a partner and role-play. Then switch roles.

   Partner A, who has a solar energy company in Masdar, offers partner B a job. Partner A must tell about all the advantages Masdar has to offer.

   Partner B asks several questions about the city in order to decide whether or not he or she wants to move there, such as, "Why won't I need a car? How will I get to work?"

3. Take a poll to see how many in the class would accept an opportunity to live and work in Masdar.

Learn the Vocabulary

> ## Strategy
>
> ### Using Word Cards: Changing Order and Grouping
>
> You can change the order of your word cards. If you always study the words in the same order, it will be hard to remember each word on its own. You should change the order of your cards every time you study them.
>
> You can also group them in many different ways. For example, you can make two groups of cards, one for words that you remember easily and the other for words that you often forget. Then you can review the words you forget more often than the other words. A third way to group cards is to select the words that you will need for your daily life and put those in a special group to study.

A. Make cards for the words from Chapters 19 and 20 that were new to you when you started the unit. Include target words and words that you wrote on page 236.

B. Review your new cards one time with a partner. As your partner quizzes you, he or she will put your cards into two groups: one group for the words you remembered and one group for the words you didn't remember. Review the words you didn't remember a second time.

C. Add your cards from Units 1–9 to the new cards. Now look through all your cards. Choose twenty to thirty words that you think are the most useful for you in real life. For the next three days, review these words twice a day. Review the second group of cards (the remaining words) once a day. Remember to change the order of the cards in each group before you review them. Each time you review your cards, make a check (✓) in the chart.

Day one	Day two	Day three
Group 1: _____ / _____ Group 2: _____	Group 1: _____ / _____ Group 2: _____	Group 1: _____ / _____ Group 2: _____

D. After three days, put the two groups back together, change the order, and review all of the cards with your partner in class. How many words did you remember this time?

E. Go back to the vocabulary list at the beginning of each chapter. What did you learn about the target words? Add your numbers to the lists.

Vocabulary Practice 10, see page 246.

Multitasking:
Can You Handle It?

▷ THINK BEFORE YOU READ

A. Work with a partner. Look at the picture. Ask and answer the questions. If you don't know a word in English, ask your partner or look in your dictionary. Then write your new words on page 236.

1. What do you see in the picture? Describe the details.

2. Why do you think the woman is multitasking? How does she feel?

3. Are people busier today than they were in the past? Explain.

B. Work in small groups. Ask and answer the questions.

1. Of the activities in the box, which can you do at the same time? Circle them.

cook dinner	drive a car	play a video game	surf the Internet	watch TV
do homework	listen to music	read	talk on the phone	write an e-mail

2. What jobs require people to multitask?

3. Is multitasking an effective way to work? Explain.

CHAPTER 21

Keeping an Eye on the Sky

 PREPARE TO READ

A. Look at the words (and phrases) in the list. Write the number(s) next to each word to show what you know. You may be able to write more than one number next to some of the words. You will study all of these words in this chapter.

1. I can use the word in a sentence.

2. I know <u>one meaning</u> of the word.

3. I know <u>more than one meaning</u> of the word

4. I know how to pronounce the word.

B. Work with a partner. Look at the picture. Ask and answer the questions. If you don't know a word in English, ask your partner or look in your dictionary. Then write your new words on page 236.

1. What do you see in the picture? Describe the details.

2. What duties do air traffic controllers perform?

3. Do air traffic controllers have to multitask? Explain.

_____ channel

_____ distorted

_____ distracted

_____ drawback

_____ exception

_____ impair

_____ on the go

_____ readily

_____ recollection

_____ rural

_____ simultaneously

_____ switch

C. Scan "Keeping an Eye on the Sky," an aviation magazine writer's interview with an air traffic controller. Check your answer from Exercise B, question 3.

> ## READ

Read "Keeping an Eye on the Sky." Check your answer from Exercise B, question 2.

Keeping an Eye on the Sky

1 ***What made you want
to become an air traffic
controller?***

As a child, I was always
5 fascinated by airplanes. My
parents used to take my
brother and me to a park
near the airport, and we
would sit there for hours
10 watching the planes take
off and land. I loved the
size and the noise of the planes and wanted
to be a pilot when I grew up. I later realized
that being a controller would allow me to stay
15 in one place. The problem with being a pilot is
that you are always **on the go**.

Where do you work?
Dulles International Airport in Washington,
D.C. I've been there about seven years.

20 ***How did you get to this point?***
Well, lots of training. I graduated from
the University of Oklahoma with degrees in
aeronautics[1] and air traffic.

***What is the most important skill a
25 controller needs?***
I think, more than anything, you need the
ability to do more than one thing at once,
to multitask. To be more specific, you need

multidimensional awareness[2]—when you have
30 planes coming at you from all sides, you need
not only to know where each one is, but also
where each one is going to be in thirty seconds'
time. You have to work with the different pilots
simultaneously. At a single moment, you might
35 have three planes coming in to land, three more
waiting to take off, and a couple of helicopters
flying just a couple hundred yards[3] away from
the arriving planes. You can't let yourself get
distracted by any one situation, no matter
40 what's happening. Sometimes we'll deal with an
emergency landing, but we can't lose track of
the other planes.

***It seems that you would need a good
memory.***
45 Yes, you need a perfect **recollection** of
where each plane is at all times.

***What other skills do you need besides the
ability to multitask?***
Good communication skills. If you
50 misunderstand a single word a pilot says, it
can lead to disaster. We use a one-way radio
channel, so pilots and controllers can't speak
at the same time. Otherwise, the messages
could combine and get **distorted**. There's a
55 certain procedure we have to follow when
communicating. A big part of our training
focuses on that. In addition to that, you need

(continued on next page)

---

[1] **aeronautics:** the science of designing and flying airplanes

[2] **multidimensional awareness:** knowledge or understanding of many things happening at the same time

[3] **yard:** a unit for measuring length or distance, equal to 3 feet or 0.91 meters

the ability to follow the rules but at the same time be flexible and able to make **exceptions** when necessary.

Can you give an example of that?

Well, when a pilot is in trouble you have to do whatever is necessary to get him or her home safe. One time I guided a pilot who was low on fuel in bad weather to land on a **rural** highway. That's not an everyday situation but one you have to be prepared for.

I've heard being a controller is the most stressful job in the world. Is it true?

Well, you have to **readily** work under pressure. My sister is a stockbroker,[4] and we often argue about who has the more stressful job. I always say, if a stockbroker makes a mistake, she stands to lose some money. If a controller makes a mistake, we stand to lose a whole lot more. The responsibility is enormous.

What's a typical day like for you?

No day is really that typical. Weather really affects us, and we have to deal with equipment breaking all the time. Our work schedule changes a lot, too. Our day can start at 7 A.M., at 2 P.M., or even at 11 at night. My actual duties vary as well. I work with five other controllers in the tower. Each person does a different job; for example, one person will be assigning gates to planes that have landed, while another person will be clearing flights to take off. The most difficult job is local control, where you are responsible for actual planes in the air. We **switch** jobs every ninety minutes to keep our minds fresh.

It sounds like the job requires a lot of teamwork.

Oh, absolutely. The other controllers and I work as a team. We're all in the same boat. If one of us makes a mistake it's everybody's problem. We completely rely on each other and are in constant communication. We joke around a little bit, but getting distracted is out of the question.

What are the biggest advantages to the job?

You get a good salary and benefits, and you must retire by age fifty-six. I get to be around airplanes all day, and I love the excitement. Even after all these years, watching an airplane take off is still incredible. Plus, the view from the tower is great.

Why is the retirement age so early?

Well, there are a few reasons. Studies show it gets more difficult to multitask, to have the multidimensional perception that controllers need, once you reach a certain age. That and the stress get to people eventually.

I see. Are there any drawbacks to the career?

Well, aside from the stress and the unpredictable work schedule, there aren't that many. One interesting thing is that there are a lot of medications we are not allowed to take. Basically, anything that might **impair** our reaction time even slightly is forbidden, so, for example, I can't take any cold medications that have antihistamines[5] in them.

What advice would you have for someone who wants to be a controller?

Do it! It's a great job you can take with you if you move to a new city. With a mandatory retirement age of fifty-six, this career always has a need for new talent.

---

[4] **stockbroker:** someone whose job is to buy and sell stocks, bonds, etc. for other people

[5] **antihistamine:** a drug that is used to treat an allergy (a physical reaction to a substance, such as a particular plant, food, or animal, that causes no problem to most other people)

Vocabulary Check

A. Write the letter of the correct definition next to the word. Be careful. There are two extra definitions.

_____ **1.** channel

_____ **2.** distorted

_____ **3.** readily

_____ **4.** switch

_____ **5.** impair

a. quickly and easily

b. changed so that it is strange or unclear

c. very big, fast, powerful, etc.

d. to change from doing or using one thing to doing or using another

e. a particular range of sound waves that can be used to send and receive radio messages

f. describe the character of someone or something in a particular way

g. to damage something or make it not as good as it should be

B. Circle the letter of the correct answer to each question.

1. How do you describe a person who is not listening to directions?

   a. distracted   **b.** distorted   **c.** fascinated

2. What do you call someone who is the only person who doesn't have to follow a rule?

   a. a switch   **b.** a recollection   **c.** an exception

3. What word do you use to say that two people are doing something at the same time?

   a. readily   **b.** simultaneously   **c.** exceptionally

4. Which word is associated with remembering something?

   a. rural   **b.** channel   **c.** recollection

5. What do you call something that might be a problem?

   a. a recollection   **b.** an exception   **c.** a drawback

6. What do you call an area that is far away from the city?

   a. a drawback   **b.** rural   **c.** distorted

7. What would you say about a man who is very busy and active?

   a. He is distorted.   **b.** He is always on the go.   **c.** He is skilled.

READ AGAIN

Read "Keeping an Eye on the Sky" again and complete the comprehension exercises. As you work, keep the reading goal in mind.

> 📖 **READING GOAL:** To write a job description for an air traffic controller

Comprehension Check

A. Find the sentences in the reading. What do the underlined words refer to? Circle the letter of the correct answer. The numbers in parentheses are the paragraphs where you can find the sentences.

1. How did you get to <u>this point</u>? (3)
   a. graduating from the University of Oklahoma
   b. being fascinated by airplanes
   c. working at Dulles International Airport

2. You can't let yourself get distracted by any one <u>situation</u>, no matter what's happening. (4)
   a. joking around with other air traffic controllers
   b. an airplane or helicopter landing or taking off
   c. dealing with equipment breaking or bad weather

3. In addition to <u>that</u>, you need the ability to follow the rules but at the same time be flexible and able to make exceptions when necessary. (6)
   a. good communication skills
   b. degrees in aeronautics and air traffic
   c. multidimensional awareness

4. <u>That</u>'s not an everyday situation, but one you have to be prepared for. (7)
   a. working under pressure
   b. an emergency landing
   c. bad weather

5. Well, aside from the stress, and the unpredictable work schedule, there aren't that <u>many</u>. (13)
   a. prohibited medications
   b. the stress and unpredictable schedule
   c. drawbacks

B. Work with a partner. Talk about the following aspects of being an air traffic controller. Mention as many details as you can. Don't look back at the reading.

- training
- skills
- work environment
- benefits
- drawbacks

C. On a separate sheet of paper, write a job description for an air traffic controller. Explain the necessary training and skills. Describe the work environment, benefits, and drawbacks. Use your answers from Exercise B to help you.

⟩ DISCUSS

Work with a partner. Partner A is applying for a job as an air traffic controller. Partner B is the interviewer. Use the questions below and add two of your own. Then practice the interview. Switch roles when you have finished.

1. What makes you feel that you would be a good air traffic controller?

2. Tell me about a situation in which you successfully multitasked or in which you successfully dealt with a stressful situation.

3. How do you feel about the fact that your work schedule changes frequently?

4. _____

5. _____

The Effects of Multitasking

> PREPARE TO READ

A. Look at the words (and phrases) in the list. Write the number(s) next to each word to show what you know. You may be able to write more than one number next to some of the words. You will study all of these words in this chapter.

1. I can use the word in a sentence.

2. I know <u>one meaning</u> of the word.

3. I know <u>more than one meaning</u> of the word.

4. I know how to pronounce the word.

B. Work with a partner. Look at the picture. Ask and answer the questions. If you don't know a word in English, ask your partner or look in your dictionary. Then write your new words on page 236.

1. When you are talking to someone on the phone, can you tell whether or not that person is doing something else at the same time? How?

2. Do you think multitasking is good or bad? If you wanted to find out the answer, how would you research this question?

_____ audibly

_____ build up

_____ consistently

_____ in favor of

_____ inefficiency

_____ long-term

_____ on a regular basis

_____ operate

_____ perception

_____ range

_____ rotate

_____ run risks

Reading Skill: Understanding APA and MLA Style

In academic texts, writers often use information from other people's writing (outside sources) to support their main ideas. Unless the information is a general fact, writers need to give credit to, or cite, the source of the information. Writers use *parenthetical citations* to do this. A parenthetical citation appears immediately before or after information from an outside source and includes basic source information in parentheses. At the end of the text, the writer gives complete source information. The complete source information is called a *reference.*

Two common styles of parenthetical citation are APA (American Psychological Association) and MLA (Modern Language Association). It is important to understand the APA and MLA styles when you read or write academic texts.

Study the sample in-text citation and end-of-text reference in APA format below.

EXAMPLES:

APA in-text citation:
Air traffic controllers must retire at age 56 (Watson, 2004).

APA end-of-text reference:
Watson, E. (2004). *The life of a controller.* New York, NY: Pearson.

In APA style, the in-text citation tells the last name of the person and the year of publication. The reference is organized as follows: author's last name, initial of first name, year of publication, title, place of publication, and publishing company, and if the source was found online, the web address. If you see *et al.* (Latin for *and others*), you know that there are other authors who are not listed.

Now, study the same citation and reference in MLA style.

EXAMPLES:

MLA in-text citation:
Air traffic controllers must retire at age 56 (Watson, 163).

MLA end-of-text reference:
Watson, Emily, *The Life of a Controller.* New York, NY: Pearson, 2004. Print.

In MLA style, the in-text citation tells the last name of the person whose work is being cited and the page in his or her book from which the information came. The reference is organized as follows: the person's last name, first name, title, place of publication, publishing company, year of publication, and format (for example, print or online). If you see *et al.,* you know that there are other authors who are not listed.

C. Read the first three paragraphs of the academic paper "The Effects of Multitasking" on the next page. Answer the questions.

1. Whose information is cited?

2. What information is taken from an outside source?

Read "The Effects of Multitasking." Pay attention to the citations.

The Effects of Multitasking

1 In psychology, a great deal of research has been done on multitasking. Multitasking can be defined as "performing more than one task at a time." As multitasking has become
5 more common, psychologists have sought to understand how it affects the brain. This paper will summarize the findings of research on multitasking.

Most studies show that multitasking has
10 negative effects. The effects depend on the type of tasks being performed and can **range** from temporary **inefficiency** to **long-term** problems.

Multitasking is not necessarily harmful. It is well known that people can readily perform
15 two simple tasks at the same time. For example, one can walk down the street while having a conversation. The key to successful multitasking is that activities be "highly practiced skills." Pashler (2000) pointed out
20 that people can easily combine a **perception** skill, such as watching or listening, with physical movement or mental planning.

Multitasking becomes much less efficient, however, when one attempts two complex tasks
25 at the same time. Spelke, Hirst, & Neisser (1976) found that people could learn to take dictation and read at the same time but only after an enormous amount of practice. In most cases, people simply fail to multitask. Instead,
30 their brains quickly switch focus between the two challenging tasks. With each switch, the brain stops processing information so that it can re-focus (Just, Carpenter, Keller, Emery, Zajac, & Thulborn, 2001).
35 This finding that the brain is not really suited to multitasking has led many researchers to say that multitasking is a myth. People may believe they are performing a number of tasks at once, but in fact they are just switching their
40 attention between them.

With each switch, more time is lost, and over time inefficiency **builds up**. Rubinstein, Meyer, & Evans (2001) showed that the more complex the tasks, the more inefficient the
45 multitasking. When trying to solve math problems and classify objects simultaneously, test subjects did very poorly. Subjects performed the worst when switching between unfamiliar tasks. Miller has argued that the
50 effects of multitasking are comparable to a ten-point drop in IQ[1] (Lapowski, 2009).

The drop in efficiency also occurs with familiar tasks, however. Just et al. (2001) tested people's ability to visually and **audibly**
55 multitask. Subjects listened to sentences while watching and comparing two **rotating** objects. The study showed that multitasking caused visual performance to decrease by 29 percent. Listening comprehension dropped 53 percent.
60 Rubinstein et al. (2001) stated that the drop in performance is greatest when multitasking involves the same task type. Trying to perform two listening tasks at the same time, for example, is much more difficult than listening
65 while writing.

Another drawback is that multitasking leads to errors. A study by Stanford University tested "heavy multitaskers" against "light multitaskers," or people who do not usually
70 do two tasks at once. Both groups were tested on their ability to recognize patterns, remember information, and classify objects. In each test, the heavy multitaskers made far more errors than the light multitaskers. The
75 researchers blamed the low performance of the heavy multitaskers on their lack of focus.

---

[1] **IQ:** Intelligence Quotient; your level of intelligence, measured by a special test, with 100 being the average result

The heavy multitaskers were easily distracted, even when they tried to ignore certain pieces of information **in favor of** others (Ophir, Nass, & Wagner, 2009).

Some psychologists believe this loss of focus makes multitasking dangerous. A commonly cited example is the effect it has on driving performance. A study by Virginia Tech discovered that 80 percent of car accidents were caused by distracted drivers (Bagg, 2006). Common driver distractions included talking on cell phones and **operating** car radios.

In addition to **running risks** such as being in a car accident, multitaskers may also suffer in the long-term. Foerde, Knowlton, & Poldrack (2006) suggest that multitasking changes how the brain learns. The researchers compared the brain activity of multitaskers and non-multitaskers with magnetic resonance imaging (MRI)[2] technology. They found that when subjects focused on a single task, a part of the brain called the hippocampus was most active. The hippocampus is associated with long-term memory and storage of facts. When subjects focused on multiple tasks, a different part of the brain called the striatum was most active. The striatum is associated with the learning of skills. Other experiments have shown that knowledge acquired through the striatum is not as easy to remember as information learned through the hippocampus. Thus, **consistently** learning while multitasking may impair the memory (Arden, 2002).

Despite the warnings from the scientific community, multitasking is becoming more common. Office surveys show that 54 percent of people read e-mails while talking on the phone (Faw, 2006). Research on families uncovers similar trends, with parents performing more and more duties at one time (Wallis, 2006).

Studies show that young people are the most likely to multitask. According to the Pew Research Center, 33 percent of teenagers multitask "most of the time," and as many as 82 percent multitask **on a regular basis** (Wallis, 2006). Young people often have a positive attitude about multitasking. Many think it is a valuable life skill.

More research will need to be done to determine exactly how multitasking affects the brain. Of particular importance are studies on multitasking's effects on learning. Future studies may show whether multitasking's effects on the memory are permanent or only temporary.

---

[2] **MRI:** a picture of the inside of someone's body produced with Magnetic Resonance Imaging equipment

References:

Arden, J. (2002). *Improving your memory for dummies*. New York: Wiley Publishing, Inc.

Bagg C. (2006). Multitasking and driving don't mix. *Research Magazine, Winter Edition.*

Faw B. (2006, October 12). *The myth of multitasking*. NBC News. Retrieved from http://www.msnbc.msn.com/id/15225042/

Foerde, K., Knowlton, B.J., & Poldrack, R.A. (2006). Modulation of competing memory systems by distraction. *Proceedings of the National Academy of Sciences, 103,* 11778-83.

Gibson, M (2005). Multi-tasking in practice: Coordinated activities in the computer supported doctor–patient consultation. *International Journal of Medical Informatics, 74, Issue 6,* 425-436.

Just, M., Carpenter P., Keller T., Emery, L., Zajac, H., & Thulborn, K. (2001). *Interdependence of nonoverlapping cortical systems in dual cognitive tasks.* NeuroImage, 14, 417-426.

Lapowski I. (2009, August 13). Stop the multitasking madness. *New York Daily News.*

Ophir, E., Nass, C., and Wagner, A. (2009, September 15). Cognitive control in media multitaskers, *Proceedings of the National Academy of Sciences of the United States of America.* Retrieved from http://www.pnas.org/content/106/37/15583

Pashler, H. (2000). Task switching and multitask performance. Monsell, S., and Driver, J. (editors). *Attention and Performance XVIII: Control of mental processes.* Cambridge, MA: MIT Press.

Rubinstein J., Meyer D., & Evans J. (2001). Executive control of cognitive processes in task switching. *Journal of Experimental Psychology: Human Perception and Performance, 27, No.4.*

Spelke E., Hirst W., & Neisser U. (1976). Skills of divided attention. *Cognition,* 4, 3, 215-230.

Wallis C. (2006, March 19). The multitasking generation. Retrieved from http://www.time.com/time/magazine/article/0,9171,1174696-1,00.html

Vocabulary Check

A. Work with a partner. Ask and answer the questions. The boldfaced words are the target words.

1. What computer tasks do you do **on a regular basis**?

2. Do you agree that multitaskers are **running the risk** of making a mistake?

3. Is the author of the reading **in favor of** multitasking?

4. What are two of your **long-term** goals?

5. Why do some people say that Internet access creates **inefficiency** in the workplace?

6. Do you ever feel that your technology use **builds up** to the point that it interferes with the rest of your life? Explain.

B. Read the definitions. Write the correct boldfaced word from the reading next to the definition.

1. _____ = loudly enough for you to hear it

2. _____ = always having the same beliefs, behavior, attitudes, quality

3. _____ = using or controlling a machine or a piece of equipment

4. _____ = the way you understand or think of something and your beliefs about what it is like

5. _____ = a number of things that all are different but of the same general type

6. _____ = turning with a circular movement around a central point

Comprehension Check

A. Are the statements facts or opinions? Write *F* (for fact) or *O* (for opinion).

_____ **1.** Multitasking is a myth.

_____ **2.** People can learn to take dictation and read at the same time.

_____ **3.** The effects of multitasking are comparable to a ten-point drop in IQ.

_____ **4.** The more complex the tasks, the more inefficient the multitasking.

_____ **5.** Multitasking is dangerous.

_____ **6.** Most car accidents are caused by distracted drivers.

_____ **7.** Multitasking changes how the brain learns.

_____ **8.** Knowledge acquired through the striatum is not as easy to remember as information learned through the hippocampus.

_____ **9.** Young people like to multitask.

_____ **10.** Multitasking is a valuable life skill.

B. Work with a partner. Compare your answers from Exercise A. Underline the information in the reading that supports your answers.

C. Work in small groups. Study the list of activities in *Think Before You Read*, Exercise B, on page 195. Then answer the questions. Use information in the reading to support your answers.

1. Which activities will be most difficult to do at the same time?

2. Which activities will be most dangerous to do at the same time?

3. Which activities will be easiest to do at the same time?

4. Which activities, if done at the same time, might lead to long-term problems?

D. Work with a partner. Ask and answer the questions.

1. Does the reading use APA or MLA style?

2. Of the sources cited in the reading, which is the oldest publication?

3. How many of the sources cited in the reading had multiple authors?

4. In paragraph 7, which groups of authors are referred to for a second time with *et al.*?

5. Study the references page for the reading on page 206. How many of the sources for the reading were found online?

⟩ DISCUSS

Work in groups of three. Share your answers to the following questions.

1. Talk about one time when you multitasked and answer the questions.
   a. What did you do?
   b. Why were you multitasking?
   c. What was the result? Did you complete all the tasks effectively and efficiently?
   d. How did you feel afterwards?
   e. If you had it to do over would you multitask or not?

2. In your opinion does multitasking make you more productive or less productive why?

3. What percentage of your group is in favor of multitasking? What percentage is against it? (Share results as a class.)

> VOCABULARY SKILL BUILDING

Vocabulary Skill: The Prefix *multi-*

The prefix *multi-* means more than one; many.

EXAMPLE:

multifamily = several families together.

We went on a multifamily camping trip.

A. Write the letter of the correct definition next to the word. When you finish, check your answers in a dictionary.

_____ **1.** multitask

_____ **2.** multimillionaire

_____ **3.** multinational

_____ **4.** multilingual

_____ **5.** multicultural

_____ **6.** multicolored

a. having people, factories, offices, business activities, etc., in many different countries

b. to do several tasks at once

c. having many different colors

d. a person who has several millions of dollars

e. a person who can speak several languages

f. involving people or ideas from many different countries, races, or religions

B. Answer the questions on a separate sheet of paper.

1. What would you do if you were a multimillionaire?

2. What kind of ice cream is multicolored?

3. When do you multitask?

4. What is an example of a multicultural family?

5. What languages would you want to learn in order to be multilingual?

6. What are some examples of multinational corporations?

Learn the Vocabulary

A. Act out the phrases that reflect things that people feel and do.

1. switch a light on and off

2. multitask by talking on the phone and typing on the computer

3. be deeply engaged in a conversation

4. make a hand signal that shows that you like something

5. look distracted

B. Make cards for the words that were new to you when you started the unit. Include target words and words that you wrote on page 236. Use them for the following activities.

1. Put all the cards down and organize them into alphabetical order.

2. Turn over two cards. Try to come up with one sentence that includes both words.

3. Turn over four to eight cards and arrange them in a circle. Start a story by creating a sentence with one of the cards. Move around the circle, including each word in your story.

4. Organize the words into columns according to the first letter of each word.

5. Take the cards to a place you have never studied before: For example, go to a different part of the building. Review your cards. Then choose a new location and review your cards there. Do this in three different places.

C. Go back to the vocabulary list at the beginning of each chapter. What did you learn about the target words? Add your numbers to the lists.

Vocabulary Practice 11, see page 247.

> THINK BEFORE YOU READ

A. Work with a partner. Look at the pictures. Ask and answer the questions. If you don't know a word in English, ask your partner or look in your dictionary. Then write your new words on page 236.

   1. What do you see in the pictures? Describe the details.

   2. Where do you think each shopping area is?

   3. How is shopping in each area different?

   4. What products would you expect to find in each shopping area?

B. Work in small groups. Ask and answer the questions.

   1. Look at the unit title and the pictures. What do you think the readings in this unit will be about?

   2. What does "the developing world" mean? What kinds of things do people in the developing world buy?

The Next Billion

> PREPARE TO READ

A. Look at the words (and phrases) in the list. Write the number(s) next to each word to show what you know. You may be able to write more than one number next to some of the words. You will study all of these words in this chapter.

1. I can use the word in a sentence.

2. I know <u>one meaning</u> of the word.

3. I know <u>more than one meaning</u> of the word.

4. I know how to pronounce the word.

B. Work with a partner. Look at the picture. Ask and answer the questions. If you don't know a word in English, ask your partner or look in your dictionary. Then write your new words on page 236.

1. What do you see in the picture? Describe the details.

2. How much do you think the laptops in the picture cost?

3. How do the laptops help the students in the picture?

4. What problem(s) do you think the laptops help solve?

_____ accordingly

_____ conventional

_____ devoted

_____ durable

_____ end user

_____ enterprising

_____ household name

_____ in debt

_____ install

_____ nutritious

_____ plug in

_____ roll up (their) sleeves

_____ run by

_____ sole

_____ strike a deal

Reading Skill: Making Connections

Some readings have very complete main idea statements that tell you which examples you will read about and how each example is related to the others. In other readings, the main idea is only stated very generally. In such readings, it is important to make connections. You make connections when you notice the various ways the examples in a reading are related to each other.

To make connections while reading, ask yourself:

1. How is each example similar to the previous examples?

2. What basic ideas are true about every example the author mentions?

It is much easier to summarize the main ideas in a reading if you have made connections among the examples.

C. Skim the magazine article "The Next Billion" on the next page. Find the two paragraphs that describe the product in the picture on page 213. Check your answers from Exercise B.

D. In what ways do you think this laptop will be similar to the other products mentioned in the reading? Check (✓) the connections you think you will be able to make.

_____ **1.** has a low cost

_____ **2.** is available only to a limited number of rich people

_____ **3.** meets the specific needs of people in developing countries

_____ **4.** has many expensive, high-tech features

_____ **5.** helps solve problems people in developing countries face

READ

Read "The Next Billion." Pay attention to how the examples in the reading are connected.

The Next Billion

1   Companies are always looking for new markets where they can sell their products. These days, however, more and more consumers around the world are **in debt**. As a result,
5   they're cutting back on spending. What, then, can established companies do to stay profitable? What can young **enterprising** companies do to cover their start-up costs and build their business? They all can **roll up their**
10   **sleeves** and look to what economists call "the next billion."

The "next billion" refers to consumers living in developing countries,[1] places where most incomes are low but populations are large.
15   Multinational corporations have traditionally ignored these places, making their **sole** focus "the first billion," the wealthiest 15 percent of the world's population. These days, however, a number of innovative firms are developing
20   products specially designed for consumers in developing countries. As a result, these companies can help not only themselves but others as well. Some say that these companies are engaging in a practice known as "doing
25   right by doing good."

Some companies are doing right by doing good by expanding the market for computer products. Worldwide, about 1.2 billion people— the world's wealthiest people—have computers.
30   **Accordingly**, most computer products cost a lot. For example, Microsoft's software program[2]

MS Office Professional sells for $499.95, more than a person in a developing country might earn in a single year. Microsoft is a **household**
35   **name**, as more than 90 percent of computers use the company's software. To compete with the well-known computer giant, other high-tech firms have realized they need to find customers in new places.
40   Nicholas Negroponte, a computer expert and professor at the Massachusetts Institute of Technology, decided to do just that. Negroponte founded One Laptop Per Child (OLPC), a program **devoted** to providing
45   children in developing countries with information technology.[3] OLPC makes a special laptop called the XO. The company has **installed** thirty educational programs in the XO so it is ready for children to use. Already, OLPC
50   has delivered more than one million of the cute green and white laptops to children in thirty-one countries, and another one million are on the way. The small, lightweight machines sell for only $188, and OLPC hopes to reduce the
55   price to $75 as orders increase. Although the XO's **end users** are children, its customers are governments and aid organizations seeking to improve the quality of education.

The success of the XO results not only from
60   its low price, but also from OLPC's ability to meet the needs of children. The **durable** laptop can survive a 5-foot drop to the ground, and

---

[1] **developing country:** a poor country that is trying to increase its industry and trade and improve life for its people

[2] **software program:** a set of written rules that tell a computer what to do

[3] **information technology:** the use of electronic processes for gathering information, storing it, and making it available, using computers

it can be used outdoors in direct sunlight. The rechargeable battery runs on as little as 2 watts[4]
65 (a **conventional** laptop, by comparison, may need 45 watts). The laptop also supports wireless networking,[5] allowing a classroom full of XOs to share a single connection to the Internet.

Just as OLPC has reinvented the computer
70 for the next billion consumers, entrepreneur Adam Grosser has remade the refrigerator for this market. A refrigerator may seem like an everyday item, but 1.6 billion people live without electricity and thus without
75 refrigeration. As a result, food and medicine spoil quickly, and malnutrition and disease spread. With these problems in mind, Grosser invented a new type of refrigerator, a device that can keep things cold without needing to
80 be **plugged in**.

The new refrigerator is a blue 8-pound cylinder that Grosser calls his "sustainable fridge." When the handheld device is placed over a fire, heat activates a special chemical
85 inside the cylinder. This chemical causes the fridge to drop in temperature. The cold fridge can then go into a larger container (3 gallons/ 15 liters) and keep it cold for over twenty-four hours, even in the warmest climates. Grosser
90 hopes to sell his sustainable fridge for as little

as $25. "We think we can make refrigeration something that everyone will have," he says.

Other companies are changing not only their products but also the way they do business.
95 French food-maker Danone has **struck a deal** with economist Muhammad Yunus in India to create a "social business enterprise." Their goal is to build fifty factories that will produce low-cost, **nutritious** yogurt. The factories will be **run by**
100 local workers, and they will use local ingredients. In addition to providing a food source that will sell for only 7 cents or so per cup, each factory will provide employment for approximately 1,600 local people. Danone employees say that the
105 project has a promising future.

"It's really a growth strategy for our company," says Danone CEO[6] Franck Riboud. "We are convinced that in this world . . . it would be crazy to think only about the peak of
110 the pyramid."

Whether they are the next billion shoppers to purchase yogurt, laptops, or something else, consumers in developing countries are finding they now have more and better options than
115 before. For both these shoppers and global businesses, the partnership couldn't have come at a better time.

---

[4] **watt:** a measure of electrical power

[5] **wireless networking:** a system of communication that uses radio signals over the air instead of wires

[6] **CEO:** Chief Executive Officer; the person with the most authority in a large company

Vocabulary Check

A. Work with a partner. Ask and answer the questions. The boldfaced words are the target words.

1. If something isn't **durable**, what is it likely to do?

2. Who are the **end users** of cooking equipment?

3. Microsoft is a **household name**. Can you name three other companies that are household names?

4. What are some reasons someone might be **in debt**?

5. What are some differences between a school **run by** the government and one that is private?

6. What words would you use to describe an **enterprising** person?

7. What are three **nutritious** foods?

B. Complete the sentences with the boldfaced words from the reading.

1. The CEO does not only want to make money. He cares about his country and is _____ to the cause of providing products that will improve people's lives.

2. They needed to find new places to sell products; _____, they began looking outside their usual market.

3. The refrigerator did not work because it was not _____.

4. After his partner died, he became the _____ owner of the business.

5. She needed more supplies so she _____ with another company to trade services for materials.

6. In order to increase productivity, they _____ three new machines at the factory.

7. For such a big job, they just have to _____ and get to work.

8. Internet connections through a _____ phone line are usually very slow.

 READ AGAIN

Read "The Next Billion" again and complete the comprehension exercises on the next page. As you work, keep the reading goal in mind.

READING GOAL: To make connections among the examples

Comprehension Check

A. Work with a partner. Check your answers from *Prepare to Read*, Exercise D.

B. Complete the chart with information from the reading.

Product	Cost	Specific needs it meets	Problems it solves
	currently $188, the price may drop to $75 as orders increase		
		keeps things cold without needing to be plugged in; works for 24 hours in even the warmest climates	
			reduces unemployment: 1,600 new jobs are created per factory

C. On a separate sheet of paper, write a paragraph explaining the similarities of the products mentioned in the reading. Start with a general main idea sentence. Then give specific examples and details about the products. Use your answers from Exercise B to help you.

> DISCUSS

Work in small groups. Choose one of the needs below. Design a product that you think will be useful in meeting that need. Then answer the questions.

Need

- Schools need electricity.

- People need protection from mosquitoes and flies that spread disease.

- People need fuel for cooking.

- Families need housing.

- Farmers need a way to deliver food.

- Farmers need a way to grow crops with very little water.

1. What is the name of your product?

2. What problem(s) will it solve?

3. Who will be the end users of your product?

4. How will your product be different from conventional versions?

5. What will you do to make sure the product has a low cost?

Listen to other groups describe their products. Then vote for your favorite. Don't vote for your group's product.

CHAPTER 24

A Company Prospers by Saving Poor People's Lives

> PREPARE TO READ

A. Look at the words in the list. Write the number(s) next to each word to show what you know. You may be able to write more than one number next to some of the words. You will study all of these words in this chapter.

1. I can use the word in a sentence.

2. I know <u>one meaning</u> of the word.

3. I know <u>more than one meaning</u> of the word.

4. I know how to pronounce the word.

B. Work with a partner. Look at the picture. Ask and answer the questions. If you don't know a word in English, ask your partner or look in your dictionary. Then write your new words on page 236.

1. What do you see in the picture? Describe the details.

2. What is the purpose of the product in the picture?

3. Who do you think makes this product?

_____ backpacking

_____ cave

_____ charitable

_____ coup

_____ daring

_____ disclose

_____ entertain

_____ filter

_____ insecticide

_____ refugee

_____ soaked

_____ supplier

_____ transmit

_____ version

C. Read the first four paragraphs of the newspaper article, "A Company Prospers by Saving Poor People's Lives." Check your answers from Exercise B.

> READ

Read "A Company Prospers by Saving Poor People's Lives." Pay attention to the products described in the reading.

A Company Prospers by Saving Poor People's Lives

1   NY Times, Tuesday, Feb. 3, 2009
By Donald G. McNeil Jr.

It all started with mosquito nets. Or, before that, with a million yards[1] of wool[2] in the
5   mountains of Sweden.

Or, taken back another generation, to uniforms for hotel and supermarket workers.

There are plenty of **charitable** foundations and public agencies devoted to helping the
10   world's poor, many with instantly recognizable names like UNICEF or the Bill and Melinda Gates Foundation.

But private companies with that as their sole focus are rare. Even the best-known is not . . . a
15   household name: Vestergaard-Frandsen.

Its products are in use in **refugee** camps and disaster areas all over the third world:[3] PermaNet, a mosquito net [**soaked**] with **insecticide**; ZeroFly, a tent tarp that kills flies;
20   and the LifeStraw, a **filter** worn around the neck that makes filthy water safe to drink.

Some are not only life-saving but even beautiful. The turquoise and navy blue LifeStraw is in museum design collections.

25   "Vestergaard is just different from other companies we work with," said Kevin Starace, malaria[4] adviser for the United Nations Foundation. "They think of the end user as a consumer rather than as a patient or a victim."

30   For example, he said, they have added a cell phone pocket to [the PermaNet] and make window curtains [on the ZeroFly] that kill bugs.

The company begun in Denmark fifty-one years ago to make work uniforms is now run by
35   Mikkel Vestergaard-Frandsen, the grandson of the founder.

After finishing high school in 1991, he said he had "no interest in growing the market for men's shirts." Instead, he went **backpacking**
40   through India and Africa, **entertaining** thoughts of going to Kuwait to fight the oil field fires set during the Gulf War.[5]

. . . In Egypt, he met two Nigerians who told him he could make good money in their country
45   importing used cars from Europe.

"When you're nineteen, you don't have much of a business plan," he said. "So I ended up in Lagos, selling cars and truck engines and buses."

---

[1] **yard:** a unit for measuring length and distance, equal to 3 feet or 0.91 meters

[2] **wool:** material made from the soft thick hair of sheep and goats

[3] **third world:** the poorer countries of the world that are not industrially developed

[4] **malaria:** a disease common in hot countries that happens when an infected mosquito bites you

[5] **Gulf War:** a war which began in 1991 when Iraq attacked Kuwait and took control of it

But a **coup** in 1993 sent him back to
50 Denmark.

Meanwhile, his father, Torben, had struck a
deal to buy a million yards of old, olive-gray wool
cloth from Sweden's civil defense [supplies].

"Sweden had mountain **caves** full of
55 everything you need in case of World War
III, but they decided the risk was not so great
anymore," the elder Mr. Vestergaard-Frandsen
said. "This was for military uniforms. It was
good quality, very expensive wool, but it
60 looked so bad that no housewife would have it
on her couch."

Mikkel agreed to take a desk at the back of
the factory and work on the next step: having
it cut into blankets and sold to the Red Cross.
65 Much of it, he said, ended up in Rwanda and
Kurdistan.

Meanwhile, the company's main business
was facing competition from Asia, and
both he and his father found relief work[6]
70 more interesting. Exporting used clothes for
distribution in refugee camps was profitable.
And there was a market in tsetse fly[7] traps;
the flies which **transmit** sleeping sickness are
drawn to blue light, so the company had to
75 make [its tent tarps with] the right shade that
did not fade in sunlight.

The company also recreated an idea from
nomads[8] in [Western Africa]: packing the filter
into a short plastic pipe so the user could lie
80 down and drink from any puddle.[9]

That pipe was the inspiration for the
LifeStraw, a 10-inch plastic cylinder that filters
out or kills bacteria, parasites,[10] and some
viruses and can be made for less than $3.
85 [Relief] agencies have bought tens of
thousands for use after the Myanmar cyclone[11]
and earthquakes in Asia. The company now
makes a bigger **version** that filters 5 gallons an
hour and will last a typical family three years.
90 While Torben is sometimes described as
the company's mad scientist,[12] Mikkel has
gone beyond being a **supplier** to helping set
global policy. Mr. Starace of the United Nations
Foundation [said] "[Mikkel's] always the most
95 [**daring**] thinker in the room. And he's willing
to roll up his sleeves or even throw his own
employees at a problem. He lent Roll Back
Malaria his chief financial officer. . . . Nobody
else would do that."
100 Vestergaard-Frandsen, which is family-
owned, does not **disclose** financial data, but it
has sold 165 million nets and makes a profit,
Mikkel said.

But he also has a passion for the work, he
105 said, and the challenge of trying to invent a new
product each year.

"Very few companies take the attitude that
doing good is good money," he said. "They
make a net, or they make a filter, and sell it. But
110 make no mistake—as soon as we've proven this
is a good idea, they'll come in. They're sitting
there right now, watching us."

---

[6] **relief work:** giving money, food, and clothes to people who need them, especially after a disaster

[7] **tsetse fly:** an African fly that sucks the blood of people and animals and spreads serious diseases

[8] **nomad:** a member of a tribe that travels from place to place, especially to find fields for their animals

[9] **puddle:** a small pool of water, especially rainwater, on a path, street, etc.

[10] **parasite:** a plant or animal that lives on another plant or animal and gets food from it

[11] **cyclone:** a very strong wind that moves very fast in a circle

[12] **mad scientist:** a character in popular fiction who works on unlikely ways to save the world

Vocabulary Check

A. Work with a partner. Ask and answer the questions. The boldfaced words are the target words.

1. What would you take with you to go **backpacking** in the mountains?

2. What sports do you have to be **daring** to try?

3. Where are two places where you would use **insecticide**?

4. What do you find inside **caves**?

5. A bad hurricane can cause people to become **refugees**. What are other events that can cause people to become refugees?

6. What is one idea you **entertained** but then rejected?

7. What is one way that a person can **transmit** the flu to another person?

B. Rewrite the sentences with the target words from the list.

charitable	coup	disclose	filter	soaked	~~supplier~~	version

EXAMPLE:

The manager can give you the name of the company that sells to us.

The manager can give you the name of our supplier.

1. She gives money to organizations that help people.

   _____

2. He agreed to make information about his company's finances public.

   _____

3. The original software had problems, but the next type of software was better.

   _____

4. There was a change of government after the military took control of the government.

   _____

5. They put the dried tomatoes in water and then cooked them with oil and garlic.

   _____

6. He poured the water through a special cloth to remove the bacteria.

   _____

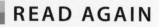

READ AGAIN

Read "A Company Prospers by Saving Poor People's Lives" again and complete the comprehension exercises. As you work, keep the reading goal in mind.

> 📖 **READING GOAL:** To write a descriptive paragraph about the company

Comprehension Check

A. Write the letter of the product(s) each statement refers to. Some statements may refer to more than one product. Write *P* (PermaNet), *Z* (ZeroFly), *L* (LifeStraw), or *W* (wool blankets).

_____ **1.** made out of material that came from Sweden

_____ **2.** in use in refugee camps and disaster areas

_____ **3.** is colored a shade of blue

_____ **4.** is in museums

_____ **5.** has a cell phone pocket

_____ **6.** has a window curtain that kills flies

_____ **7.** mostly ended up in Rwanda and Kurdistan

_____ **8.** kills insects or infectious parasites

_____ **9.** 165 million have sold

_____ **10.** replicates an idea by West African nomads

B. Put the events from the reading into the order in which they happened. Don't look back at the reading. Write *1* next to the first event, *2* next to the second, and so on.

_____ **a.** The company Vestergaard-Frandsen starts to focus on relief products.

_____ **b.** Mikkel goes backpacking through India and Africa.

_____ **c.** Mikkel returns to Denmark to work for the company.

_____ **d.** Vestergaard-Frandsen starts helping to set global policy.

_____ **e.** Mikkel's grandfather founds a company that makes uniforms.

_____ **f.** Relief agencies buy tens of thousands of LifeStraws.

C. Work with a partner. Compare your answers from Exercise B.

D. On a separate sheet of paper, write a descriptive paragraph about Vestergaard-Frandsen. Briefly explain the company's history, the types of products they sell, and what makes them special. Use your answers from Exercises A and B to help you.

> **DISCUSS**

Work in small groups. Ask and answer the questions.

1. What are three words that describe Mikkel Vestergaard-Frandsen? Why do they fit him?

2. Do you agree or disagree with the statement *Vestergaard-Frandsen is doing right by doing good*? Why or why not?

3. What is one way that you think Vestergaard-Frandsen got ideas for products? Can you think of any others?

4. Do you agree that creating products for the developing world is good business? Explain.

> **VOCABULARY SKILL BUILDING**

Vocabulary Skill: Expressions

An expression is a group of words that are frequently used together to generate an image or communicate an idea.

Sometimes they have a figurative meaning; that is, they are used to describe a situation in a colorful way, but they are not meant to be taken literally.

EXAMPLE:

Roll up your sleeves = prepare for hard work

You may or may not actually roll up the sleeves of your shirt, but you are certainly going to put a lot of energy and attention to completing a job or task.

*He's willing to **roll up his sleeves** and stay up all night to get the job done.*

Other times, expressions can have a literal meaning; that is, they are used to describe the actual action in a colorful way.

EXAMPLE:

Eat your fill = eat as much as you want or until you are full

Literally, you will fill your stomach.

*After we had **eaten our fill** we rested in front of the fire.*

A. Work with a partner. Read the example sentences (a and b). Discuss the meaning of the boldfaced expression. Then read the last sentence (c) and decide if it uses the expression correctly or not. Put a check (✓) if the expression is used correctly or an *X* if it is not.

1. **a.** We want to remodel our house, but we need to borrow money from the bank in order to **cover our costs**.

   b. Many restaurant owners cannot **cover their costs** during the winter when business is slow.

   _____ **c.** We have to **cover the costs** so no one will find out how much we spent.

2. **a.** We are hoping to **strike a deal** with the suppliers so that we can get a discount on the materials.

   b. I **struck a deal** with my roommate. She will cook, and I will clean up.

   _____ **c.** Our business agreement stopped when we **struck a deal** to buy goods from them.

3. **a.** Our household has agreed to **cut back on** electricity use, so we do not turn on the heat unless it gets very cold.

   b. In order to lose weight, he is trying to **cut back on** sweets and fried foods.

   _____ **c.** I couldn't sleep very well, so I **cut back on** coffee, tea, and caffeinated soda.

4. **a.** After we had **eaten our fill**, we relaxed and talked about the good times we had had over the years.

   b. The harvest season is a time when people can **eat their fill** of special foods that are not always available during the rest of the year.

   _____ **c.** You look hungry. Go ahead and **eat your fill**. We have plenty of food.

5. **a.** The discovery and use of fossil fuels **changed the course of** human history.

   b. The war **changed the course of** events and created difficulty for some nations but opportunities for others.

   _____ **c.** The scientist who finds a cure for cancer could **change the course of** medicine.

6. **a.** The hurricane was heading toward our country, so we decided to **keep out of harm's way** by going to my cousin's house in California.

   b. As a war photographer, he can't **keep out of harm's way**.

   _____ **c.** Most risk-takers are excited to **keep out of harm's way**.

B. On a separate sheet of paper, write short answers to the questions below. The boldfaced words are target words from previous chapters.

1. How does an advertising salesperson feel when he or she **strikes a deal** with a big company?

2. What is a program that you are **in favor of**? Explain what it does.

3. How might an athlete **run the risk of** injury?

4. When did you have to **roll up your sleeves** and work very hard?

5. When are actors and musicians **in the same boat**?

6. What is something you like to **make from scratch**?

7. When you are buying a car, is it best to offer a low price and **hold your ground**, or should you just pay the price the dealer is asking?

8. What does a student who cheats **stand to lose**?

9. When have you **gone out on a limb**? Explain.

Learn the Vocabulary

A. Scan a few of the sentences that were found when the phrase "on the way" was entered into an online concordancer. Pay attention to how the phrase is used. Circle any prepositions or words that can occur next to or near the phrase.

1. . . . dine at a restaurant on the shores of the Aegean. **On the way** out, Mr. Sakellariadis detoured up a . . .

2. I fainted and woke up in an ambulance **on the way** to the hospital with a lump on my head.

3. "I'll walk," Doc said. "I've got to run an errand **on the way**. See you in about an hour."

4. I wonder if we shouldn't just leave, and grab a bite **on the way** instead, a sandwich or something.

5. Go straight to nan's, call **on the way** back. If it isn't too late.

B. Complete the sentences by adding *on the way*. If it does not make sense, leave it out.

1. We were _____*on the way*_____ to the meeting when we got a flat tire.

2. She parked under a tree _____ and dented the car.

3. He had a successful trip, but _____ back he lost his computer at the airport.

4. She was _____ and we could not get past her.

5. We decided to stop at the store _____ home.

6. We do not have time to cook. Let's get some food _____ to the movies.

C. Type three more phrases into a concordancer and write down the patterns you see on your word cards. Pay careful attention to prepositions and pronouns or other words that appear between the words in your phrase.

D. Review your cards. Try to create new sentences with your phrases.

E. Go back to the vocabulary list at the beginning of each chapter. What did you learn about the target words? Add your numbers to the lists.

Vocabulary Practice 12, see page 248.

FLUENCY PRACTICE 4

Fluency Strategy

To become a more fluent reader, you need to read materials in English as frequently as possible, ideally every day. The material should be very easy for you, but you need to read extensively. Choose longer readings over short ones. Ask your teacher to help you find readings that are at the appropriate level of difficulty. Guided readers—simplified versions of classic novels—are a good place to start. There are also many magazines, websites, and newspapers with an appropriate reading level for fluency practice. Set yourself a goal of a certain number of pages every week. For example, you can start by reading fifty pages a week. Then increase the number of pages by ten pages every week, so that in the second week you are reading sixty pages, seventy in the third week, and so on.

> READING 1

Before You Read

Preview "A Cleaner Way to Shop?" on the next page. Then circle the letter of the correct answer to each question.

1. What is the main topic of the reading?
   a. online shopping
   b. environmental scientists
   c. overnight delivery

2. What is the main idea of the reading?
   a. Online shopping is bad for the environment.
   b. Environmental scientists say we shouldn't shop in big stores.
   c. Overnight delivery is a cleaner and faster way to shop.

Read

A. Read "A Cleaner Way to Shop?" Time yourself. Write your start and end times and your total reading time. Then calculate your reading speed (words per minute) and write it in the progress chart on page 249.

Start time: _____ **End time:** _____ **Total time:** _____ (in seconds)

Reading speed:

706 words ÷ _____ (total time in seconds) x 60 = _____ words per minute

A Cleaner Way to Shop?

1   Need to buy something? Why get in your car and go to a store? Just buy it on the Internet! Need it now? Why wait? Order it for next-day delivery! Each day, more and more people try
5 online shopping. Business analysts say that online sales have doubled in the last ten years. Americans alone spend well over $150 billion a year buying goods and services on the web. For online merchants, this is a dream come true.
10 But not everyone shares their excitement. Many scientists are now arguing that all this online shopping is bad for the environment.

    This seems to go against conventional wisdom. "With online shopping, people think,
15 'I don't need to drive, and the business doesn't need to build a store, so there will be less pollution,'" says Nuria Prost, an environmental scientist. "But it really is not so simple. The truth is online shopping generates a lot of
20 waste. It also adds to air pollution."

    Historically, the Internet has not always been a good friend to the environment. For example, most people thought that the Internet would help offices use less paper and other materials.
25 But paper use increased by 33 percent between 1986 and 1997. With the increased demand for paper, more and more trees have been cut down. This leads to deforestation. "[Online shopping] could have similarly negative effects," says Nevil
30 Cohen, a professor of environmental science.

    Part of the problem is what people are buying these days. In the past, people bought things on the Internet that did not require much packing material. Many of the first generation
35 of online stores sold small goods. Amazon.com, for example, sold books, and other websites offered flower delivery or magazine subscriptions. But since then a new wave of Internet businesses has appeared, offering an
40 almost unlimited selection of products. People now shop online for large, heavy products such as computers, televisions, even furniture. These products require tremendous amounts of plastic and paper shipping materials. The larger the
45 product, the more waste is created.

    "People forget how efficient regular stores are," says business advisor Linda Eggers. "They have had years to perfect their model. Online retailers are still figuring it out." A conventional
50 store can take one large, single shipment and distribute it to local customers. With online shopping, small shipments of individually packed products may travel long distances. "So what you get is one book, in one box, traveling
55 one hundred miles, instead of a hundred books in one box traveling one mile," Eggers explains.

    Perhaps the biggest drawback of online shopping is its link to air pollution. As online shopping has grown in popularity, companies
60 have increased their air shipping. Airplanes use much more fuel than cars and produce more carbon dioxide. Next-day delivery, which requires overnight flights, causes particular problems. Studies show that night flights create twice as
65 much pollution as day flights. Without sunlight to reflect carbon dioxide into space, it stays in the atmosphere and traps heat. This leads to greater warming and further environmental problems.

    When people buy a lot of different things
70 from different online businesses, this creates even more travel by airplanes. As the popularity of online shopping continues to grow, experts predict air shipping will increase as well.

    Online product returns are also a factor in
75 the problem. For example, an online shoe store may allow customers to return shoes for free if they are the wrong size. While this pleases customers, it doubles the packing materials and number of airplane trips required to sell one
80 pair of shoes. Even worse is when customers abuse the policy and order three to four pairs of shoes with the intention of keeping only one pair and returning all the others.

    "If people want to protect the environment,
85 they need to think before they shop," says Prost. "People need to put things in perspective: Is this the exact thing I want? Is this thing so important that I really need it tomorrow, or will I be OK if I wait?" Online stores can
90 also charge customers for returns. This may lead people to shop more carefully. "Online shopping is fast and easy," says Prost, "but we can't forget the long-term negative effect it has on the environment."

B. Read "A Clearer Way to Shop?" again, a little faster this time. Write your start and end times and your total reading time. Then calculate your reading speed (words per minute) and write it in the progress chart on page 249.

Start time: _____   **End time:** _____   **Total time:** _____ (in seconds)

Reading speed:

706 words ÷ _____ (total time in seconds) x 60 = _____ words per minute

Comprehension Check

A. Read the statements about the reading. Write *T* if the statement is true and *F* if the statement is false.

_____ **1.** Online shopping is becoming more popular, but it is also wasteful.

_____ **2.** Most customers know that online shopping is bad for the environment.

_____ **3.** In the past, customers shopped online for products that were big and weighed a lot.

_____ **4.** The delivery of heavy products requires a lot of materials.

_____ **5.** An airplane creates more pollution than a car.

_____ **6.** "Next day delivery" is helpful for the environment.

_____ **7.** If online stores charge a fee for returns, customers might shop more carefully.

_____ **8.** Nuria Prost tells shoppers *not* to buy products on the Internet.

B. Answer the questions on a separate sheet of paper. Try not to look back at the reading.

1. What problem does online shopping cause?

2. What are some reasons for the problem? List three.

C. Check your answers for the comprehension questions in the Answer Key on page 251. Then calculate your score and write it in the progress chart on page 249.

_____ (my number correct) ÷ 10 x 100 = _____%

➤ READING 2

Before You Read

Preview "Your Second Life." Circle the letter of the correct answer to each question.

1. What is *Second Life*?

   a. a book

   b. a video game

   c. a company

2. What process does the reading explain?

   a. how *Second Life* was written

   b. how to make money by playing *Second Life*

   c. how *Second Life* grew from a small company to a global business

Read

A. Read "Your Second Life." Time yourself. Write your start and end times and your total reading time. Then calculate your reading speed (words per minute) and write it in the progress chart on page 249.

Start time: _____   **End time:** _____   **Total time:** _____ (in seconds)

Reading speed:

763 words ÷ _____ (total time in seconds) x 60 = _____ words per minute

Your Second Life

1   As far as we know, humans are the only creatures on Earth with the ability to imagine lives that are different from the ones we have. Some people enter the world of imagination
5 through books and stories. Others watch television or movies. Children bring their toys to life with the power of their imagination. Today, the Internet makes it easier than ever for both children and adults to enter imaginary
10 worlds. But what happens when the real world and the world of the imagination start to come together? To find out, all you need to do is go on the Internet and enter the virtual world of *Second Life*.

15   First of all, to understand Second Life, let's meet someone who lives and works there, Nyla Cheeky. Cheeky is an enterprising young fashion designer. She designs and makes women's clothing and then sells it in her
20 own stores. Cheeky's clothes are surprisingly inexpensive. Her original designs range in price from 25 cents to $6.00. How can she afford to sell things at such low prices? She has a tremendous number of customers. In fact,
25 thousands of people visit her stores every day.

    Now meet Canadian fashion designer Nyla Kazakoff. Kazakoff's designs are very similar to Cheeky's. However, they cost significantly

(continued on next page)

more. For example, both designers sell a similar dress. Cheeky's dress costs about $5.35. Kazakoff's costs $1,500. Kazakoff needs to sell her designs at high prices because she can create and sell only a few of them every month.

Have you guessed the secret of the two Nylas yet? They are both the same person. Nyla Kazakoff is a real life fashion designer. Nyla Cheeky is a fashion designer too, but she doesn't live in the real world. She lives in the online world of the virtual reality game Second Life. The clothes in her stores are virtual, not real. But the money she makes is undeniably real.

To play Second Life, you create a computer character, or *avatar*, as it is called in the gaming world. Nyla Cheeky is Nyla Kazakoff's avatar. When your avatar enters Second Life, he or she does many of the same things people do in the real world. For example, avatars go to nightclubs, drive cars, and play games. And like people in the real world, avatars love to shop on a regular basis. This is where fashion designer Nyla Kazakoff comes in. Designer fashions are very popular among Second Life avatars. The real-world Nyla Kazakoff creates online digital copies of her real-world clothes. Then Second Life Nyla Cheeky sells the virtual clothing in stores that she operates in Second Life. Customers pay for her designs with money called Lindens. Second Life players exchange real money for Lindens.

Up to this point, Second Life might not sound very different from other online games. But this is where things get interesting. The unique thing about Second Life is that players like Kazakoff create things and sell them in Second Life. They then exchange the Lindens that they make for real money. For example, imagine that someone buys one of Kazakoff/Cheeky's designs for 500 Lindens. Those Lindens go into Kazakoff/Cheeky's Second Life account. After Kazakoff/Cheeky pays Second Life expenses such as the rent on her stores, any remaining Lindens are hers. She can then exchange them for real dollars.

Currently, Kazakoff is making about two-thirds of her income from real-world sales of her designs, and one-third from Cheeky's sales in Second Life. And Kazakoff isn't the only one making real money in the virtual world. Some Second Life players have done so well that they have devoted themselves entirely to their Second Life careers. In fact, there is at least one Second Life player who has become rich developing and then selling property such as land, homes, and office buildings in Second Life.

But wait a minute! Why would anyone pay real money for imaginary clothing or property? Probably for the same reason that a little girl saves her birthday money to buy clothing and a house for her favorite doll. She dresses her doll in clothing that she can't wear in real life and puts her in a house where adults can't tell her what to do. Through her doll, the little girl experiences a reality that is different from her own. The same is true of adults playing Second Life. Through their avatars, they have a chance to experience a "second life," with a better standard of living. And they are happy to pay real money to bring that imaginary world to life.

B. Read "Your Second Life" again, a little faster this time. Write your start and end times and your total reading time. Then calculate your reading speed (words per minute) and write it in the progress chart on page 249.

Start time: _____   **End time:** _____   **Total time:** _____ (in seconds)

Reading speed:

763 words ÷ _____ (total time in seconds) x 60 = _____ words per minute

Comprehension Check

A. Read the statements about the reading. Write *T* if the statement is true and *F* if the statement is false.

_____ **1.** Nyla Cheeky is a real person.

_____ **2.** Nyla Kazakoff is a real person.

_____ **3.** Nyla's virtual and real-world designs sell for similar prices.

_____ **4.** Some *Second Life* players pay rent.

_____ **5.** A purpose of the game *Second Life* is to make money.

_____ **6.** Some *Second Life* players create digital houses, land, or other things and sell them to other players.

_____ **7.** *Second Life* uses the same currency as the United States, dollars.

_____ **8.** Most *Second Life* players are adults.

B. Answer the questions in your own words on a separate sheet of paper.

1. Who is Nyla Cheeky?

2. How are businesses in *Second Life* similar to real-world businesses?

3. How are *Second Life* players similar to a child playing with a doll house?

C. Check your answers for the comprehension questions in the Answer Key on page 251. Then calculate your score and write it in the progress chart on page 249.

_____ (my number correct) ÷ 11 x 100 _____ %

New Words

UNIT 1

UNIT 2

UNIT 3

UNIT 4

UNIT 5

UNIT 6

New Words

UNIT 7

UNIT 8

UNIT 9

UNIT 10

UNIT 11

UNIT 12

THINK ABOUT MEANING

Circle the letter of the correct answer(s) to complete each sentence. There may be more than one answer. The boldfaced words are the target words.

1. People **get rid of** _____.
  a. old clothes
  b. science
  c. broken plates

2. A person can **activate** a _____.
  a. machine
  b. plan
  c. scientist

3. Computers can **function** as _____.
  a. video cameras
  b. communication tools
  c. home theaters

4. _____ is **offensive**.
  a. A swim team
  b. A terrible smell
  c. Impolite behavior

5. A person can be **susceptible** to a _____.
  a. disease
  b. lie
  c. job

6. A(n) _____ is a useful **device**.
  a. cell phone
  b. bottle opener
  c. airplane

7. Students are sometimes **subjected** to _____.
  a. good grades
  b. boring talks
  c. stressful tests

8. _____ are a **phenomenon** that often occur in California.
  a. Earthquakes
  b. Noises
  c. Innovations

PRACTICE A SKILL: Parts of Speech

Read the sentences. Are the underlined words nouns, verbs, adjectives, or adverbs. Write *N, V, Adj,* or *Adv.*

_____ **1.** She comes in for help quite <u>frequently</u>.

_____ **2.** If you take too much medicine the effect could be <u>lethal</u>.

_____ **3.** When the alarm sounded, the noise was <u>deafening</u>.

_____ **4.** I like the <u>tune</u>, but I cannot understand the words.

_____ **5.** In the summer, insects <u>invade</u> the garden and eat the tomato leaves.

_____ **6.** My dentist often <u>hums</u> to himself while he is working on my teeth.

_____ **7.** The Web site is <u>temporarily</u> unavailable. Check back later.

_____ **8.** She has a <u>high-pitched</u> voice that is effective in getting people's attention.

_____ **9.** A virus <u>infected</u> my computer, which caused a delay.

_____ **10.** Influenza can be <u>lethal</u>, especially when the victims are old or sick.

PRACTICE A STRATEGY: Making Word Cards

Make word cards for 12 more words that you learned this week. Add them to the cards that you made for this unit. Review your cards for a few minutes several times a day. Always change the order of your cards before you review them.

VOCABULARY PRACTICE 2

THINK ABOUT MEANING

Circle the word(s) that has the same meaning as the boldfaced target word.

1. She patted the dog **affectionately** but kept her eyes on the road ahead.
   a. cautiously   **b.** lovingly   **c.** warmly

2. The sunlight **faded**.
   a. slowly disappeared   **b.** diminished   **c.** brightened

3. I'll tutor you in math **in exchange for** an hour of language practice.
   a. as a trade for   **b.** as a consequence for   **c.** as a payment for

4. I grew up in a five-**story** apartment building.
   a. room   **b.** floor   **c.** level

5. The children **clamored** for food.
   a. called   **b.** noisily asked   **c.** whispered

6. I must have looked at him **uncomprehendingly** because he laughed and started explaining again.
   a. confusedly   **b.** desperately   **c.** dangerously

PRACTICE A SKILL: Similes vs. Metaphors

Read the sentences. Are the underlined phrases similes or metaphors? Write *S* or *M*.

1. The child grew <u>like a weed</u> during her sixth grade year.

2. We all sat down hungrily admiring <u>the gorgeous mountains of food</u>.

3. The first part of the paper is very well organized, but then <u>it wanders off topic</u>.

4. When it is in bloom, the jasmine flower is <u>as fragrant as a perfume</u>.

5. The grass was swaying in the wind <u>like the fur of a giant moving cat</u>.

6. <u>My city is an urban paradise</u> because of the gardens, trees, and classical architecture.

7. Those children were brought up <u>like wild animals</u>.

8. Fresh vegetables contain vitamins and minerals that will keep you <u>as healthy as a horse</u>.

PRACTICE A STRATEGY: Using Word Cards with Example Sentences

Review your word cards for this unit. Look up the words in your dictionary. Find and copy an example sentence from the dictionary or your reading. Study the example sentences as you review your word cards. Try to make up new example sentences.

THINK ABOUT MEANING

Look at each group of words. Cross out the one word in each group that does not belong.

1. helpless   weak   vulnerable   kind
2. writhe   shake   sing   twist
3. jerk   move   twitch   sit
4. moan   groan   purchase   sigh
5. authoritative   wonderful   powerful   strong
6. proceed   continue   take   go
7. remedy   solve   fix   expect
8. wail   cry   chew   scream
9. grief   sorrow   excitement   sadness
10. steady   balance   adjust   sell

PRACTICE A SKILL: Understanding Phrasal Verbs

Circle the word or phrase that correctly completes each sentence.

1. A child / chair can straighten up.
2. A student tries to figure out problems / skills.
3. A passenger can whip out a ticket / suitcase.
4. People sometimes lose track of their phones /services.
5. It is difficult for a child to cut down on sweets / trees.
6. You need to bend down to pick up a rock / see a sunset.
7. A good student does not settle for a bad grade /a lot of homework.
8. The losers in a race usually give up hope / problems early on.
9. When their children act up, parents are usually happy /upset.
10. Students get tired of studying /getting good grades

PRACTICE A SRATEGY: Guessing Meaning from Context

Review the phrasal verbs you studied in this unit. Type each phrasal verb into a search engine to find example sentences. Write the sentences on your word cards. Think about what the phrasal verb means in the sentences.

THINK ABOUT MEANING

Complete the sentences with the words from the list. The boldfaced words are the target words. There are two extra words.

alert	desperately	emerge	grab	penetrate
assumed	diameter	gap	gravity	rot

1. The rabbit tried to escape through the fence, but I was able to _____ her just in time.

2. Years of bad weather had caused the wood to _____, so the stairs were not safe.

3. In the spring, tiny plants began to _____ from the wet brown Earth.

4. We _____ that they would agree with us, so were surprised when they didn't.

5. The faint light could not _____ the darkness for more than a few feet.

6. Hail stones that are five inches in _____ are not unheard of, but they are very rare.

7. His safety rope broke, and he reached _____ for a branch just above his head.

8. There is no _____ in space.

PRACTICE A SKILL: Using Nouns as Adjectives and Verbs

A. Underline the nouns used as adjectives. Then check (✓) the sentences where the noun used as an adjective creates a logical statement.

_____ **1.** We ordered a bush cutter to clear out the plants we did not want.

_____ **2.** Naturalists can become foliage experts.

_____ **3.** It is possible to measure a diameter circle.

_____ **4.** Three hundred years ago, Alaska was frontier country.

B. Underline the nouns used as verbs. Then check (✓) the sentences where the noun used as a verb creates a logical statement.

_____ **1.** Children can tangle ropes.

_____ **2.** You can gravity a rock.

_____ **3.** You can layer lettuce and tomato.

_____ **4.** You can diameter a circle.

PRACTICE A STRATEGY: Choosing Which Words to Study

Make a list of 10 words from this unit that you think are important to learn. Write example sentences that use two of your vocabulary words in a particular context. For example, if you think *leap* and *gap* share a context, you might write *Frogs like to leap over gaps between rocks.* Remember to avoid pairing words that are similar in spelling, sound, or meaning.

THINK ABOUT MEANING

Are the meanings of the two sets of words or phrases similar or different? Write *S* or *D*.

_____ **1.** digit/number

_____ **2.** simplicity/reality

_____ **3.** seriously/solemnly

_____ **4.** pursue/chase

_____ **5.** volunteer/expect

_____ **6.** flexibility/adaptability

_____ **7.** extra/spare

_____ **8.** skin/mind

_____ **9.** anticipate/look forward to

_____ **10.** drain/remove

PRACTICE A SKILL: Numerical Prefixes

Answer the questions.

1. How many sports are there in a decathlon? _____

2. How many millimeters are there in a meter? _____

3. How many sides does a pentagram have? _____

4. Does a polyglot speak one language or many? _____

5. How many degrees does a centigrade thermometer show between freezing and boiling?

_____

6. If a family has triplets, how many children are there? _____

7. How many feet does a biped have? _____

8. How many rulers are there in a monarchy? _____

9. If something is unilateral, how many sides does it have? _____

PRACTICE A STRATEGY: Finding the Core Meaning

Choose 10 words from this unit that you want to learn. Look up each word in the dictionary and study the different meanings and example sentences. Compare the meanings given in the dictionary and write a core definition for each one of your words.

THINK ABOUT MEANING

Look at the words and phrases in the list. Think about their meanings, and decide where to put them in the chart. Some of the words can go in more than one place in the chart. Be ready to explain your decisions.

Cooks in a kitchen	Workers at a building site	Politicians in a meeting

acre	objection
advocate	on the defensive
defrost	organic
exhort	remodel
grain	spacious
made from scratch	stock

PRACTICE A SKILL: Using Prefixes

Write the words from the list next to their descriptions. You will not use every word.

antiaging	antismoking	defeat	relight
antibiotic	antiwar	depersonalize	remake
antifashion	debrief	deplane	rewrite
antiplane	decriminalize	reappear	

1. when something can stop you from aging = _____

2. someone who is against smoking = _____

3. a person who hates the fashion industry = _____

4. to write a second or third time = _____

5. someone who works to stop war = _____

6. to make impersonal = _____

7. to make something legal = _____

8. to come back into view = _____

PRACTICE A STRATEGY: Learning for Different Purposes

Make a list of 10 words from this unit that you want to learn. Then think about what you need to learn about each word: meaning, pronunciation, grammatical features, or other members of the word family. Make a card for each word. Look up each word in the dictionary and copy the information you want onto your card. For meaning and writing purposes, always include example sentences to help you. For pronunciation, use the phonetic alphabet or your own symbols, and do not forget to mark the stress.

THINK ABOUT MEANING

Complete the sentences with the words from the list. The boldfaced words are the target words.

activate	assumed	emerged	on the defensive	penetrate
advocate	device	gravity	oxygen	phenomenon

1. The moon **orbits** Earth because of Earth's _____.

2. The **probe** was able to _____ the planet's thick atmosphere.

3. Many astronomers _____ spending more money to research our **vast galaxy**.

4. The door to the UFO opened, and an **extraterrestrial being** slowly _____.

5. One _____ you might find at a **planetarium** is a telescope.

6. After his theory was attacked by **skeptics**, the astronomer went _____.

7. The rocket is ready to **launch**; _____ the engines!

8. Because the UFO witness was a scientist, I _____ his **account** was **credible**.

9. The birth of a star is a _____ **worthy** of study.

10. The **essential criteria** for life are water and _____.

PRACTICE A SKILL: Prefixes *inter-* and *extra-*

Circle the letter of the word that best completes each sentence.

1. It is difficult for John to make friends; he has no _____ skills.
   a. interchangeable   **b.** interpersonal   **c.** intergalactic

2. Scientists want to see if the planet has _____ life.
   a. extramarital   **b.** extracurricular   **c.** extraterrestrial

3. Either car part will fit in the engine; they are _____.
   a. interchangeable   **b.** interpersonal   **c.** intergalactic

4. At my school, astronomy is offered as an _____ course.
   a. extramarital   **b.** extracurricular   **c.** extraterrestrial

PRACTICE A STRATEGY: Choosing Which Words to Study

Study the new words from *Practice a Skill*. Decide which words are most useful to you in real life. Make word cards for those words.

VOCABULARY PRACTICE 8

THINK ABOUT MEANING

Circle the letter of the correct answer(s) to complete each sentence. There may be more than one answer. The boldfaced words are the target words.

1. A common **domestic** animal is a _____.
   a. cat
   b. bear
   c. dog

2. _____ **float** in water.
   a. Rocks
   b. Tree branches
   c. People

3. People can be **displaced** by a _____.
   a. war
   b. layout
   c. storm

4. _____ are **radiant**.
   a. Clouds
   b. Birds
   c. Stars

5. A drought means a **shortage** of _____.
   a. land
   b. water
   c. air

6. _____ require **maintenance**.
   a. Cars
   b. Travels
   c. Buildings

7. If you drive _____, your license may be **suspended**.
   a. carefully
   b. dangerously
   c. frequently

8. The city wants to **tear down** the old _____.
   a. stadium
   b. park
   c. wall

PRACTICE A SKILL: Knowing Root Meanings

Complete the words in the sentences with a root from the list. Each root may be used more than once.

cred	dom	flect	man	radi

1. The people who trust you enough to loan you money are your _____itors.

2. Real estate agents need a lot of wis_____ about the housing market.

3. Building a house requires a lot of _____ual labor.

4. I want to sing better, so I'm trying to improve the in_____ion of my voice.

5. When his father died, the prince took control of the king_____.

6. This company _____ufactures safety equipment.

7. Don't stand too close to the X-ray machine. It releases _____ation.

8. I installed windows that de_____ some of the sunlight.

PRACTICE A STRATEGY: Adding a Picture for Example Sentences

Review your word cards for this unit. If a word is difficult for you to remember, add an example sentence to the back of the card. Then draw a picture under the sentence.

THINK ABOUT MEANING

Look at the words in the list. Circle the words that have a positive meaning (something good), and underline the words that have a negative meaning (something bad).

come clean	foe	frailty	menacing	petrifying
despair	formidable	fury	outlast	spine-chilling

PRACTICE A SKILL: Onomatopoeia

Answer the questions on a separate sheet of paper.

1. When does a balloon make a **puff** sound?

2. When does a balloon make a **hissing** sound?

3. If you stomach starts to **growl**, what should you do?

4. When does the audience at a sporting event **roar**?

5. Which types of drinks **fizz** when you open them?

6. In what situations do animals **snarl**?

7. What pieces of furniture would make you **grunt** if you picked them up?

8. In what situations do people **snort** when they laugh?

PRACTICE A STRATEGY: Using Word Parts to Guess Meaning

Study the boldfaced words. Pay attention to roots and prefixes. Write your definition for the word on the space provided. Then check your definitions in your dictionary.

1. I think I was **overcharged** for my ticket to the zoo. My friend paid only $5.00.

    overcharge = _____

2. It is not easy to **domesticate** a wild animal.

    domesticate = _____

3. When I saw the lion standing in my backyard, I was **incredulous**.

    incredulous = _____

4. If you see a lion sleeping in the wild, don't come within a 200 foot **radius** of it.

    radius = _____

5. Before you feed the tiger, be sure to **debone** the meat.

    debone = _____

6. To look young, I use an **antiaging** cream.

    antiaging = _____

THINK ABOUT MEANING

Look at the words in the list. Think about their meanings, and decide where to put them in the chart. Some of the words can go in more than one place in the chart. Be ready to explain your decisions.

Climate	City	Energy

breeze   outskirts

drought   pedestrian

dust   renewable

generate   resources

harsh   self-sufficient

humid   settlement

PRACTICE A SKILL: Collocations

Complete the sentences with the words from the list. The words in the list form collocations with the boldfaced words. There are two extra words.

action	deeply	environmentally	run	support
current	demand	face	show	take

1. Many people want to live in a way that is _____ **friendly**.

2. The damage that has been done to the environment is _____ **troubling**.

3. More and more people are **taking** _____ to protect the environment.

4. **Research** will _____ that we are depleting our resources.

5. These days, there is **rising** _____ for solar panels.

6. In the automobile industry, smaller cars are the _____ **trend**.

7. Many people are learning to _____ shorter **showers** to conserve water.

8. In the future, it will take less electricity to _____ **the appliances** in your home.

PRACTICE A STRATEGY: The Keyword Technique

Review the words from this unit that were new to you. If a word is difficult to remember, think of a keyword from your first language that sounds similar to that word. Imagine a picture where the meaning of the new word and the meaning of the keyword are connected in some way. Draw the picture on the back of your word card.

THINK ABOUT MEANING

The sentences below do not make sense. Replace each underlined word with a word from the list so the sentences make sense. The boldfaced words are the target words.

consciousness	go out on a limb	out of the question	overhaul	shift
follow suit	linked to	outskirts	reluctantly	suspended

1. One **drawback** of multitasking is that it is <u>unrelated to</u> **long-term** memory problems.

2. All students must take the test; there are no **exceptions**. So missing the test is <u>possible</u>.

3. If you are arrested for driving while **impaired**, your driver's license may be <u>approved</u>.

4. I have no **recollection** of the accident; I must have lost <u>interest</u>.

5. My office has a **rotating** work schedule; every week my working hours <u>stay the same</u>.

6. I don't **readily** attend the theater; I'm <u>eagerly</u> going to a play this weekend.

7. My brother **switched** phone companies and saved money. Maybe I should <u>not do that</u>.

8. The system is **inefficient** and doesn't work **consistently**. Let's <u>keep</u> the system.

PRACTICE A SKILL: The Prefix *multi-*

A. Make new words by adding the prefix *multi-* to some of the words below. If you cannot add the prefix *multi-* to a word, write *X*. If you are not sure, look in your dictionary.

	multi - + word?		*multi -* + word?
1. attractive	_____ *X* _____	5. media	_____
2. lingual	_ *multilingual* _	6. purpose	_____
3. colored	_____	7. roof	_____
4. helpful	_____	8. billionaire	_____

B. Complete each sentence with a new word from Exercise A.

1. Shania's _____ presentation included music, a video, and some great photos.

2. I really loved the _____ roses in the botanical garden.

3. The owner of the company is a _____.

4. Janet is _____; at the moment she's studying Korean.

5. This device is _____; it can be a phone, a music player, a camera, and more.

PRACTICE A STRATEGY: Changing the Order and Grouping of Word Cards

Review your cards every day. If you remember a word correctly three times, remove that card and put it in a safe place. Then after a few days, put that card back with the other cards, change the order, and review all of your cards again.

VOCABULARY PRACTICE 12

THINK ABOUT MEANING

Circle the letter of the correct answer(s) to complete each sentence. There may be more than one answer. The boldfaced words are the target words.

1. A **conventional** mode of transportation is a _____.
   a. car
   b. hot air balloon
   c. train

2. To function, _____ need to be **plugged in**.
   a. airplanes
   b. televisions
   c. refrigerators

3. _____ are very **nutritious**.
   a. Donuts
   b. Apples
   c. Sodas

4. _____ are the **end users** of educational products.
   a. Textbooks
   b. Exams
   c. Students

5. A **daring** activity is _____.
   a. cleaning
   b. skydiving
   c. swimming

6. You can **entertain** _____.
   a. ideas
   b. storms
   c. guests

PRACTICE A SKILL: Expressions

Complete each sentence with an expression from the list. You will not use every expression.

changed the course of	eat their fill	make from scratch	strike a deal
cover their costs	go out on a limb	roll up their sleeves	
cut back on	hold his ground	stand to lose	

1. They have a lot of work to do; they'd better _____ and get started.

2. If the project is unsuccessful, the investors _____ a lot of money.

3. My friends love buffet style restaurants; they can _____ for a low price.

4. I love to bake. Cake and apple pie are two things I can _____.

5. The creation of the Internet has undoubtedly _____ human history.

6. If Trent is ever going to lose some weight, he'd better _____ sweets.

7. Jim openly criticized his boss at the meeting; I guess he's not afraid to _____.

8. You have a car to sell, and I need to buy one; maybe we can _____.

PRACTICE A STRATEGY: Using an Online Concordancer

Type three or four of the expressions from *Practice a Skill* into a concordancer. Write the patterns you see on your word cards. Pay careful attention to prepositions and pronouns or other words that appear between the words in your expressions.

Fluency Progress Charts

FLUENCY PRACTICE 1

	Words per Minute	
	First Try	Second Try
Reading 1		
Reading 2		
Comprehension Check Score _____%		

FLUENCY PRACTICE 2

	Words per Minute	
	First Try	Second Try
Reading 1		
Reading 2		
Comprehension Check Score _____%		

FLUENCY PRACTICE 3

	Words per Minute	
	First Try	Second Try
Reading 1		
Reading 2		
Comprehension Check Score _____%		

FLUENCY PRACTICE 4

	Words per Minute	
	First Try	Second Try
Reading 1		
Reading 2		
Comprehension Check Score _____%		

Fluency Practice Answer Key

Fluency Practice 1

Reading 1

Comprehension Check, p. 56

A.

1. b   4. c
2. c   5. c
3. c   6. a

B.

1. *Answers may vary but should include three of the following:* by making tools, by learning behavior and teaching it to other crows, by planning and solving problems, by developing advanced social skills, by manipulating situations to their advantage, by being able to be trained
2. *Answers may vary but should include a fact about crows' intelligence, a fact about dogs' intelligence, and a statement explaining why crows are or are not as intelligent as dogs.*

Reading 2

Comprehension Check, p. 59

A.

1. T   4. F
2. T   5. T
3. F   6. T

B.

1. c   4. b
2. a   5. d
3. e

Fluency Practice 2

Reading 1

Comprehension Check, p. 116

A.

1. a   5. a
2. c   6. c
3. b   7. c
4. b

B.

1. long   3. in high mountains
2. big business   4. spiritually enlightened

Reading 2

Comprehension Check, p. 120

A.

1. Culinary tourism   4. Storm chasing
2. Dark tourism   5. Ecotourism
3. Extreme tourism

B.

1. Extreme tourism   4. Ecotourism
2. Dark tourism   5. Culinary tourism
3. Dark tourism

Fluency Practice 3

Reading 1

Comprehension Check, p. 175

A.

True statements: 2, 4, 5, 6, 7

B.

1. *Answers may vary but should include the following:* Shyness is very common. Almost 80 percent of people report feeling shy at some point.
2. *Answers may vary but should include four of the following:* troubling social experiences, genetics, family size, place of birth, technology
3. *Answers may vary but should include some of the following:* People often overcome shyness by going through a significant life step, such as starting a career, getting married, or buying a home. People can also take certain steps, such as being conscious of negative thoughts, shifting their attention to other people, practicing conversational strategies, and remembering that many people are shy.

Reading 2

Comprehension Check, p. 177

A.

1. b   5. b
2. c   6. c
3. c   7. a
4. c

B.

1. They have chosen lifestyles that distinguish them from others.
2. They all come from different backgrounds and have different motivations for their behavior.

Fluency Practice 4

Reading 1
Comprehension Check, p. 231

A.

1. T   5. T
2. F   6. F
3. F   7. T
4. T   8. F

B.

1. Online shopping is bad for the environment. It causes waste and air pollution.
2. Large items: require a lot of plastic and paper shipping materials
   Next-day delivery by airplanes: causes a great deal of air pollution and global warming
   Online product returns: doubles the packing materials and number of airplane trips

Reading 2
Comprehension Check, p. 234

A.

1. T   5. T
2. F   6. T
3. F   7. F
4. T   8. T

B.

1. Nyla Cheeky is an enterprising young fashion designer.
2. Both businesses sell products and make money, and both have expenses such as rent.
3. *Second Life* players have a chance to experience a "second life" with a better standard of living.

Pronunciation Table

Vowels

Symbol	Key Word
i	beat, feed
ɪ	bit, did
eɪ	date, paid
ɛ	bet, bed
æ	bat, bad
ɑ	box, odd, father
ɔ	bought, dog
oʊ	boat, road
ʊ	book, good
u	boot, food, student
ʌ	but, mud, mother
ə	banana, among
ɚ	shirt, murder
aɪ	bite, cry, buy, eye
aʊ	about, how
ɔɪ	voice, boy
ɪr	beer
ɛr	bare
ɑr	bar
ɔr	door
ʊr	tour

/*t*/ means that /*t*/ may be dropped.

/*d*/ means that /*d*/ may be dropped.

/'/ shows main stress.

/ˌ/ shows secondary stress.

Consonants

Symbol	Key Word
p	pack, happy
b	back, rubber
t	tie
d	die
k	came, key, quick
g	game, guest
tʃ	church, nature, watch
dʒ	judge, general, major
f	fan, photograph
v	van
θ	thing, breath
ð	then, breathe
s	sip, city, psychology
z	zip, please, goes
ʃ	ship, machine, station, special, discussion
ʒ	measure, vision
h	hot, who
m	men, some
n	sun, know, pneumonia
ŋ	sung, ringing
w	wet, white
l	light, long
r	right, wrong
y	yes, use, music
t̬	butter, bottle
t̚	button

Vocabulary Index

The numbers following each entry are the pages where the word appears. All words followed by asterisks* are on the Academic Word List.

A

abandon* /əˈbændən/ 180, 182
abuse /əˈbyuz/ 180, 183, 229
accordingly /əˈkɔrdɪŋli/ 212, 214
account /əˈkaʊnt/ 129, 131, 141
acoustic /əˈkustɪk/ 12, 14
acre /ˈeɪkɚ/ 104, 106, 182
activate /ˈæktəˌveɪt/ 12, 14, 56, 215
advocate* /ˈædvəˌkeɪt/ 104, 106, 119
affair /əˈfer/ 26, 29
affectionately /əˈfɛkʃənɪtli/ 20, 21, 28
alert /əˈlɚt/ 68, 70, 116
anticipate* /ænˈtɪsəˌpeɪt/ 85, 88
assume* /əˈsum/ 62, 64, 70, 115, 132
audibly /ˈɔdəbli/ 202, 204
authoritative* /əˈθɔrəˌteɪtɪv, əˈθɑr-/ 44, 46

B

backpacking /ˈbækpækɪŋ/ 220, 221
beam /bim/ 12, 14
being /ˈbiɪŋ/ 123, 126
bloom /blum/ 20, 22, 29
breakthrough /ˈbreɪkθru/ 85, 88
breeze /briz/ 188, 190
bring up /brɪŋ ʌp/ 26, 29, 39
builds up /bɪldz ʌp/ 202, 204
bush /bʊʃ/ 68, 70, 115, 158

C

catchy /ˈkætʃi/ 2, 4, 5, 14
cave /keɪv/ 220, 222
channel* /ˈtʃænl/ 196, 197
charge /tʃɑrdʒ/ 157, 158, 164
charitable /ˈtʃærətəbəl/ 220, 221
cite* /saɪt/ 104, 105, 205
clamor /ˈklæmɚ/ 20, 21, 55
clear one's throat /klɪr wʌnz θroʊt/ 44, 46
collapse* /kəˈlæps/ 180, 182
come clean /kʌm klin/ 163, 165
come down with /kʌm daʊn wɪθ, -wɪð/ 79, 81
consciousness /ˈkɑnʃəsnɪs/ 2, 5, 132
consideration /kənˌsɪdəˈreɪʃən/ 38, 40, 105
consistently* /kənˈsɪstəntli/ 202, 205
consumption* /kənˈsʌmpʃən/ 104, 105, 106, 182, 183
conventional* /kənˈvɛnʃənəl/ 213, 216, 230

coup /ku/ 220, 222
credible /ˈkrɛdəbəl/ 123, 126, 130
criteria* /kraɪˈtɪriə/ 123, 126
curriculum /kəˈrɪkyələm/ 97, 99
cylinder /ˈsɪləndɚ/ 68, 70, 216, 222

D

daring /ˈderɪŋ/ 220, 222
deafening /ˈdɛfənɪŋ/ 12, 14
dedicated /ˈdɛdəˌkeɪtɪd/ 97, 98, 106, 115
defrost /dɪˈfrɔst/ 97, 98, 119
despair /dɪˈsper/ 163, 165, 173
desperately /ˈdɛsprɪtli, -pərɪtli/ 68, 71
device* /dɪˈvaɪs/ 2, 4, 14, 56, 159, 215
devoted* /dɪˈvoʊt̬ɪd/ 213, 215, 221, 233
diameter /daɪˈæmət̬ɚ/ 62, 63
digest /daɪˈdʒɛst, dɪ-/ 104, 105
digit /ˈdɪdʒɪt/ 79, 81, 87
disclose /dɪsˈkloʊz/ 220, 222
disfiguring /dɪsˈfɪgyɚɪŋ/ 79, 81
dismiss /dɪsˈmɪs/ 123, 126, 131, 132
displace* /dɪsˈpleɪs/ 139, 141, 147
distorted* /dɪˈstɔrtɪd/ 196, 197
distracted /dɪˈstræktɪd/ 196, 197, 198, 204, 205
domestic* /dəˈmɛstɪk/ 139, 141, 148, 164, 165
dose /doʊs/ 26, 28, 130
drain /dreɪn/ 79, 81, 88
drawback /ˈdrɔbæk/ 196, 198, 204, 230
drought /draʊt/ 180, 183
drudgery /ˈdrʌdʒəri/ 20, 22, 29
durable /ˈdʊrəbəl/ 213, 215
dust /dʌst/ 188, 189

E

ecosystem /ˈikoʊˌsɪstəm/ 62, 64, 106, 119
emerge* /ɪˈmɚdʒ/ 62, 64, 70, 115
end user /ɛnd yuzɚ/ 213, 215, 221
enterprising /ˈɛntɚˌpraɪzɪŋ/ 213, 215, 232
entertain /ˌɛntɚˈteɪn/ 220, 221
envy /ˈɛnvi/ 123, 126
essential /ɪˈsɛnʃəl/ 123, 125, 174, 177
exception /ɪkˈsɛpʃən/ 196, 198
exhort /ɪgˈzɔrt/ 97, 98, 105
extraterrestrial /ˌɛkstrətəˈrɛstriəl/ 123, 126, 131, 132

F

fabric /ˈfæbrɪk/ 129, 131
fade /feɪd/ 20, 21, 28, 221
familiar /fəˈmɪlyɚ/ 2, 4, 14, 173, 204
field of vision /fild əv ˈvɪʒən/ 44, 45, 59
filter /ˈfɪltɚ/ 220, 221, 222
flexibility* /ˌflɛksəˈbɪləṭi/ 85, 87, 142, 148
float /floʊt/ 146, 148
flush out /flʌʃ aʊt/ 188, 190
foe /foʊ/ 157, 160, 165
foliage /ˈfoʊliɪdʒ/ 68, 70, 119
follow suit /ˈfɑloʊ sut/ 97, 99
formidable /ˈfɔrmədəbəl, fɔrˈmɪdə-/ 157, 158, 165
fossil fuel /ˈfɑsəl ˈfyuəl, -fyul/ 97, 99, 106, 183
frailty /ˈfreɪlti/ 157, 159, 165
frequency /ˈfrikwənsi/ 12, 14
frontier /frʌnˈtɪr/ 62, 64, 119
function* /ˈfʌŋkʃən/ 2, 5, 14, 56
fundamental* /ˌfʌndəˈmɛntəl/ 129, 132, 158, 174
fury /ˈfyʊri/ 163, 164

G

galaxy /ˈgæləksi/ 123, 126
gap /gæp/ 68, 70
gaze /geɪz/ 157, 164
generate* /ˈdʒɛnəˌreɪt/ 188, 190, 229
get rid of /gɛt rɪd əv/ 2, 4, 22, 55
giant /ˈdʒaɪənt/ 62, 63, 64, 70, 164, 214
gorgeous /ˈgɔrdʒəs/ 26, 29, 63, 119
grab /græb/ 68, 70, 71, 147
grain /greɪn/ 104, 106
gravity /ˈgrævəṭi/ 68, 71
grief /grif/ 38, 40, 46
growl /graʊl/ 163, 164
grunt /grʌnt/ 157, 158, 165

H

harsh /hɑrʃ/ 180, 183, 189, 190
helpless /ˈhɛlplɪs/ 38, 40, 55
high-pitched /haɪ-/pɪtʃt/ 12, 13
hold your ground /hoʊld /yɚ graʊnd/ 157, 159, 160
household name /ˈhaʊshoʊld, ˈhaʊsoʊld neɪm/ 213, 215, 221
hum /hʌm/ 2, 4, 14, 58
humid /ˈhyumɪd/ 188, 190

I

impair /ɪmˈpɛr/ 196, 198, 205
impose on /ɪmˈpoʊz ɔn, -ən/ 146, 147, 177

impulsive /ɪmˈpʌlsɪv/ 38, 39, 55
in debt /ɪn dɛt/ 213, 215
in exchange for /ɪn ɪksˈtʃeɪndʒ fɚ/ 26, 29, 40, 46, 56, 119
in favor of /ɪn feɪvɚ əv/ 202, 204
in sum /ɪn sʌm/ 85, 88
in the same boat /ɪn ðə seɪm boʊt/ 163, 165, 174
inefficiency /ˌɪnəˈfɪʃənsi/ 202, 204
infect /ɪnˈfɛkt/ 2, 4
innovation* /ˌɪnəˈveɪʃən/ 13, 148, 182
insecticide /ɪnˈsɛktəˌsaɪd/ 220, 221
insight* /ˈɪnsaɪt/ 79, 81, 115
install /ɪnˈstɔl/ 213, 215
intently /ɪnˈtɛntli/ 163, 164
invade /ɪnˈveɪd/ 2, 5
itch /ɪtʃ/ 2, 4, 5

J

jerk /dʒɚk/ 44, 46, 58

L

launch /lɔntʃ, lɑntʃ/ 123, 125, 131
layer* /ˈleɪɚ/ 68, 70
layout /ˈleɪaʊt/ 139, 141, 147
lean /lin/ 70, 81
leap /lip/ 68, 70, 119
lethal /ˈliθəl/ 12, 14
likelihood /ˈlaɪkliˌhʊd/ 85, 87
limb /lɪm/ 62, 64, 70, 71, 125
linked to /lɪŋkt tu/ 180, 182, 230
literally /ˈlɪṭərəli/ 129, 132
long-term /lɔŋ-tɚm/ 202, 204, 205, 230
look back /lʊk bæk/ 79, 81,190
lose track of /luz /træk əv/ 26, 28,197

M

made from scratch /meɪd frəm skrætʃ/ 97, 98, 119
mainstream /ˈmeɪnstrim/ 123, 125, 130, 176
maintenance* /ˈmeɪntˈn-əns/ 139, 142
majestic /məˈdʒɛstɪk/ 157, 160, 165, 176
manage to /ˈmænɪdʒ tu/ 62, 63, 64, 70, 115
manipulate* /məˈnɪpyəˌleɪt/ 38, 40, 55, 56
manners /ˈmænɚz/ 38, 39, 40, 106
mating season /meɪtɪŋ sizən/ 157, 159, 164
menacing /ˈmɛnɪsɪŋ/ 157, 159, 164, 173
microclimate /ˈmaɪkroʊˌklaɪmɪt/ 188, 190
mineral /ˈmɪnərəl/ 26, 28, 64
moan /moʊn/ 44, 45, 165
mount /maʊnt/ 146, 147
movement /ˈmuvmənt/ 139, 141, 142, 176

spacious /ˈspeɪʃəs/ 97, 98, 106, 119

spare /spɛr/ 85, 88

spine-chilling /spaɪn ˈtʃɪlɪŋ/ 157, 158, 165

spray /spreɪ/ 180, 182

standard of living /ˈstændəd əv ˈlɪvɪŋ/ 180, 182, 232

starvation /starˈveɪʃən/ 180, 182

steady /ˈstɛdi/ 44, 46

stock /stak/ 97, 99, 106

storage /ˈstɔrɪdʒ/ 139, 141, 148, 205

story /ˈstɔri/ 20, 21, 64, 70, 141, 147, 190

straighten up /ˈstreɪtʼn ʌp/ 44, 46

strain /streɪn/ 20, 21, 28, 58

strenuous /ˈstrɛnyuəs/ 85, 87, 115, 116

strike a deal /straɪk ə dil/ 213, 216, 222

subjected /səbˈdʒɛktɪd/ 2, 4, 14

supplier /səˈplaɪə/ 220, 222

susceptible /səˈsɛptəbəl/ 2, 5

suspend* /səˈspɛnd/ 146, 148

sway /sweɪ/ 20, 22, 29

swing /swɪŋ/ 68, 70, 119

switch /swɪtʃ/ 196, 198, 204

T

take over /teɪk ˈouvə/ 188, 190

take up /teɪk ʌp/ 85, 88

tame /teɪm/ 163, 165

tangle /ˈtæŋgəl/ 68, 71

tear down /tɛr daʊn/ 146, 148

temporarily* /ˌtɛmpəˈrɛrəli/ 12, 14, 55

texture /ˈtɛkstʃə/ 104, 106

trail off /treɪl ɔf/ 26, 28

transformation* /ˌtrænsfəˈmeɪʃən/ 146, 148, 174

transmit* /trænzˈmɪt/ 220, 222

transplant /trænsˈplænt/ 26, 29

tune /tun/ 2, 4, 5, 14

turn (ten) /tən/ 79, 81

twitch /twɪtʃ/ 163, 164

U

uncomprehendingly /ˌʌnkamprɪˈhɛndɪŋli/ 26, 28

urban /ˈəbən/ 20, 22, 55, 69, 176, 177

V

vast /væst/ 129, 131, 132, 141, 176

version* /ˈvəʒən/ 220, 222

volunteer* /ˌvalənˈtɪr/ 85, 87, 88, 115

W

wail /weɪl/ 38, 40, 46

wander /ˈwandə/ 20, 22, 28, 29, 106

weed /wid/ 20, 22, 28, 29

willing /ˈwɪlɪŋ/ 104, 106, 115, 119, 221

with ease /wɪθ, wɪð iz/ 44, 45, 58, 88

wizard /ˈwɪzəd/ 79, 81

work one's way /wək wʌnz weɪ/ 68, 71

worthy /ˈwəði/ 129, 132

writhe /raɪð/ 38, 40, 46, 59

MP3 Audio Tracking Guide